AUTODESK® 3DS MAX 2014

ESSENTIALS

Randi L. Derakhshani

Dariush Derakhshani

 :SK®

 **SYBEX®**

A Wiley Brand

Acquisitions Editor: Mariann Barsolo
Development Editor: Tom Cirtin
Technical Editor: Jon McFarland
Production Editor: Rachel Gunn
Copy Editor: Judy Flynn
Editorial Manager: Pete Gaughan
Production Manager: Tim Tate
Vice President and Executive Group Publisher: Richard Swadley
Vice President and Publisher: Neil Edde
Book Designer: Happenstance Type-O-Rama
Compositor: Craig W. Johnson, Happenstance Type-O-Rama
Proofreader: Candace Cunningham
Indexer: Nancy Guenther
Project Coordinator, Cover: Katherine Crocker
Cover Designer: Ryan Sneed
Cover Image: Randi L. Derakhshani

Copyright © 2013 by John Wiley & Sons, Inc., Indianapolis, Indiana
Published simultaneously in Canada
ISBN: 978-1-118-57514-7
ISBN: 978-1-118-72366-1 (ebk.)
ISBN: 978-1-118-75025-4 (ebk.)
ISBN: 978-1-1187-2364-7 (ebk.)

Dear Reader,

Thank you for choosing *Autodesk® 3ds Max® 2014 Essentials.* This book is part of a family of premium-quality Sybex books, all of which are written by outstanding authors who combine practical experience with a gift for teaching.

Sybex was founded in 1976. More than 30 years later, we're still committed to producing consistently exceptional books. With each of our titles, we're working hard to set a new standard for the industry. From the paper we print on, to the authors we work with, our goal is to bring you the best books available.

I hope you see all that reflected in these pages. I'd be very interested to hear your comments and get your feedback on how we're doing. Feel free to let me know what you think about this or any other Sybex book by sending me an email at nedde@wiley.com. If you think you've found a technical error in this book, please visit http://sybex.custhelp.com. Customer feedback is critical to our efforts at Sybex.

Best regards,

NEIL EDDE
Vice President and Publisher
Sybex, an Imprint of Wiley

To Max Henry

Acknowledgments

We are thrilled to be a part of the team working to publish *Autodesk® 3ds Max® 2014 Essentials*, a complete update and style change to our previous *Introducing Autodesk® 3ds Max®* series. Education is an all-important goal in life and should always be approached with eagerness and earnestness. We would like to show appreciation to the teachers who inspired us; you can always remember the teachers who touched your life, and to them we say thanks. We would also like to thank all of our students, who taught us a lot during the course of our many combined academic years.

Special thanks go to Mariann Barsolo, Thomas Cirtin, Rachel Gunn, and Pete Gaughan, our editors at Sybex who have been professional, courteous, and ever patient. Our appreciation also goes to technical editor Jon McFarland, who worked hard to make sure this book is of the utmost quality. We could not have done this revision without their help.

In addition, thanks to Dariush's mother and brother for their love and support, not to mention the life-saving babysitting services.

Writing on the HP EliteBook

Having a good computer system is important with this type of work, so a special thank you goes to HP for keeping us on the cutting edge of workstation hardware by providing us with a fully decked-out EliteBook 8760w, which was our primary computer in writing this book. What struck us about the laptop was that it was not only portable, making it easy for a writing team to collaborate; it was also powerful enough to run truly demanding tasks. It takes a special machine to run graphics-intensive applications, such as Autodesk 3ds Max, and we were thrilled to write this book on the HP EliteBook.

Running an Intel i7 CPU alongside 16 GB of RAM and an Nvidia Quadro 5010M (with a whopping 6 GB of memory) gave us the muscle we needed to run multiple applications alongside 3ds Max splendidly. Dual 320 GB hard drives gave us plenty of space for Windows 7 Professional and its applications and still left lots of room for renders. We opted out of the RAID option to mirror the drives (you can also stripe them for performance), but that doesn't mean we neglected our backup duties with this machine! The 8760w was easily integrated into a Gigabit network in the home office, and on fast Wi-Fi everywhere else, so we had constant access to the home network and the hundreds upon hundreds of files necessary to write this book (and all their backups!).

And since we are so very image conscious (as in the screen!), we wondered if the images we created and captured for this book would be done justice on "just a laptop screen." The EliteBook has a stunning 17″ 30-bit IPS display panel that put those questions to rest very quickly! The HP EliteBook screen is no less than professionally accurate and calibrated for optimum image clarity and correct color. Barely a handful of high-end mobile workstations could even come close to meeting the demands image professionals put on their gear. But this note-book HP DreamColor display is remarkable—there's just no other way to put it—going as far as besting any of our desktop screens in color and vibrancy.

With performance at such a high level, and in a nice portable form, we were easily convinced that we should perform all of our intensive work for this book on the EliteBook. Going back to a desk-bound tower quickly became a non-option. Thanks, HP!

About the Authors

Randi L. Derakhshani is an Autodesk Certified Instructor and a staff instructor with The Art Institute of California–Los Angeles. She began working with computer graphics in 1992 and was hired by her instructor to work at Sony Pictures Imageworks, where she developed her skills with the Autodesk 3ds Max program and Nuke, among many other programs. A teacher since 1999, Randi enjoys sharing her wisdom with young talent and watching them develop at The Art Institute. Currently, she teaches a wide range of classes, from Autodesk® 3ds Max®, Autodesk® Maya®, and ZBrush to compositing with The Foundry's Nuke. Juggling her teaching activities with caring for a little boy makes Randi a pretty busy lady.

Dariush Derakhshani is an Autodesk Certified Instructor and Certified Evaluator, a visual-effects supervisor, a writer, and an educator in Los Angeles, California, as well as Randi's husband. Dariush used Autodesk® AutoCAD® software in his architectural days and migrated to using 3D programs when his firm's principal architects needed to visualize architectural designs in 3D on the computer. Dariush started using Alias PowerAnimator version 6 when he enrolled in USC Film School's animation program, and he has been using Alias/Autodesk animation software for the past 14 years. He received an MFA in Film, Video, and Computer Animation from the USC Film School in 1997. He also holds a BA in Architecture and Theater from Lehigh University in Pennsylvania. He worked at a New Jersey architectural firm before moving to Los Angeles for film school. He has worked on feature films, music videos, and countless commercials as a 3D animator, as a CG/VFX supervisor, and sometimes as a compositor. Dariush also serves as an editor and is on the advisory board of *HDRI 3D*, a professional computer graphics magazine from DMG Publishing.

CONTENTS AT A GLANCE

Introduction   *xv*

CHAPTER 1   The 3ds Max Interface   1

CHAPTER 2   Your First 3ds Max Project   19

CHAPTER 3   Modeling in 3ds Max: Architectural Model Part I   57

CHAPTER 4   Modeling in 3ds Max: Architectural Model Part II   79

CHAPTER 5   Introduction to Animation   111

CHAPTER 6   Animation Principles   131

CHAPTER 7   Character Poly Modeling: Part I   143

CHAPTER 8   Character Poly Modeling: Part II   169

CHAPTER 9   Character Poly Modeling: Part III   193

CHAPTER 10   Introduction to Materials: Interiors and Furniture   209

CHAPTER 11   Textures and UV Workflow: The Soldier   235

CHAPTER 12   Character Studio: Rigging   263

CHAPTER 13   Character Studio: Animation   291

CHAPTER 14   Introduction to Lighting: Interior Lighting   305

CHAPTER 15   3ds Max Rendering   331

CHAPTER 16   mental ray   357

APPENDIX   Autodesk® 3ds Max® Certification   385

Index   *389*

CONTENTS

Introduction   *xv*

CHAPTER 1   The 3ds Max Interface   1

The Workspace 1
    User-Interface Elements. 2
    Viewports 4
    ViewCube 6
    Mouse Buttons 7
    Quad Menus 7
    Display of Objects in a Viewport 8
    Viewport Navigation. 10
Transforming Objects Using Gizmos 11
Graphite Modeling Tools Set 12
Command Panel 14
    Object Parameters and Values 15
    Modifier Stack 15
    Objects and Sub-Objects 16
Time Slider and Track Bar 16
File Management 16
    Setting a Project. 17
    Version Up! 18
The Essentials and Beyond. 18

CHAPTER 2   Your First 3ds Max Project   19

Setting Up a Project Workflow 19
    Ready, Set, Go…Set Project! 20
    Ready, Set, Reference! 20
Time to Model a Clock! 25
    Modeling in Sub-Object Mode 26
    Bring on the Bevel 30
    Chamfer Time. 32
In Splines We Trust. 38
    One Lathe to Make a Whole. 45
    Introducing the Dynamic Duo: Extrude & Bevel 49
Bringing It All Together 54
The Essentials and Beyond. 56

CHAPTER 3   Modeling in 3ds Max: Architectural Model Part I   57

Units Setup 58
Importing a CAD Drawing 59
Creating the Walls. 61
Creating the Doors 64
Creating the Window 68
Adding a Floor and Ceiling. 70
    Creating Baseboard Moldings 72
The Essentials and Beyond. 78

CHAPTER 4   Modeling in 3ds Max: Architectural Model Part II   79

Modeling the Couch 79
    Blocking Out the Couch Model 80
    Using NURMS to Add Softness 82
    Adding Details to the Couch 85
    The Chaise Lounge. 89
    Creating the Couch Feet 90
Modeling the Lounge Chair 93
    Creating Image Planes. 93
    Adding the Materials 94
    Building the Splines for the Chair Frame. 95
    Creating the Chair Cushion. 101
    Creating the Lounge Chair's Base. 103
    Bringing It All Together. 108
The Essentials and Beyond. 110

CHAPTER 5   Introduction to Animation   111

Animating the Ball 112
    Copying Keyframes 113
    Using the Track View–Curve Editor 114
    Reading Animation Curves 116
Refining the Animation 118
    Editing Animation Curves. 119
    Squash and Stretch 121
    Setting the Timing. 123
    Moving the Ball Forward 124
    Using the XForm Modifier 127
    Animating the XForm Modifier. 128
The Essentials and Beyond. 130

CHAPTER 6	**Animation Principles**	**131**

Anticipation and Momentum in Knife Throwing 131

    Blocking Out the Animation 131

    Trajectories. 134

    Adding Rotation 135

    Adding Anticipation 137

    Following Through. 139

    Transferring Momentum to the Target. 140

The Essentials and Beyond. 142

CHAPTER 7	**Character Poly Modeling: Part I**	**143**

Setting Up the Scene 143

    Creating Image Planes. 144

    Adding the Material to the Image Plane 145

Beginning the Soldier Model 146

    Forming the Torso 147

    Creating the Arms 158

    Creating the Legs. 161

    Fixing Up the Body. 166

The Essentials and Beyond. 168

CHAPTER 8	**Character Poly Modeling: Part II**	**169**

Completing the Main Body. 169

Creating the Accessories. 173

    Utility Belt. 173

    Pouch 174

    Vest 177

    Leg Strap 178

    Gun Holster 182

Putting on the Boots 183

Creating the Hands. 188

The Essentials and Beyond. 192

CHAPTER 9	**Character Poly Modeling: Part III**	**193**

Creating the Head. 193

    Outlining the Head 196

    Rounding Out the Face 203

    Creating the Back of the Head. 205

    Mirroring the Head 206

Merging and Attaching the Head's Accessories 207
The Essentials and Beyond 208

CHAPTER 10   **Introduction to Materials: Interiors and Furniture   209**

The Slate Material Editor 210
Material Types 211
    Standard Materials 211
mental ray Material Types 212
Shaders 212
Mapping the Couch and Chair 213
    Creating a Standard Material 213
    Applying the Material to the Couch 214
    Adding a Bitmap 216
    Introduction to Mapping Coordinates 218
    Applying the Material to the Lounge Chair 223
Mapping the Window and Doors 228
    Creating a Multi/Sub-Object Material 228
The Essentials and Beyond 233

CHAPTER 11   **Textures and UV Workflow: The Soldier   235**

UV Unwrapping 236
    Pelting the Arms UVs 242
    Unwrapping and Using Pelt for the Head 245
Seaming the Rest of the Body 249
    Unfolding the Rest of the Body 250
Applying the Color Map 257
Applying the Bump Map 258
Applying the Specular Map 261
The Essentials and Beyond 262

CHAPTER 12   **Character Studio: Rigging   263**

Character Studio Workflow 263
    General Workflow 264
Associating a Biped with the Soldier Model 266
    Creating and Modifying the Biped 266
    Adjusting the Torso and Arms 272
    Adjusting the Neck and Head 274

Applying the Skin Modifier 275
Tweaking the Skin Modifier. 278
Controlling the View 287
The Essentials and Beyond. 290

CHAPTER 13 Character Studio: Animation 291

Animating the Soldier 291
Adding a Run-and-Jump Sequence. 292
Adding Freeform Animation 294
Modifying Animation in the Dope Sheet 299
The Essentials and Beyond. 304

CHAPTER 14 Introduction to Lighting: Interior Lighting 305

Three-Point Lighting 305
3ds Max Lights 306
Standard Lights 307
Target Spotlight 307
Target Direct Light. 309
Free Spot or Free Direct Light 310
Omni Light. 311
Lighting a Still Life in the Interior Space 312
Selecting a Shadow Type 319
Shadow Maps 320
raytraced Shadows 320
Atmospheres and Effects 321
Creating a Volumetric Light 321
Adding Shadows. 323
Excluding an Object from a Light 324
Adding a Volumetric Effect 327
Volume Light Parameters 329
Light Lister 329
The Essentials and Beyond. 330

CHAPTER 15 3ds Max Rendering 331

Rendering Setup 331
Common Tab 333
Choosing a Filename 334
Rendered Frame Window. 334

Render Processing 334

Assign Renderer 336

Rendering the Bouncing Ball 336

Cameras. 338

Creating a Camera 339

Using Cameras 339

Talk Is Cheap! 340

Animating a Camera 341

Clipping Planes. 342

Safe Frames. 343

Raytraced Reflections and Refractions 345

Raytrace Material 345

Raytrace Mapping. 347

Refractions Using the Raytrace Material. 348

Refractions Using Raytrace Mapping 351

Rendering the Interior and Furniture. 353

Adding Raytraced Reflections 353

Outputting the Render. 355

The Essentials and Beyond. 356

CHAPTER 16   mental ray   357

mental ray Renderer 357

Enabling the mental ray Renderer 357

mental ray Sampling Quality 358

Final Gather with mental ray. 360

Basic Group 361

Advanced Group. 363

The mental ray Rendered Frame Window. 364

mental ray Materials. 364

Using Arch & Design Material Templates 366

Creating Arch & Design Materials. 369

Multi/Sub-Object Material and Arch & Design. 370

3ds Max Photometric Lights in mental ray Renderings. 372

3ds Max Daylight System in mental ray Renderings 378

The Essentials and Beyond. 384

APPENDIX   Autodesk® 3ds Max® Certification   385

Index   389

INTRODUCTION

Welcome to Autodesk® 3ds Max® 2014 Essentials. The world of computer-generated (CG) imagery is fun and ever changing. Whether you are new to CG in general or are a CG veteran new to 3ds Max designing, you'll find this book the perfect primer. It introduces you to the Autodesk 3ds Max software and shows how you can work with the program to create your art, whether it is animated or static in design.

This book exposes you to all facets of 3ds Max by introducing and plainly explaining its tools and functions to help you understand how the program operates—but it does not stop there. This book also explains the use of the tools and the ever-critical concepts behind the tools. You'll find hands-on examples and tutorials that give you firsthand experience with the toolsets. Working through them will develop your skills and the conceptual knowledge that will carry you to further study with confidence. These tutorials expose you to various ways to accomplish tasks with this intricate and comprehensive artistic tool. These chapters should give you the confidence you need to venture deeper into the feature set in 3ds Max, either on your own or by using any of the software's other learning tools and books as a guide.

Learning to use a powerful tool can be frustrating. You need to remember to pace yourself. The major complaints CG book readers have are that the pace is too fast and that the steps are too complicated or overwhelming. Addressing those complaints is a tough nut to crack, to be sure. No two readers are the same. However, this book offers the opportunity to run things at your own pace. The exercises and steps may seem confusing at times, but keep in mind that the more you try and the more you fail at some attempts, the more you will learn how to operate the 3ds Max engine. Experience is king when learning the workflow necessary for *any* software program, and with experience come failure and aggravation. But try and try again. You will find that further attempts will always be easier and more fruitful.

Above all, however, this book aims to inspire you to use the 3ds Max program as a creative tool to achieve and explore your own artistic vision.

Who Should Read This Book

Anyone who is interested in learning to use the 3ds Max tools should start with this book.

If you are an educator, you will find a solid foundation on which to build a new course. You can also treat the book as a source of raw materials that you can adapt to fit an existing curriculum. Written in an open-ended style, *Autodesk 3ds Max 2014 Essentials* contains several self-help tutorials for home study as well as plenty of material to fit into any class.

What You Will Learn

You will learn how to work in CG with Autodesk 3ds Max 2014. The important thing to keep in mind, however, is that this book is merely the beginning of your CG education. With the confidence you will gain from the exercises in this book, and the peace of mind you can have by using this book as a reference, you can go on to create your own increasingly complex CG projects.

What You Need

Hardware changes constantly and evolves faster than publications can keep up. Having a good solid machine is important to a production, although simple home computers will be able to run the 3ds Max software quite well. Any laptop (with discrete graphics; not a netbook) or desktop PC running Windows XP Professional, Windows 7, or Windows 8 (32- or 64-bit) with at least 2 GB of RAM and an Intel Pentium Core 2 Duo/Quad or AMD Phenom or higher processor will work. Of course, having a good video card will help; you can use any hardware-accelerated OpenGL or Direct3D video card. Your computer system should have at least a 2.4 GHz Core 2 or i5/i7 processor with 2 GB of RAM, a few GBs of hard-drive space available, and a GeForce FX or ATI Radeon video card. Professionals may want to opt for workstation graphics cards, such as the ATI FirePro or the Quadro FX series of cards. The following systems would be good ones to use:

 ▶ Intel i7, 4 GB RAM, Quadro FX 2000, 400 GB 7200 RPM hard disk

 ▶ AMD Phenom II, 4 GB RAM, ATI FirePro V5700, 400 GB hard disk

You can check the list of system requirements at the following website: www.autodesk.com/3dsmax.

FREE AUTODESK SOFTWARE FOR STUDENTS AND EDUCATORS

The Autodesk® Education Community is an online resource with more than five million members that enables educators and students to download—for free (see website for terms and conditions)—the same software used by professionals worldwide. You can also access additional tools and materials to help you design, visualize, and simulate ideas. Connect with other learners to stay current with the latest industry trends and get the most out of your designs. Get started today at www.autodesk.com/joinedu.

What Is Covered in This Book

Autodesk® 3ds Max® 2014 Essentials is organized to provide you with a quick and essential experience with 3ds Max to allow you to begin a fruitful education in the world of computer graphics.

Chapter 1, "The 3ds Max Interface," begins with an introduction to the interface for 3ds Max 2014 to get you up and running quickly.

Chapter 2, "Your First 3ds Max Project," is an introduction to modeling concepts and workflows in general. It shows you how to model using 3ds Max tools with polygonal meshes and modifiers to create a retro alarm clock.

Chapter 3, "Modeling in 3ds Max: Architectural Model Part I," takes your modeling lesson from Chapter 2 a step further by showing you how to use some of the Architecture Engineering and Construction (AEC) tools to build an interior space using a room from an image.

Chapter 4, "Modeling in 3ds Max: Architectural Model Part II," continues with the interior space from Chapter 3 by adding some furniture. The main focus of this chapter is the Graphite Modeling Tools tab and its many tools.

Chapter 5, "Introduction to Animation," teaches you the basics of 3ds Max animation techniques and workflow by animating a bouncing ball. You will also learn how to use the Track View–Curve Editor to time, edit, and finesse your animation.

Chapter 6, "Animation Principles," rounds out your animation experience by showing the animation concepts of weight, follow-through, and anticipation when you animate a knife thrown at a target.

Chapter 7, "Character Poly Modeling: Part I," introduces you to the first of three chapters on creating a low-polygon mesh character model of a soldier. In this chapter, you begin by blocking out the primary parts of the body.

Chapter 8, "Character Poly Modeling: Part II," continues the soldier model, focusing on using the Editable Poly toolset. You will finish the body and add hands and boots.

Chapter 9, "Character Poly Modeling: Part III," finishes the model of the soldier started in Chapter 7. You will create the head and merge in elements such as goggles and a face mask and integrate them into the scene.

Chapter 10, "Introduction to Materials: Interiors and Furniture," shows you how to assign textures and materials to your models. You will learn to texture the couch, chair, and window from Chapter 4 as you learn the basics of working with 3ds Max materials and UVW mapping.

Chapter 11, "Textures and UV Workflow: The Soldier," furthers your understanding of materials and textures and introduces UV workflows in preparing and texturing the soldier.

Chapter 12, "Character Studio: Rigging," covers the basics of Character Studio in creating a biped system and associating the biped rig to the soldier model.

Chapter 13, "Character Studio: Animation," expands on Chapter 12 to show you how to use Character Studio to create and edit a walk cycle using the soldier model.

Chapter 14, "Introduction to Lighting: Interior Lighting," begins by showing you how to light a 3D scene with the three-point lighting system. It then shows you how to use the tools to create and edit 3ds Max lights for illumination, shadows, and special lighting effects. You will light the furniture to which you added materials in Chapter 10.

Chapter 15, "3ds Max Rendering," explains how to create image files from your 3ds Max scene and how to achieve the best look for your animation by using proper cameras and rendering settings when you render the interior scene.

Chapter 16, "mental ray and HDRI," shows you how to render with mental ray. Using Final Gather, you will learn how to use indirect lighting.

The companion web page to this book at www.sybex.com/go/3dsmax2014essentials provides all the sample images, movies, and files that you will need to work through the projects in *Autodesk 3ds Max 2014 Essentials*.

> **NOTE**
>
> This book is a great primer for Autodesk 3ds Max. If you're interested in taking the Autodesk Certification exams for 3ds Max, go to www.autodesk.com/certification for information and resources.

The Essentials Series

The Essentials series from Sybex provides outstanding instruction for readers who are just beginning to develop their professional skills. Every Essentials book includes these features:

- ▶ Skill-based instruction with chapters organized around projects rather than abstract concepts or subjects

- ▶ Suggestions for additional exercises at the end of each chapter, where you can practice and extend your skills

- ▶ Digital files (via download) so you can work through the project tutorials yourself. Please check the book's web page at www.sybex.com/go/3dsmax2014essentials for these companion downloads.

You can contact the authors through Wiley or on Facebook at www.facebook.com/3dsMaxEssentials.

CHAPTER 1

The 3ds Max Interface

The Autodesk 3ds Max® software interface is where you view and work with your scene. This chapter explains its basic operations and tools. You can use this chapter as a reference as you work through the rest of this book, although the following chapters and their exercises will orient you to the 3ds Max user interface (UI) quickly. It's important to be in front of your computer when you read this chapter so you can try out techniques as we discuss them in the book.

This chapter includes the following topics:

▶ **The workspace**

▶ **Transforming objects using gizmos**

▶ **Graphite Modeling Tools set**

▶ **Command panel**

▶ **Time slider and track bar**

▶ **File management**

The Workspace

The following sections present a brief rundown of what you need to know about the UI and how to navigate in the 3D workspace.

In this version of 3ds Max they have rolled out a new Enhanced Menus workspace that defines the look of interface. When you first open the program, you will see the Default Workspace. Throughout this book, however, we have opted to use the Enhanced Menus workspace instead. The differences between the two are seen mainly in the menus and the ribbon. We believe the Enhanced Menu workspace is a smoother workflow for new users to the program. To use the Enhanced Menu workspace, go to the Quick Access toolbar located at the top of the interface, and in the Workspaces drop-down list, choose the Enhanced Menus workspace, as shown here.

User-Interface Elements

Figure 1.1 shows the 3ds Max UI. (See Table 1.1 for explanations of the UI elements.) At the very top left of the application window is an icon ( ) called the Application button; clicking it opens the Application menu, which provides access to many file operations. Also running along the top is the Quick Access toolbar, which provides access to common commands, and the InfoCenter, which offers to access many product-related information sources. Some of the most important commands in the Quick Access toolbar are file management commands such as Save File and Open File. If you do something and then wish you hadn't, you can click the Undo Scene Operation button ( ) or press Ctrl+Z. To redo a command or action that you just undid, click the Redo Scene Operation button ( ) or press Ctrl+Y.

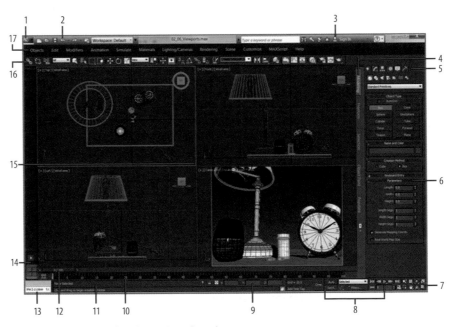

FIGURE 1.1   The 3ds Max interface elements

TABLE 1.1   The 3ds Max interface elements*

	Element	Function
1	Application button	Opens the Application menu, which provides file management commands.
2	Quick Access toolbar	Provides some of the most commonly used file management commands as well as Undo Scene Operation and Redo Scene Operation.
3	InfoCenter	Provides access to 3ds Max product-related information.
4	The ribbon	Provides access to a wide range of tools to make building and editing models in 3ds Max fast and easy. In Figure 1.1, the ribbon is shown in a vertical orientation.
5	Command panel tabs	Where all the editing of parameters occurs; provides access to many functions and creation options; divided into tabs that access different panels, such as Create panel, Modify panel, etc.
6	Rollout	A section of the command panel that can expand to show a listing of parameters or collapse to just its heading name.
7	Viewport navigation controls	Icons that control the display and navigation of the viewports; icons may change depending on the active viewport.
8	Animation Time/ Keying controls	Controls for animation keyframing and animation playback controls.
9	Coordinate display area	Allows you to enter transformation values.
10	Track bar	Provides a timeline showing the frame numbers; select an object to view its animation keys on the track bar.
11	Prompt line and status bar controls	Prompt and status information about your scene and the active command.
12	Time slider	Shows the current frame and allows for changing the current frame by moving (or scrubbing) the time bar.
13	MAXScript Mini Listener	A command prompt window for the MAXScript language. The window is useful for performing interactive work and developing small code fragments.
14	Viewport Layout tab bar	This is an easy access tab for quickly changing viewport layouts. Preset layouts can be added to the menu on the tab bar.

(Continues)

TABLE 1.1 *(Continued)*

	Element	Function
15	Viewports	You can choose different views to display in these four viewports as well as different layouts from the viewport label menus.
16	Main toolbar	Provides quick access to tools and dialog boxes for many of the most common tasks.
17	Menu bar	Provides access to commands grouped by category.

*The numerals in the first column refer to labels in Figure 1.1.

Just below the Quick Access toolbar is the menu bar, which runs across the top of the interface. The menus give you access to a ton of commands—from basic scene operations, such as Duplicate and Group under the Edit menu, to advanced tools such as those found under the Modifiers menu. Immediately below the menu bar is the main toolbar. It contains several icons for functions, such as the three transform tools: Select And Move, Select And Rotate, and Select And Uniform Scale ( ).

When you first open 3ds Max, the workspace has many UI elements. Each is designed to help you work with your models, access tools, and edit object parameters.

Viewports

You'll be doing most of your work in the viewports. These windows represent 3D space using a system based on Cartesian coordinates. That is a fancy way of saying "space on X, Y, and Z axes."

You can visualize X as left-right, Y as in-out (into and out of the screen from the Top viewport), and Z as up-down within the Perspective and Camera viewports. In the orthographic viewports, you visualize Y as up-down and Z as in-out. The coordinates are expressed as a set of three numbers, such as (0, 3, –7). These coordinates represent a point that is at 0 on the X-axis, 3 units up on the Y-axis, and 7 units back on the Z-axis.

Four-Viewport Layout Tab Bar

The viewports in 3ds Max are the windows into your scene. By default, there are four views: Front, Top, Left, and Perspective. The first three—Front, Top, and Left—are called orthographic views. They are also referred to as modeling windows. These windows are good for expressing exact dimensions and size relationships, so they are good tools for sizing up your scene objects and fine-tuning their layout. The default viewport layout has the four views, but this can be changed. The Viewport Layout tab bar, which is located at the lower-left corner of the interface, is a tab bar that allows you to switch between many different viewport layout configurations with a single click. When you click the arrow button on the tab bar, the Standard Viewport Layouts menu gives you access to choose a layout. It will then be added to the tab bar for easy access, as shown in Figure 1.2.

The General viewport label menus ([+]) in the upper-left corner of each viewport provide options for overall viewport display or activation, as shown in Figure 1.3. It also gives you access to the Viewport Configuration dialog box.

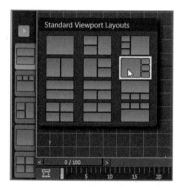

FIGURE 1.2 Viewport Layout tab bar

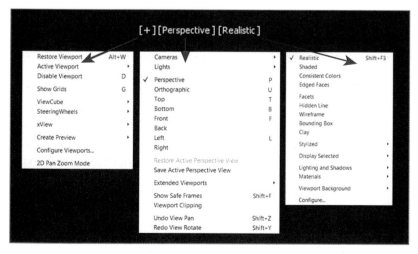

FIGURE 1.3 Viewport label menus showing the General Viewport, Point-of-View, and Shading Viewport menus.

The Perspective viewport displays objects in 3D space using perspective. Notice in Figure 1.1 how the distant objects seem to get smaller in the Perspective viewport. In actuality, they are the same size, as you can see in the orthographic viewports. The Perspective viewport gives you the best representation of what your output will be.

To make a viewport active, click in a blank part of the viewport (not on an object). If you do have something selected, it will be deselected when you click in the blank space.

When active, the view will have a mustard-yellow highlight around it. If you right-click in an already active viewport, you will get a pop-up context menu called the quad menu. You can use the quad menu to access some basic commands for a faster workflow. We will cover this topic in the section "Quad Menus" later in this chapter.

> You can also right-click anywhere in an inactive viewport to activate it without selecting or deselecting anything.

ViewCube

The ViewCube® 3D navigation control, shown in Figure 1.4, provides visual feedback of the current orientation of a viewport; it lets you adjust the view orientation and allows you to switch between standard and isometric views.

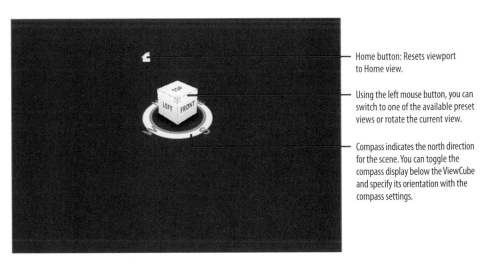

Home button: Resets viewport to Home view.

Using the left mouse button, you can switch to one of the available preset views or rotate the current view.

Compass indicates the north direction for the scene. You can toggle the compass display below the ViewCube and specify its orientation with the compass settings.

FIGURE 1.4   ViewCube navigation tool

The ViewCube is displayed by default in the upper-right corner of the active viewport; it is superimposed over the scene in an inactive state to show the orientation of the scene. It does not appear in camera or light views. When you position your cursor over the ViewCube, it becomes active. Using the left mouse button, you can switch to one of the available preset views, rotate the current view, or change to the Home view of the model. Right-clicking over the ViewCube opens a context menu with additional options.

Mouse Buttons

Each of the three buttons on your mouse plays a slightly different role when manipulating viewports in the workspace. When used with modifiers such as the Alt key, they are used to navigate your scene, as shown in Figure 1.5.

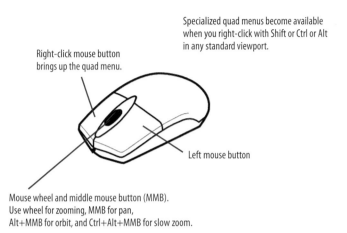

Specialized quad menus become available when you right-click with Shift or Ctrl or Alt in any standard viewport.

Right-click mouse button brings up the quad menu.

Left mouse button

Mouse wheel and middle mouse button (MMB).
Use wheel for zooming, MMB for pan,
Alt+MMB for orbit, and Ctrl+Alt+MMB for slow zoom.

FIGURE 1.5 Breakdown of the three mouse buttons

Quad Menus

When you click the right mouse button anywhere in an active viewport, except on the viewport labels and the ViewCube, a quad menu is displayed at the location of the mouse cursor, as shown in Figure 1.6. The quad menu can display up to four quadrant areas with various commands without your having to travel back and forth between the viewport and rollouts on the command panel (the area of the interface to the right—more on this later in the section "Command Panel").

The right quadrant of the default quad menu displays generic commands, which are shared between all objects. The left quadrant contains context-specific commands, such as mesh tools and light commands. You can also repeat your last quad menu command by clicking the title of the quadrant.

The quad menu contents depend on what is selected. The menus are set up to display only the commands that are available for the current selection; therefore, selecting different types of objects displays different commands in the quadrants. Consequently, if no object is selected, all of the object-specific commands will be hidden. If all of the commands for one quadrant are hidden, the quadrant will not be displayed.

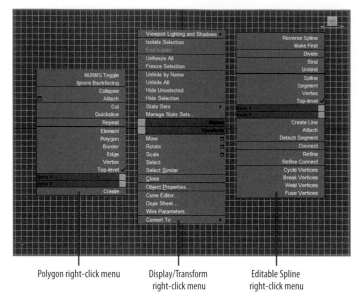

Polygon right-click menu   Display/Transform   Editable Spline
                                right-click menu   right-click menu

F I G U R E   1 . 6   Quad menus

Cascading menus display submenus in the same manner as a right-click menu. The menu item that contains submenus is highlighted when expanded. The submenus are highlighted when you move the mouse cursor over them.

To close the menu, right-click anywhere on the screen or move the mouse cursor away from the menu and click the left mouse button. To reselect the last-selected command, click in the title of the quadrant of the last menu item. The last menu item selected is highlighted when the quadrant is displayed.

> Some of the selections in the quad menu have a small icon next to them. Clicking this icon opens a dialog box where you can set parameters for the command.

Display of Objects in a Viewport

Viewports can display your scene objects in a few ways. If you click the viewport's name, you can switch that panel to any other viewport angle or point of view. If you click the Shading Viewport label, a menu appears to allow you to change the display driver. The display driver names differ depending on the graphics drive mode you selected when you first start 3ds Max. This book uses the default display mode Nitrous.

Wireframe mode   Wireframe mode displays the edges of the object, as shown on the left in Figure 1.7. It is the fastest to use because it requires less computation on your video card.

Realistic mode   The Realistic mode is a shaded view in which the objects in the scene appear solid. It shows realistic textures with shading and lighting, as shown in the middle in Figure 1.7.

Each viewport displays a ground plane grid, called the *home grid*. This is the basic 3D-space reference system where the X-axis is red, the Y-axis is green, and the Z-axis is blue. It's defined by three fixed planes on the coordinate axes (X, Y, Z). The center of all three axes is called the origin, where the coordinates are (0, 0, 0). The home grid is visible by default, but it can be turned on and off in the right-click General Viewport Label Menu or by pressing the G key.

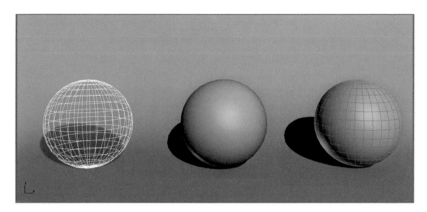

FIGURE 1.7   Viewport rendering options with the default Nitrous driver modes

Selecting Objects in a Viewport

Click an object to select it in a viewport. If the object is displayed in Wireframe mode, its wireframe turns white while it is selected. If the object is displayed in a Shaded mode, a white bracket appears around the object.

To select multiple objects, hold down the Ctrl key as you click additional objects to add to your selection. If you Alt+click an active object, you will deselect it. You can clear all your active selections by clicking in an empty area of the viewport.

Changing/Maximizing the Viewports

To change the view in any given viewport—for example, to go from a Perspective view to a Front view—click the current viewport's name. From the menu, select the view you want to have in the selected viewport. You can also use keyboard shortcuts. To switch from one view to another, press the appropriate key on the keyboard, as shown in Table 1.2.

If you want to have a larger view of the active viewport than is provided by the default four-viewport layout, click the Maximize Viewport Toggle icon ( ) in the lower-right corner of the 3ds Max window.

> You can also use the Alt+W keyboard shortcut to toggle between the maximized and four-viewport views. ◀

TABLE 1.2 Viewport shortcuts

Viewport	Keyboard shortcut
Top view	T
Bottom view	B
Front view	F
Left view	L
Camera view	C
Orthographic view	U
Perspective view	P

Viewport Navigation

3ds Max allows you to move around its viewports by using either key/mouse combinations, which are highly preferable, or the viewport controls found in the lower-right corner of the 3ds Max UI. An example of navigation icons is shown for the Top viewport in Figure 1.8, though it's best to become familiar with the key/mouse combinations.

FIGURE 1.8
Viewport navigation controls are handy, but the key/mouse combinations are much faster to use for navigation in viewports.

Open a new, empty scene in 3ds Max. Experiment with the following controls to get a feel for moving around in 3D space. If you are new to 3D, using these controls may seem odd at first, but it will become easier as you gain experience and should become second nature in no time.

Pan   Panning a viewport slides the view around the screen. Using the middle mouse button (MMB), click in the viewport and drag the mouse pointer to pan the view.

Zoom   Zooming moves your view closer to or farther away from your objects. To zoom, press Ctrl+Alt and MMB+click in your viewport and then drag the mouse up or down to zoom in or out. The zoom will occur around the cursor location. You may also use the scroll wheel to zoom.

Orbit   Orbit will rotate your view around your objects. To orbit, press Alt and MMB+click and drag in the viewport. By default, 3ds Max will rotate about the center of the viewport.

Transforming Objects Using Gizmos

Using gizmos is a fast and effective way to transform (move, rotate, and/or scale) your objects with interactive feedback. When you select a transform tool such as Move, a gizmo appears on the selected object. Gizmos let you manipulate objects in your viewports interactively to transform them. Coordinate display boxes at the bottom of the screen display coordinate, angular, or percentage information on the position, rotation, and scale of your object as you transform it. The gizmos appear in the viewport on the selected object at their pivot point as soon as you invoke one of the transform tools, as shown in Figure 1.9.

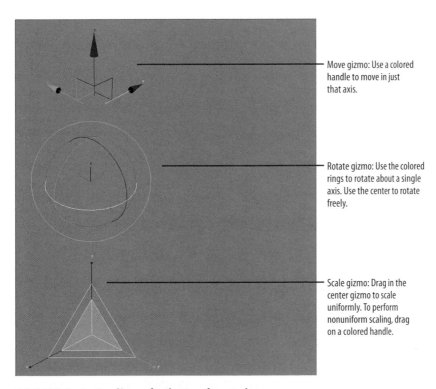

Move gizmo: Use a colored handle to move in just that axis.

Rotate gizmo: Use the colored rings to rotate about a single axis. Use the center to rotate freely.

Scale gizmo: Drag in the center gizmo to scale uniformly. To perform nonuniform scaling, drag on a colored handle.

FIGURE 1.9   **Gizmos for the transform tools**

You can select the transform tools by clicking the icons in the main toolbar's Transform toolset ( ) or by invoking shortcut keys:

W for Move

E for Rotate

R for Scale

In a new scene, create a sphere by choosing Create ➢ Standard Primitives ➢ Sphere. In a viewport, click and drag to create the sphere object. Follow along as we explain the transform tools next.

Move   Invoke the Move tool by pressing W (or accessing it through the main toolbar), and your gizmo should look like the top image in Figure 1.9. Dragging the X-, Y-, or Z-axis handle moves an object on a specific axis. You can also click on the plane handle, the box between two axes, to move the object in that two-axis plane.

Rotate   Invoke the Rotate tool by pressing E, and your gizmo will turn into three circles, as shown in the middle image in Figure 1.9. You can click on one of the colored circles to rotate the object on the axis only, or you can click anywhere between the circles to freely rotate the selected object in all three axes.

Scale   Invoke the Scale tool by pressing the R key, and your gizmo will turn into a triangle, as shown in the bottom image of Figure 1.9. Clicking and dragging anywhere inside the yellow triangle will scale the object uniformly on all three axes. By selecting the red, green, or blue handle for the appropriate axis, you can scale along one axis only. You can also scale an object on a plane between two axes by selecting the side of the yellow triangle between two axes.

Graphite Modeling Tools Set

The ribbon interface is a toolbar containing these tabs: Modeling, Freeform, Selection, Object Paint, and Populate. Each tab comprises a number of panels and tools whose availability depends on the context. The ribbon can be oriented horizontally or vertically. The default for the ribbon is vertical, docked immediately to the left of the command panel, as shown earlier in Figure 1.1. The Modeling tab provides you with a wide range of modeling tools to make building and editing models in 3ds Max fast and easy. All the available tools are organized into separate panels for convenient access. In the following chapters, you will make copious use of the Modeling tab, which is shown in Figure 1.10.

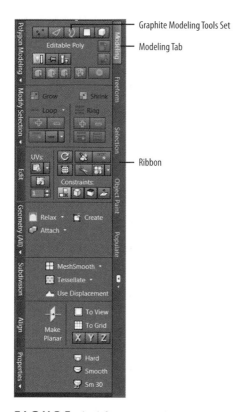

FIGURE 1.10
The Modeling tab found in the ribbon

The following panels are found in the Graphite Modeling Tool set:

▶ Polygon Modeling panel

▶ Modify Selection panel

▶ Edit panel

▶ Geometry (All) panel

▶ [Sub-Object] panel

▶ Loops panel

▶ Additional panels

One easy way to customize the ribbon is by using the Minimum/Maximum toggle switch as shown in Figure 1.11. By clicking on the button, you toggle the minimum/maximum options; when you maximize the ribbon, you are able to view most of the controls. The Minimize drop-down list, which is the small arrow next to the Minimum/Maximum toggle switch, gives access to different ribbon states.

Min/Max toggle switch
Minimize drop-down list

FIGURE 1.11 The Minimum/Maximum toggle for the Graphite Modeling Tools set

Command Panel

Everything you need to create, manipulate, and animate objects can be found in the command panel running vertically on the right side of the UI (Figure 1.1). The command panel is divided into tabs according to function. The function or toolset you need to access will determine which tab you need to click. When you encounter a panel that is longer than your screen, 3ds Max displays a thin vertical scroll bar on the right side. Your cursor also turns into a hand you can use to click and drag the panel up and down.

You will be exposed to more panels as you progress through this book. Table 1.3 is a rundown of the command panel functions and what they do.

TABLE 1.3 Command panel functions

Icon	Name	Function
	Create panel	Create objects, lights, cameras, etc.
	Modify panel	Apply and edit modifiers to objects
	Hierarchy panel	Adjust the hierarchy for objects and adjust their pivot points
	Motion panel	Access animation tools and functions

TABLE 1.3 *(Continued)*

Icon	Name	Function
	Display panel	Access display options for scene objects
	Utilities panel	Access several functions of 3ds Max, such as motion capture utilities and the Asset Browser

Object Parameters and Values

The command panel and all its tabs give you access to an object's parameters. Parameters are the values that define a specific attribute of or for an object. For example, when an object is selected in a viewport, its parameters are shown in the Modify panel, where you can adjust them. When you create an object, that object's creation parameters are shown (and editable) in the Create panel.

Modifier Stack

In the Modify panel you'll find the modifier stack, as shown in Figure 1.12. This UI element lists all the modifiers that are active on any selected object. Modifiers are actions applied to an object that change it somehow, such as bending or warping. You can stack modifiers on top of each other when creating an object and then go back and edit any of the modifiers in the stack (for the most part) to adjust the object at any point in its creation. You will see this in practice in the following chapters.

Modifier Stack

FIGURE 1.12 The modifier stack in the Modify panel

Objects and Sub-Objects

An object or mesh in 3ds Max is composed of polygons that define the surface. For example, the facets or small rectangles on a sphere are *polygons*, all connected at common edges at the correct angles and in the proper arrangement to make a sphere. The points that generate a polygon are called *vertices*. The lines that connect the points are called *edges*. Polygons, vertices, and edges are examples of sub-objects and are all editable so that you can fashion any sort of surface or mesh shape you wish.

> To edit a sub-object, you have to convert it to an editable poly object, which you will learn how to do in the following chapters.

Time Slider and Track Bar

Running across the bottom of the 3ds Max UI are the time slider and the track bar, as shown earlier in Figure 1.1. The time slider allows you to move through any frame in your scene by scrubbing (moving the slider back and forth). You can move through your animation one frame at a time by clicking the previous frame and next frame arrows on either side of the time slider or by pressing the shortcut keys.

You can also use the time slider to animate objects by setting keyframes. With an object selected, right-click the time slider to open the Create Key dialog box, which allows you to create transform keyframes for the selected object.

The track bar is directly below the time slider. The track bar is the timeline that displays the timeline format for your scene. More often than not, the track bar is displayed in frames, with the gap between each tick mark representing frames. On the track bar, you can move and edit your animation properties for the selected object. When a keyframe is present, right-click it to open a context menu where you can delete keyframes, edit individual transform values, and filter the track bar display.

The Animation Playback controls in the lower right of the 3ds Max UI ( ) are similar to the ones you would find on a VCR (how old are you?) or DVD player.

File Management

Different kinds of files are saved in categorized folders under the project folder. For example, scene files are saved in a Scenes folder and rendered images are saved in a Render Output folder within the project folder. The projects are set up according to what types of files you are working on, so everything is neat and organized from the get-go.

The conventions followed in this book and on the accompanying web page (www.sybex.com/go/3dsmax2014essentials) follow this project-based system so that you can grow accustomed to it and make it a part of your own workflow. It pays to stay organized.

Setting a Project

The exercises in this book are organized into specific projects, such as the Clock project that you will tackle in the next chapter. The Clock project will be on your hard drive, and the folders for your scene files and rendered images will be in that project layout. Once you copy the appropriate projects to your hard drive, you can tell 3ds Max which project to work on by clicking the Application button and choosing Manage ➢ Set Project Folder. Doing so will send the current project to that project folder. For example, when you save your scene, 3ds Max will automatically take you to the Scenes folder of the current project.

For example, if you are working on a project about a castle, begin by setting a new project called Castle. Click the Application button and choose Manage ➢ Set Project Folder, as shown in Figure 1.13. In the dialog box that opens, click Make New Folder to create a folder named Castle on your hard drive. 3ds Max will automatically create the project and its folders.

Designating a specific place on your PC or server for all your project files is important, as is having an established naming convention for the project's files and folder.

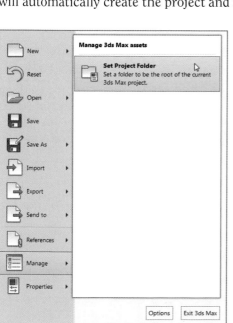

FIGURE 1.13 Choosing Set Project Folder

Once you save a scene, one of your scene filenames should look like this: `Castle_GateModel_v05.max`. This tells you right away it's a scene from your Castle project and that it is a model of the gate. The version number tells you that it's the fifth iteration of the model and possibly the most recent version. Following a naming convention will save you oodles of time and aggravation.

Version Up!

After you've spent a significant amount of time working on your scene, you will want to *version up*. This means you save your file using the same name, but you increase the version number by 1. Saving often and using version numbers are useful for keeping track of your progress and protecting yourself from mistakes and from losing your work.

To version up, you can save by clicking the Application button, choosing Save As, and manually changing the version number appended to the end of the filename. 3ds Max also lets you do this automatically by using an increment feature in the Save As dialog box. Name your scene file and click the Increment button (the + icon) to the right of the filename text. Clicking the Increment button appends the filename with 01, then 02, then 03, and so on as you keep saving your work using Save As and the Increment button.

THE ESSENTIALS AND BEYOND

In this chapter you learned about the interface and how to navigate 3D space in 3ds Max. As you continue with the following chapters, you will gain experience and confidence with the UI, and many of the features that seem daunting to you now will become second nature.

Additional Exercises

▶ From the Create panel, choose Geometry and then Standard Primitives and create each one of the primitives. Pay attention to each object's parameters to get familiar with what each object is capable of.

▶ Spend time exploring the interface, menus, and toolbars.

CHAPTER 2

Your First 3ds Max Project

In production work, setting down a plan and having clear goals for your project is very important. Without a good idea of where you need to go, you'll end up floundering and losing out on the whole experience. In any project, the beginning of the workflow starts with modeling.

Modeling in 3D programs is like sculpting or carpentry; you create objects out of shapes and forms. Even a complex model is just an amalgam of simpler parts or shapes/volumes. The successful modeler can dissect a form down to its components and translate them into surfaces and meshes. The Autodesk® 3ds Max® software modeling tools are incredibly strong for polygonal modeling, so the focus of the modeling in this book is on polygonal modeling. In this chapter, you will learn modeling concepts and how to use 3ds Max modeling toolsets.

This chapter includes the following topics:

▶ **Setting up a project workflow**

▶ **Time to model a Clock**

▶ **In splines we trust**

▶ **Bringing it all together**

Setting Up a Project Workflow

You will begin by modeling the clock body to develop your modeling muscles. This exercise introduces you to primitives and polygons. You will be modeling by editing the polygon component; it's called *editable-poly* modeling. Why buy a clock when you can just make one using 3ds Max tools?

Ready, Set, Go…Set Project!

Download the Clock project, `Clock.zip`, from the book's web page at `www.sybex`
`.com/go/3dsmax2014essentials`. Place the files on your hard drive. Open the
3ds Max 2014 program and set a 3ds Max project. Choose the `Clock` folder from
your hard drive and follow these steps:

1. Set your project folder to the Clock project you just downloaded
   (click the Application button ( ) and choose Manage ➢ Set
   Project Folder).

2. Navigate to the place on the hard drive where you saved the book
   projects.

3. Click Clock, and then click OK.

Now when you want to open a scene file, just click the Application button
and choose Open, and you will automatically be in the Clock project's `Scenes`
folder.

Ready, Set, Reference!

Using reference materials will help you efficiently create your 3D model and
achieve a good likeness in your end result. The temptation to just wing it and
start building the objects is strong, especially when time is short and you're
raring to go. This temptation should always be suppressed in deference to a well-
thought-out approach to the task. Sketches, photographs, and drawings can
all be used as resources for the modeling process. Not only are references useful
for giving you a clear direction in which to head, but you can also use references
directly in 3ds Max to help you model. Photos, especially those taken from different sides of the intended model, can be added to a scene as background images to
help you shape your model.

Go to where the Clock project folder is on your hard drive; in the `sceneassets/`
`images` folder you will see some additional reference images of the clock. These
sample reference images will give you an idea of what kind of images will be useful for a project like the clock. Of course, if this were your clock, you would have
captured tons of pictures already, right?

You're so close to modeling something! You'll want to get some sort of
reference for what you're modeling. Study the photo in Figure 2.1 for the
model.

FIGURE 2.1   The clock to be modeled

For the best in modeling references, bring in photos of your model and use the *crossing boxes* technique, which involves placing the reference images on crossing plane objects or thin boxes in the scene.

To begin the clock body, start with a new 3ds Max file:

1. Open a new 3ds Max file by clicking the Application button (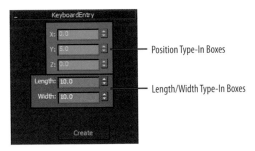) and choosing New.

    New clears the contents of the current scene without changing any of the system settings.

2. On the Create tab ( ), click the Geometry icon ( ), and in the Standard Primitives drop-down menu, click the Plane button.

    Instead of creating the plane with the click-and-drag method, you will use the Keyboard Entry rollout. This rollout allows you define both the size of the object and the X, Y, and Z positions in your scene.

3. Make sure the Front viewport is selected by right-clicking in it. This will align the plane to that viewport when it is created.

4. In the plane primitive parameters, expand the Keyboard Entry rollout.

5. Change the value in the X Position Type-In box to 0.0, the Y box to 5.0, and the Z box to 0.0, as shown in Figure 2.2. This will place the plane 5 units away from the center of the scene along the Y-axis.

FIGURE 2.2   Position Type-in in the Plane Keyboard Entry rollout

6. Change Length value to 10 and the Width value to 10 and then click the Create button.

    3ds Max creates the image plane in the Front viewport, which we will use for the Front view image plane.

    When you have an object selected, its name appears at the top of the command panel. It is a type-in that you can use to rename your object. To the right of the type-in is a small color box. Select the box and you can choose a color for your object.

7. Change the name of the Plane001object to **Front View Image**.

8. Now right-click the Left viewport to activate it. Back in the Standard Primitives drop-down menu, select the Plane button, if it is not already active from the previous steps. Expand the Keyboard Entry rollout.

9. Change the X Position Type-In to **1.8**, Y to **5.0**, and Z to **0.0**.
   This will move the plane just a bit away from the center and help with the alignment of the images when they are in place.

10. Change the Length parameter in the Keyboard Entry to 10 and the Width parameter to 10, if they are not already set that way. The parameter will stay set from the previous plane that was created.

11. Click the Create button.

12. Rename the Plane001 object **Side View Image**.

13. Go to the Viewport Label menus at the top left of the Front viewport. Click on the Shading viewport label menu and choose Shaded, as shown in Figure 2.3.

FIGURE 2.3 Shading viewport label menu

This menu lets you choose how objects are displayed in the viewport. You can also use the keyboard shortcut F3, which toggles between the last two shading modes with Realistic as the default.

14. Do the same for the Left viewport.
   This is important because if you drag and drop the image onto a plane in a wireframe viewport, it will not apply the image to the plane, but rather to the viewport.
   Use the Zoom Extents All tool on all the viewports by pressing the shortcut Ctrl+Shift+Z, or you can use the viewport navigation tool, Zoom Extents All ( ), which you will find in the lower-right corner of the interface in the viewport navigation area. This acts as a "fit in window" tool.

15. Open a Windows Explorer window; navigate to the `sceneassets\images` folder in the `Clock` folder that you downloaded to your hard drive.

In this folder, you will find two reference JPEG images, one for each of the two image planes you just created in the scene.

16. Select the front view reference image (called `Front.jpg`), drag it into the Front viewport, and then drop it onto the **Front View** image plane.

This automatically places the image onto the plane, so the image is viewable in the viewport.

17. Repeat the previous step to place the `Side.jpg` onto the **Side View** image plane in the Left viewport.

Figure 2.4 shows the image planes with the reference images applied.

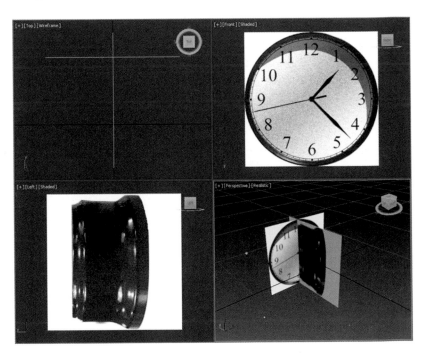

FIGURE 2.4   The image planes with the clock images applied

18. To finish, click the Application button ( ) and choose Save As. Save the file as `Clock_Body_Start.max`.

Use this file for the next section.

Time to Model a Clock!

When modeling any object, it is always best to study the object and break it up into smaller, easier-to-model components. To begin modeling the clock body, you will start with a cylinder because the clock body has a cylindrical shape as its base. For this procedure, use the `Clock_Body_Start.max` filed that was saved in the previous section. Follow these steps:

1. Select the Front viewport, which should still be set to Shaded display mode, from the previous steps.

2. Enable Edged Faces mode in the viewport by using the keyboard shortcut F4.
   Edged Faces places the wireframe over the shaded object, making the object easier to see when modeling.

3. Right-click in the Front viewport to make it the active viewport.
   This will align the cylinder to the Front viewport when it is created.

4. In the command panel, choose the Create tab, click the Geometry icon, and make sure Standard Primitives is selected.

5. In the Object Type rollout, click Cylinder, and select the Keyboard Entry rollout to expand the parameters.

6. Leave the X, Y, and Z values at 0, but enter 5.0 for Radius and –5.0 for Height, and then click the Create button.
   You could also select Cylinder from the Create panel, and in the Front viewport click and drag to create the cylinder, eyeballing the size from the Front and Left viewports.

7. Open the Modify panel ( ); this is where you go to edit the parameters of an object.

8. Change Height Segments to 1 and Sides to 30, then press Enter on your keyboard to set the new parameter. Leave all the remaining parameters at the default.

9. To turn on See-Through mode, use the keyboard shortcut Alt+X. See-Through mode will ghost out the cylinder and allow you to see through it to the image planes.

Modeling in Sub-Object Mode

To start the process of modeling the clock, you need to access the cylinder's components. All 3D objects are at their core made up of three main components: vertices, edges, and polygons. These components are the basis of polygon modeling. To access the components of any object, you need to convert it to an editable poly, which means a polygon that allows access to the components. There are many ways to do this; we will be using the Graphite Modeling Tools set, also called the *modeling ribbon*:

1. In the Graphite Modeling Tools tab ➤ Polygon Modeling. It expands and you see the Convert To Poly button. Click it, as shown in Figure 2.5.

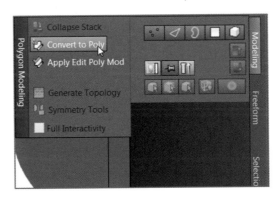

FIGURE 2.5 Converting the cylinder to an editable poly

2. Turn on Edged Faces using the keyboard shortcut F4, if it isn't already enabled. This will allow you to see the wireframe while modeling.

   In the Polygon Modeling panel is a line of icons (shown at the top of Figure 2.5). These are the components, or sub-objects, of your object.

3. Select the Polygon icon (▢) or use the keyboard shortcut by pressing 4 to enter the Polygon sub-object mode.

4. In the Perspective viewport, orbit around the cylinder so you can see the back end. Do this by clicking and dragging on any part of the ViewCube, which is the icon in the upper right of the viewport.

5. Then select the back-end polygon.

   The polygon is shaded red to indicate it is selected, as shown in Figure 2.6.

All the editable polygons have keyboard shortcuts to quickly navigate through the sub-object levels. Vertex level is 1, Edge is 2, Border is 3, Polygon is 4, Element is 5, and Ctrl+B returns to object level.

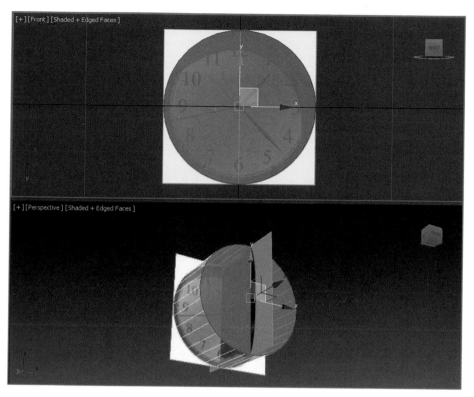

F I G U R E   2 . 6   Select the back polygon of the cylinder; it is shaded red when selected.

ORBITING IN THE VIEWPORTS

Orbiting in the viewports is a skill, and the faster you learn the many ways you can do it, the more efficient you will be as a 3D artist. You can orbit using the Orbit tool ( ), which is one of the viewport navigation tools found at the lower right of the interface. Drag the mouse on or around a view rotation "trackball," which is displayed as a yellow circle with handles placed at the quadrant points. An alternative way to orbit is to use the ViewCube. It is a great way to orbit within the viewports. Simply move your cursor to the ViewCube icon in the upper-right portion of the viewport and click+drag to rotate the current viewport. You can also use one of the preset views on the ViewCube to switch a viewport to front, back, left, right, top, or bottom. Another way to orbit is to use the keyboard/mouse shortcut Alt+MMB and drag in the viewport. As the user you need to decide which method works best for you.

6. In the Graphite Modeling Tools tab, go to the Polygons panel and click Outline. Click the arrow under the Outline button, and then select Outline Settings.

   This will open the Outline caddy, which is a dialog box to input your outline parameters.

7. Change Outline Amount to –0.75, and click the OK button (⊘). This will scale the selected polygon smaller.

   Look at the cylinder in the Left viewport. You will see that end of the cylinder now fits that end of the clock on the image plane.

8. In the Graphite Modeling Tools tab, go to the Edit panel and select the SwiftLoop tool.

   This tool places new edges that loop around the cylinder, which subdivides the sides. The subdivisions will allow for greater control of the details to be added. You will add three new subdivision, or loops, on the cylinder. To add the loops, just move the cursor over the part of the cylinder and you will see a preview loop. When the preview is where you want it, just click, and the new loop will be created.

9. Turn on Edged Faces (F4) and then view the cylinder in the Left viewport; place the loops at the positions shown in Figure 2.7.

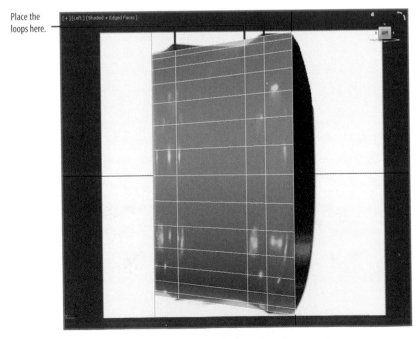

F I G U R E 2 . 7 Using the SwiftLoop tool, place three loops as shown.

5. Enter –0.25 in the Outline text box and press Enter again.

6. Click the Apply And Continue button (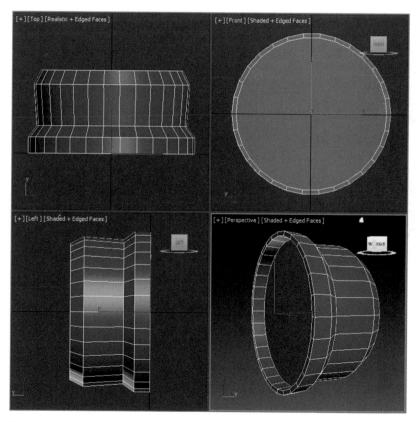). This applies the specified settings without closing the caddy.

7. Now change the Bevel caddy parameters. Enter –1.0 in the Height box, press Enter, enter 0.0 in the Outline box, press Enter again, and then click the OK button.

   The detail that you just created will be the part of the clock body where the clock face will sit. Figure 2.10 shows the clock the way it looks with the changes, shown with image planes hidden and See-Through mode turned off.

FIGURE 2.10 Clock body progress

ACCESSING MODELING TOOLS

Using the modeling ribbon is a convenient way to access modeling tools, but it isn't the only way. In most software packages, when new tools are added, the older versions of those tools aren't removed; in previous versions of the software, all poly modeling tools were accessed through the Modify panel. Many of the same buttons and functionality can be found in the Modify panel. You can also right-click on an object to access the quad menu. The quad menu allows you to find and activate most commands without having to travel back and forth between the viewport and rollouts on the command panel or main toolbar. In this book we will be using the Graphite Modeling Tools set (the modeling ribbon) to access our modeling tools.

Chamfer Time

Chamfering refers to the rounding of sharp edges or corners. For the clock, the new details on the sides are too sharp. You will be using the Chamfer tool in Edge mode. For this section, you will turn off See-Through mode and hide the image planes. Follow these steps:

1. To turn off See-Through mode, use the keyboard shortcut Alt+X.
   To hide the image planes, you will enter Isolate Selection mode.
   At the bottom of the interface, below the timeline, is an icon of a light bulb (💡). The keyboard shortcut is Alt+Q.

2. Either click the icon or use the shortcut to hide all but what is selected.

3. In the modeling ribbon, open the Polygon Modeling panel and select Edge mode (keyboard shortcut 2).

4. Select the edge shown in Figure 2.11.

5. In the Graphite Modeling Tools tab ➢ Modify Selection ➢ select Loop. This will select the entire edge loop (or use the shortcut, which is to double-click on the edge you want to loop).

6. In the main toolbar, click the Select And Move tool (✛). The keyboard shortcut is W.

7. Move the edges back toward the beveled surface, as shown in Figure 2.12.

With the new loops (or edge loops) in place, you will now edit them to change the profile of the cylinder to match the clock body.

10. In the Graphite Modeling Tools tab ➤ Modeling, select Edge mode (keyboard shortcut 2).

When you select Edge mode, the last loop you created will be selected. If it is not selected, continue with the steps 11 and 12; if it is selected, skip to step 13.

11. Select one of the edges toward the top of the cylinder; only a single edge will be selected, not the entire loop.

12. On the Modify Selection tab of the Graphite Modeling Tools tab, select Loop. This will continue the selection around the cylinder. A shortcut for the Loop tool is to double-click on an edge and the loop will be competed

13. Move your cursor to the main toolbar and select the Scale tool ( ). The keyboard shortcut is R.

14. Scale the edges up until they match the detail in the Left viewport image plane.

15. Repeat steps 10 through 12 on the other new edge loops until the cylinder matches Figure 2.8. Don't worry if it doesn't match up perfectly with the image.

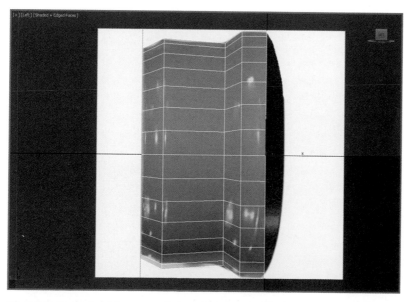

FIGURE 2.8 Edges are scaled to match the image plane.

16. This is a good time to save your file. Choose Save from the Application menu. You will use this file in the next section.

Bring on the Bevel

Now you will add detail to the front of the clock. On the clock object there is a small edge and a depression where the clock face and hands sit. To create this edge in the cylinder, you will use the Bevel tool. Beveling involves first extruding polygons and then scaling the extruded polygons with the Outline tool. The Bevel tool has three parameters:

Bevel Type   Controls how to extrude multiple polygons at once.

Height   Specifies how much extrusion to apply, based on units.

Outline Amount   Scales the outer border of the selected polygons, depending on whether the value is positive or negative.

For the Clock the bevel tool creates many of the details of the body. It allows us to create a rough model that we can refine with further tools.

1. Select the Polygon icon (▢), or use the keyboard shortcut by pressing 4 to enter the Polygon sub-object mode.

2. Select the front face of the cylinder.

3. On the Polygons panel in the modeling ribbon, click the arrow under the Bevel button. Then select Bevel Settings, as shown in Figure 2.9. This will open the Bevel caddy, which is a dialog box for inputting your bevel parameters.

FIGURE 2.9 Bevel Settings will bring up the caddy for parameter input.

4. In the Bevel caddy, enter the 0.0 in the Height text box, and then press Enter on your keyboard.

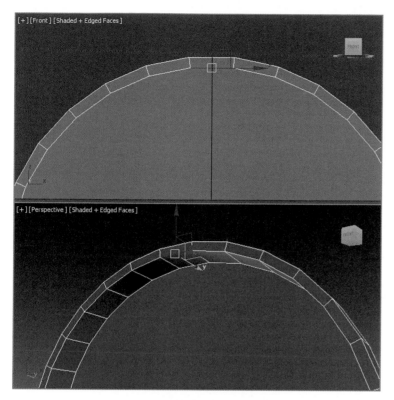

FIGURE 2.11 Select the edge shown in this image.

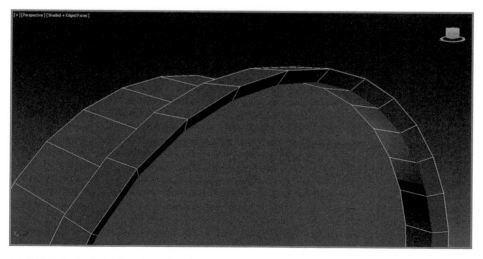

FIGURE 2.12 Move the edges back.

8. Exit Edge mode by selecting Edge mode again (or use the keyboard shortcut 2) in the Graphite Modeling Tools tab ➢ Polygon Modeling ➢ Edge button.

    This will take you to the "top level" and out of sub-object mode. Now you want the See-Through mode turned back on.

9. Select the clock body, and use the keyboard shortcut Alt+X to turn on See-Through mode.

10. To exit Isolate Selection mode, press Alt+Q or select the light bulb icon at the bottom of the interface. The image planes will reappear.

11. On the Polygon Modeling panel in the modeling ribbon, select Edge mode (keyboard shortcut 2).

12. Looking in the Left viewport, select and loop the middle edge, as shown in Figure 2.13 (Graphite Modeling Tools set ➢ Modeling ➢ Modify Selection ➢ Loop), to select the entire edge loop.

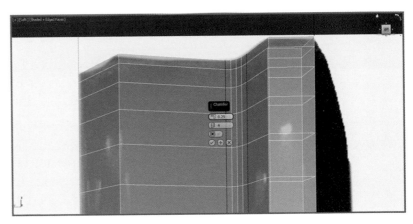

FIGURE 2.13   Select and loop the edge to prepare for chamfer.

13. Go to the Graphite Modeling Tools tab ➢ Edges ➢ Chamfer, and click on the arrow under the Chamfer button; then select Chamfer Settings. This will open the Chamfer caddy.

14. Create the smooth curve from the sharp edges. Input **0.25** for Edge Chamfer Amount (don't forget to press Enter on keyboard!) and 4 for Connect Edge Segments, and again press Enter.

15. Then click OK (✓). The results are shown in Figure 2.14.

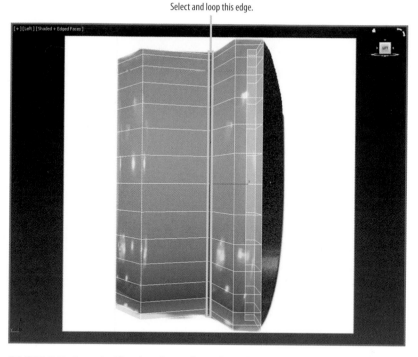

FIGURE 2.14 The chamfer performed on a looped edge

The chamfer will be repeated several times on different edges with different Chamfer parameters to achieve the correct smoothness for each curve. The next steps will chamfer the front edge and lip of the clock body.

16. On the front face of the clock, select an edge on the lip (where the clock face will be). Then hold the Ctrl key and select three more edges going towards the back of the clock, as shown in Figure 2.15 (which has See-Through mode turned off with shortcut Alt+X).

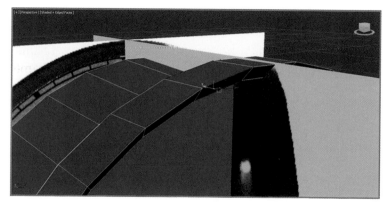

FIGURE 2.15 Select these two edges.

17. Loop the edges (Graphite Modeling Tools tab ➤ Modify Selection ➤ Loop).

18. Go to the Graphite Modeling Tools tab ➤ Polygon Modeling ➤ Edges ➤ Chamfer, and click the arrow under the Chamfer button; then select Chamfer Settings. This will open the Chamfer caddy.

19. To create the smooth curve from the sharp edges, enter 0.05 in the Edge Chamfer Amount text box, press Enter, then enter 2 in the Connect Edge Segments box and press Enter again.

20. Then click OK ( ). The results are shown in Figure 2.16.

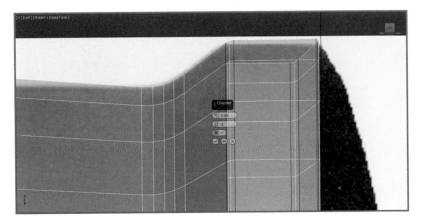

FIGURE 2.16 Chamfer result for the clock body's edge and lip.

The back side of the clock needs some special attention; its detail is a bit more intricate. First another SwiftLoop needs to be added, and then both edges need to be chamfered. Make sure you are still in Edge mode. If you are not, select Edge or the use the keyboard shortcut 2.

21. In the Graphite Modeling Tools tab ➤ Edit, select the SwiftLoop tool.

22. Add a SwiftLoop between the back edge of the clock and the loop that was added earlier, as shown in Figure 2.17.

23. In the main toolbar, select the Select And Uniform Scale tool (R), and scale down the edge loop until it matches the size in the image plane.

24. Hold down Ctrl and click on one of the edges to the right of the new edge you just created.

Add a new edge.

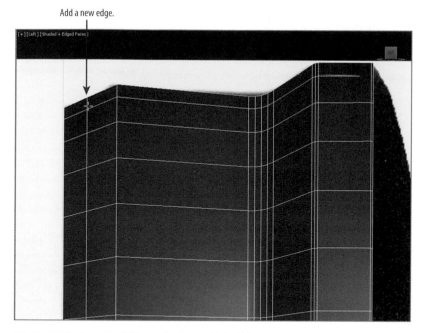

FIGURE 2.17 Add an edge loop with SwiftLoop.

25. Select the Graphite Modeling Tools tab ➤ Modify Selection panel ➤ Loop; this will select that loop also.

26. Select the Graphite Modeling Tools tab ➤ Edges panel ➤ Chamfer. Click the arrow under the Chamfer button, and then select Chamfer Settings; this will open the Chamfer caddy.

27. Enter 0.1 in the Edge Chamfer Amount text box and 3 in the Connect Edge Segments box. Then select OK; the results are shown in Figure 2.18.

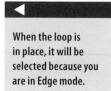

When the loop is in place, it will be selected because you are in Edge mode.

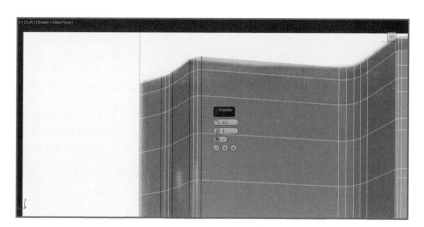

FIGURE 2.18 The two edge loops chamfered

The clock body is finished for now; there are a few tweaks that will be covered later in the chapter.

28. To finish this section, select the cylinder and rename it **Clock Body**.

29. Toggle See-Through mode off (Alt+X).

30. This time save the file using Save As, and name it `Clock_Body_End.max`.

In Splines We Trust

Now that the clock body is complete, it's time to move on to some of the clock parts. The parts that will be covered in this section are the handle, the hands, and the bell. To create these objects, you will learn a modeling technique called *spline modeling*. In computer graphics, a *spline* is a group of vertices and connecting segments that form a line or curve. Splines are used to create more complex geometry than can be found in the primitives available in 3ds Max. There are other uses for splines that will be discussed later in the book. The first clock part that you will create is the clock handle, shown in Figure 2.19.

FIGURE 2.19   **The clock handle**

Follow these steps:

1. Open `Clock_Handle_Start.max` from the `Scenes` folder of the Clock project on this book's companion web page.

This file has a full image of the front of the clock, loaded onto an image plane.

2. Start by accessing the Create panel (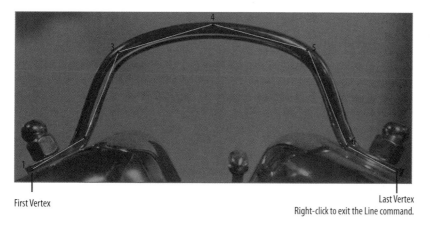), and choose the second icon from the row of icons, Shapes ( ), and from there choose Line. The following apply when you use the Line tool:

▶ A single click in a viewport creates a point with a linear segment.

▶ A click and drag creates a curved segment when you let go of the mouse.

▶ Holding the Shift key will constrain your movement to 90-degree angles; this can be very helpful in creating straight lines.

▶ A right-click exits the Line command.

Creating a line using this method can be difficult; it is easier to start with a simple shape and add more detail later. Figure 2.20 shows a simplified line that represents the clock handle.

First Vertex

Last Vertex
Right-click to exit the Line command.

FIGURE 2.20 The intended cross section for the clock handle

3. In the Front viewport, click to set a vertex and let go (refer to the first vertex in Figure 2.20).

4. Continue to click and move, following the handle around until you reach the seventh vertex; then right-click to exit the Line command.
    Now that the rough line is finished, it needs to be smoothed out and refined.

5. With the line selected, in the Modify panel's modifier stack, click the plus sign (+) to expand the list of sub-objects.

6. Select Vertex, as shown in Figure 2.21.

FIGURE 2.21 The three sub-objects of the Line command, select Vertex.

7. In the Front viewport, right-click over the middle vertex.

8. In the upper-left quadrant of the quad menu, choose Bezier, as shown in Figure 2.22.

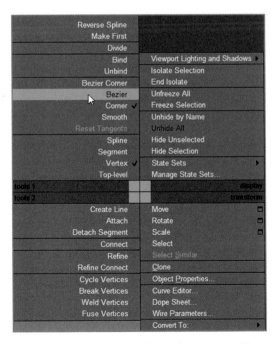

FIGURE 2.22 Use the quad menu to modify the vertex type.

VERTEX TYPES

When working on splines, you may want to change the vertex type:

Smooth   Has smooth continuous curve without tangent handles to edit.

Corner   Has sharp corners without tangent handles to edit.

Bezier   Has adjustable tangent handles that are locked.

Bezier Corner   Has adjustable tangent handles that are unlocked or broken and can adjust the curve entering and exiting the vertex independently.

There are now tangent handles coming from the vertex; the tangent handles control the amount of curve in the line. Tangents are edited using the Move tool.

9. Choose the Select And Move tool (W) and then grab one of the green boxes on either side of the vertex at the end of the tangent handle and move it until the curve matches with the handle in the image plane.

10. Right-click the vertices and change their vertex type to Bezier.

11. Adjust the tangent handles to smooth out the remaining vertices on the spline except the first and last, as shown in Figure 2.23.

Moving the handle up or down moves the segment attached to the handle in the same direction. Moving the handle closer to the vertex creates a tighter curve, and moving it farther away creates a looser curve.

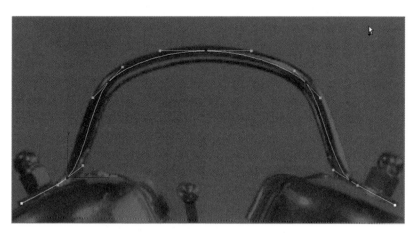

FIGURE 2.23   The line for the handle with all but the first and last vertices adjusted

12. In the Rendering rollout in the Modify panel, check the boxes Enable In Renderer and Enable In Viewport.

    These parameters control the renderability of the line, allowing you to specify thickness in the viewports and rendered scene. The default is Radial, which creates a cylindrical object along the path of the handle.

13. Change Thickness to 0.35 and leave the rest at the default, as shown in Figure 2.24.

14. Use See-Through mode (Alt+X) to ghost out the handle model; this will allow you to see the clock on the image plane.

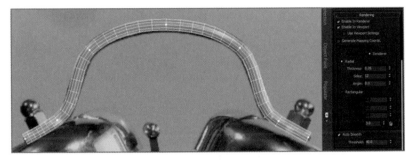

FIGURE 2.24   Rendering enabled on the clock handle line, set to Radial

The handle has the correct shape, but the area where the handle is between the bell and the bolt needs to be scaled down. This can be done easily in Vertex mode, which means you have to convert the spline to an editable polygon.

15. In the Graphite Modeling Tools tab, open the Polygon Modeling panel and choose Convert To Poly. This will keep the radial thickness and allow for component manipulations.

16. Click the Select Object tool ( )(Q) and switch to Vertex mode.

17. To make this simpler, in the main toolbar, click and hold down the Rectangular Selection Region tool; this will bring up a flyout, as shown in Figure 2.25.

18. Choose the Fence Selection Region.

19. Drag a custom selection from the end of the handle line past the seventh row of vertices, as shown in Figure 2.26.

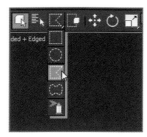

FIGURE 2.25 On the Selection Region flyout, choose the Fence Selection Region.

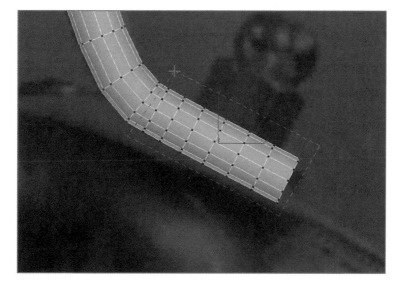

FIGURE 2.26 Use the Fence Selection Region to draw a selection around the desired vertices.

A 3D environment is defined in terms of 3D Cartesian coordinates. In 3ds Max, the main coordinate space is used to describe the scene as a whole and is known as the coordinate system. To scale the vertices correctly, you need to change the coordinate system. By default, 3ds Max uses the hybrid coordinate system View. In the View coordinate system, all orthographic views use the Screen coordinate system, while perspective views use the World coordinate system. That is all fine and good, but it won't work for vertex selection. To allow for the proper gizmo orientation for the scale, you will change the coordinate system to Local, which defines the coordinates of the object or sub-objects local center.

20. Select the Select And Scale tool (R).

In the main toolbar, to the right of the Scale tool is the Reference Coordinate System drop-down menu.

21. Click the arrow and choose Local from the list.

22. Move your cursor over the Y-axis of the Scale gizmo. Scale the vertices down until they match the image.

23. Continue selecting and scaling vertices until they match the image. Use the Select And Move tool if necessary.

24. Repeat the same process on the left side of the handle, as shown in Figure 2.27. When finished, name the object **Handle**.

FIGURE 2.27 The finished handle

25. Time to save the file, but this time choose Save As and name the file `Clock_Handle_End.max`.

One Lathe to Make a Whole

Now that the body of the clock and the handle are done, it's time to do the bells. You will use splines and a few surface creation tools new to your workflow. You are going to create a profile of the bell and then rotate the profile around its axis to form a surface. This technique is known as *lathe*, not to be mistaken for *latte*, which is a whole different deal and not covered in this book.

Open `Clock_Bell_Start.max` from the `Scenes` folder of the Clock project on the companion web page. You are going to create a cross section of the bell. To build the bell, follow these steps:

1. Select Create ➤ Shapes ➤ Line.

   Figure 2.28 shows the cross section with the vertices numbered according to their creation order.

FIGURE 2.28 The bell's profile line with the vertices numbered according to their creation order

2. Starting at the bottom-right side of the bell image, click and let go of the mouse.

   This will create the first vertex as a corner (1).

3. Now move the mouse up where the bell curves and drag out a tangent to create a Bezier vertex (2).

4. Continue the drag until the line's curve follows the bell image.

5. Again, move the mouse to the left and to the middle of the bell, and click to create a corner vertex (3).

6. Right-click to release to end the Line tool. The profile should match Figure 2.28.

7. On the Modify panel, choose Lathe from the Modifier List, as shown in Figure 2.29.

    When the lathe is added, the profile gets revolved 360 degrees around the center of the line. The bell doesn't look so good. That is because the center of the lathe is in the wrong place.

FIGURE 2.29 Choose the lathe modifier from the Modifier List.

8. To reposition the center of the Lathe, open the Lathe Parameters rollout and in the Align area, click Min.

    This should change the lathe to look more like a bell, as shown in Figure 2.30.

9. To finish the bell, create a cylinder to represent its base post. Then create another cylinder to represent a bolt above the bell and a sphere for the ball at the top, as shown in Figure 2.31 and Figure 2.32.

FIGURE 2.30   The bell with the lathe center in
the correct place

Sphere

Cylinder

Cylinder

FIGURE 2.31   The image of the bell showing the three pieces
to be created

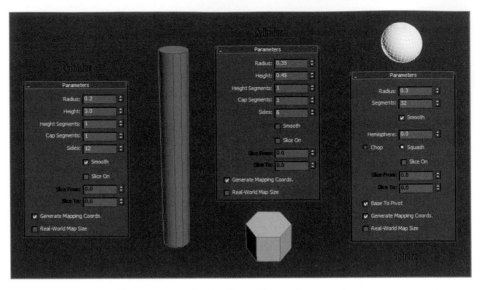

FIGURE 2.32   The parameters for the three objects to be created

Now that all the separate pieces are created, it's time to put them together.

10. Using the Move and Rotate tools, reference Figure 2.31 for placement of objects. Leave a gap where the handle goes.

11. Then select all the separate pieces, including the Bell object.
    It needs to be oriented so it fits on the clock body, which means it needs to be rotated as a whole.

12. From the Main Toolbar, select the Edit menu ➢ Group ➢ Group, as shown in Figure 2.33, and then name the group Bell.

— Group

FIGURE 2.33
Select the Group icon, and then name the group Bell.

This will allow you to orient the Bell group object to fit with the other clock objects. We are moving on, but don't worry, we will get back to the bell later in the chapter.

13. Save the file as Clock_Bell_End.max and use it for the next section.

Introducing the Dynamic Duo: Extrude & Bevel

The next step in the process is to make the clock face by creating the hour hand, the minute hand, and the second hand. This could be done by creating an image of a clock face in a graphics program like Photoshop and then applying that image as a surface onto the 3D Clock object. For this exercise, you will be creating the clock face elements, the numbers and hands, as 3D objects. This will be achieved using another set of modifiers, Extrude and Bevel. The Extrude modifier adds depth to a shape—that's it. It's simple and incredibly useful. The Bevel modifier also adds depth to a shape but allows you to add a round bevel to the edges.

Load `Clock_Face_Start.max` from the `Scenes` folder of the Clock project on the companion web page.

Creating the Clock Numbers

To create the clock numbers, follow these steps:

1. Start in the Create panel ➢ Shapes ➢ Text. Before you create the text shape, set up the text parameters.

2. Select the typeface down arrow next to the font name in the Parameters rollout.

3. Choose Times New Roman. If you do not have that typeface, just choose whichever you desire.

4. Change Size to 1.45.

5. In the Text Type-In box, type 12.
   All parameters should match Figure 2.34.

FIGURE 2.34 Text shape parameters

6. Move the mouse into the viewport over the number 12 on the image of the clock face, and then click.

7. Now open the Modify panel, and in the Modifier List, click Bevel.

8. In the Bevel Values rollout, change Level 1: Height to **0.01** and Outline to **0.01**. This will extrude the 12 shape and taper the mesh wider at the top.

9. Check the box next to Level 2 and change Height to **0.01**; leave Outline at **0.0**.

10. Check the box next to Level 3 and change Height to **0.01**; set the Outline at **-0.01**.

11. Match all bevel levels to Figure 2.35.

FIGURE 2.35 Bevel Values rollout showing all of the shape parameters for the number 12

12. Now in the Parameters rollout in the Surface group, select Curved Sides.

13. Change Segments to 2, and check the box next to Smooth Across Levels, as shown in Figure 2.36. This will give the 12 rounded smooth sides.

14. At the top of the Modify panel, change the name to 12, click the color swatch next to the Name (text field) type in and choose black.

15. To create the remaining numbers, select Create ➢ Shapes ➢ Text and place the cursor over the number 1.

Because you set up the parameters for the number 12, the text shape will repeat the same parameters for the number 1.

▶

FIGURE 2.36
Parameters for the bevel

16. Add the Bevel modifier; the same parameters you used for the number 12 will be repeated. This makes it easy to finish off the rest of the clock numbers.

17. Repeat steps 15 and 16. Then name each new number, and change the color to black.

18. Select all the numbers by holding Ctrl and clicking on each.

19. Then choose Group from the Edit menu and select Group as you did with the Bell object.

20. Name the group **Numbers**.

Creating Clock Hands

Follow these steps to create the clock hands:

1. Select the Create panel ➢ Shapes ➢ Rectangle. Create a rectangle over the minute-hand image.

2. Back in the Create panel, uncheck the box next to Start New Shape. This will allow you to create a second piece that is connected to the rectangle.

3. Select Circle and create a circle over the circle base of the minute hand.

4. Open the Modify panel, and in the modifier stack, in the Selection rollout, select Vertex mode (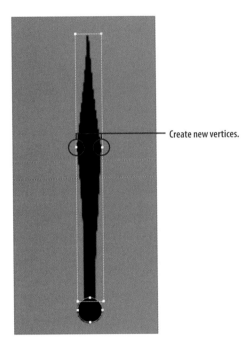).

   In the Modify Stack, you will see the rectangle and circle objects have combined into an editable spline—a 2D object that provides controls for manipulating an object's three sub-object levels: vertex, segment, and spline.

5. In the Geometry rollout, select Refine and click on each side of the rectangle in the middle, as shown in Figure 2.37.

Create new vertices.

FIGURE 2.37 Use Refine to add two vertices to the right and left sides of the rectangle.

6. Select and move the vertices to match the minute-hand image.

7. Select and move the vertices on the top of the rectangle so they come to a point. Move the vertices on the bottom so they match the image of the minute hand in the viewport.

8. Go to the Modify panel, and from the Modifier List, add the Extrude modifier.

9. Change Amount to **0.025**.

10. Change the Name to **Minute hand** and the color to black.

11. Repeat the same steps (1–10) on the hour hand. The second hand is even easier; just create a rectangle, make sure Start New Shape is still unchecked, and then create another rectangle. It doesn't matter which one you create because the final results will be the same.

12. Select and move each clock hand into the position you see on the clock image (Figure 2.38).

    Of course, you don't have to position the hands exactly as they are shown in the image.

FIGURE 2.38 The clock hands positioned to match the clock face

13. When you are finished positioning the hands, save the file as Clock_Face_End.max.

Bringing It All Together

Most of the pieces are created for the clock. Now you just have to put it all together. Each piece was created in its own 3ds Max file. To bring them all together, you will use Merge. Merge allows you to bring into one scene different 3ds Max files. You can also just build all the parts to your model in a single 3ds Max file; we will look at that technique in later chapters. Follow these steps to merge all the parts:

1. To begin, click the Application button and choose Reset. This will clear any data from previous work and reset the 3ds Max settings.

2. Click the Application button, choose Import, and click Merge, as shown in Figure 2.39.

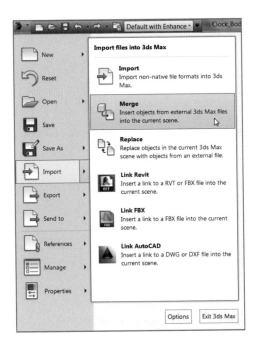

FIGURE 2.39   Merge is found in the Application menu under Import.

3. Navigate to the Scenes folder of the Clock project, and select Clock_ Body_End.max.

4. From the list in the Merge dialog box, choose the Clock Body object and click OK to close the dialog box.

In the new scene, the clock body will appear, located in the same spot as it was in the other 3ds Max file.

5. Repeat the same steps for the handle, face, and bell scenes.

6. Select the Bell group object, and from the Edit menu, choose Duplicate ➢ Clone.

This opens a Clone Options dialog box with clone options that are explained in more detail in the sidebar "The Clone Dialog Box." We prefer to use the Shift+Transform technique. This is when you use Shift+Move/Rotate/Scale to create a clone of the object. Hold Shift and move the Bell group object to the desired location. When you let go of the mouse, the Clone Options dialog box appears.

7. Select Ok to close the Clone dialog box, choose the Select And Move tool (W), and move the Bell object to the other side of the clock body.

8. Move and rotate the Bell group so it is positioned correctly on the clock body.

9. Continue with merging the Clock object into the scene. You will also need to merge the handle and clock face into the scene.

THE CLONE DIALOG BOX

Making a *copy* creates a completely separate clone from the original. An *instance* is a copy, but it is still connected to the original. If you edit the original or an instance, all of the instances change (including the original). A *reference* is dependent on the original, and the connection goes only one way; change the original, and the reference will change, but change the reference, and only it will be affected, depending on its location in the modifier stack. The changes are for modifiers and not for transforms.

Still something missing? Well, this is where we leave you. With 90 percent done, it's time to use the many tools you learned about in this chapter to finish the clock. All you have left to create are the clock feet and the bell hammer. Take a look at Figure 2.40, which is a jazzed-up version of the clock. By the time you finish this book, you will be able to create a clock exactly like the one in Figure 2.40.

FIGURE 2.40   The clock finished so far

THE ESSENTIALS AND BEYOND

In this chapter, you learned how to model with 3ds Max software. By exploring the modeling toolsets and creating a retro-style alarm clock, you saw firsthand how some of the basic 3ds Max modeling tools operate.

You learned how to create a primitive cylinder, and from that you learned to use editable polygons and the Graphite Modeling Tools set and how to use shapes, editable splines, and the Lathe, Extrude, and Bevel tools.

Additional Exercises

▶ Open the Clock_Final.max file, select the Bell group, and from the Edit menu, choose Group and click Open. Select the bolt that is holding the handle, which was made from a simple cylinder, and then select the vertical edges and chamfer them to make the sharp corners softer.

▶ Create the feet; there are many approaches you could take. One idea is to use the lathe techniques. Another is to create a cylinder and using the Graphite Modeling Tools set to add details to the feet.

▶ Use techniques learned in chapter to create the hammer for the bell.

▶ Find another object to create, something with multiple pieces. You might create another type of clock, or even a robot. Remember to use a reference image.

CHAPTER 3

Modeling in 3ds Max: Architectural Model Part I

Building models in 3D is as simple as building them out of clay, wood, stone, or metal. Using Autodesk® 3ds Max® software to model something may not be as tactile as physically building it, but the same concept applies: You have to identify how the model is shaped and figure out how to break it down into manageable parts that you can piece together into the final form.

Instead of using traditional tools to hammer or chisel or weld a shape into form, you will use the vertices of the geometry to shape the computer-generated (CG) model. As you have seen, the 3ds Max polygon toolset is quite robust.

In this chapter, you will explore the many 3ds Max architectural modeling tools by building components such as walls, doors, and windows. These objects are called *Architecture Engineering and Construction (AEC)* tools, and they are parametric to give them an advantage over imported geometry from CAD programs. There are many ways you can build an interior space—simply put, a couple of boxes and you're done—but to really create a refined and realistic interior, you will need to take time to add details.

This chapter includes the following topics:

▶ **Units setup**

▶ **Importing a CAD drawing**

▶ **Creating the walls**

▶ **Creating the doors**

▶ **Creating the windows**

▶ **Creating a floor and ceiling**

Units Setup

When you open the 3ds Max program, a system of measurement is set up to measure geometry in your scene. By default your file is set to Generic Units, where one unit is defined as 1.000 inch.

You can change the generic units to equal any system of measurement you prefer; you can use standard English units (feet and inches) or metric units. You should choose your units of measure before you begin creating your scene, not during the modeling process.

You can do so with the following steps:

1. Go to the Customize menu and choose Customization and then Units Setup, as shown in Figure 3.1.

2. Change the units from the default Generic Units to US Standard.

3. From the US Standard drop-down menu, choose Feet w/Decimal Inches, as shown in Figure 3.2.

FIGURE 3.1 Accessing the Units Setup options

FIGURE 3.2 From the US Standard drop-down menu, choose Feet w/Decimal Inches.

Importing a CAD Drawing

Using reference materials will help you efficiently create your 3D model and achieve a good likeness in your end result. The temptation to just wing it and start building the objects is strong, especially when time is short and you're raring to go. This temptation should always be suppressed in deference to a well-thought-out approach to the task. Sketches, photographs, and drawings can all be used as resources for the modeling process. Not only are references useful for giving you a clear direction in which to head, you can also use them directly in the 3ds Max software to help you model. Photos, especially those taken from different sides of the intended model, can be added to a scene as background images to help you shape your model.

For this chapter, you will be using an AutoCAD drawing as the reference and as a template to build the walls, doors, and windows. You will be supplied with a CAD drawing that will make it much easier to follow the reference.

Figure 3.3 shows the room that you will create in this chapter. There are a few changes from the original room. The opening that leads to the hallway is going to become a door. We will add a decorative element like a fancy baseboard.

FIGURE 3.3 Images of the room to be created

In the future, if you don't have a drawing using detailed measurements of a room, you can create your own layout or blueprints because proper measurements and scale are vital when creating a convincing interior space.

Here's how to import the AutoCAD drawing:

1. Select Application button (▶) ➢ Manage ➢ Set Project Folder and choose the ArchModel project, downloaded from the book's web page at www.sybex.com/go/3dsmax2014essentials.

2. Again, select the Application button and choose Import ➢ Import. Because you have already set your project to the ArchModel project, you will be taken straight to the *import* folder for that project.

3. Select the Room.dwg file. This is an AutoCAD drawing file that contains no 3D objects; it contains a drawing using 2D lines.

The AutoCAD DWG/DXF Import Options dialog box will open (Figure 3.4).

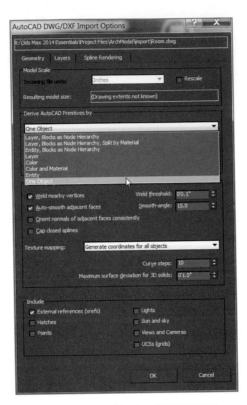

FIGURE 3.4   The AutoCAD DWG/DXF
Import Options dialog box

4. In the Derive AutoCAD Primitives By drop-down menu, choose One Object and then click OK.

   The viewport should show a 2D collection of lines making up the layout of a room. The drawing shown in Figure 3.5 has three basic parts: the walls, the window, and the doors. The figure has some colors associated with those three parts. These colors will not be reflected in the imported drawing.

5. Select the imported AutoCAD drawing, and then choose the Select And Move tool in the Main toolbar.

   At the bottom of the interface are the Transform Type-Ins and three type-in boxes with X, Y, and Z.

This is a CAD drawing of the living room and dining room of a typical house, which was created for this book by Nastasia Jorgenson, an interior design student from the Art Institute of California – Los Angeles.

Sliding Door   Door   Wall   Window

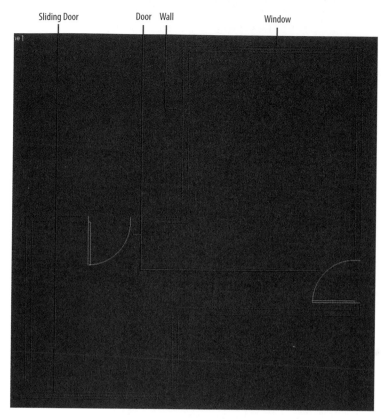

FIGURE 3.5 An AutoCAD drawing showing walls, doors, and window

6. Change the X, Y, and Z values in the type-in boxes to X: 0′0.0″, Y: 0′0.0″, and Z: 0′0.0″. This will center the AutoCAD drawing of the floor plan to the center of the environment.

7. In the command panel, go to the Create panel, and in the Name And Color rollout, rename the AutoCAD drawing **Floorplan**.

Creating the Walls

The Wall objects you will create are a part of the AEC Extended objects and are designed for use in the architectural, engineering, and construction fields. To perform this exercise, you can use your last file from the ArchModel exercise, or you can load `ArchModel_00.max` from the `Scenes` folder of the

By default the command panel is also hidden. To view the command panel, go to the Customize menu ➢ Show UI ➢ and choose Show Command Panel.

ArchModel project on the book's companion web page at www.sybex.com/go/3dsmax2014essentials. To begin, follow these steps:

1. Select and maximize the Top viewport (Alt+W).

2. In the main toolbar, click and hold the Snaps Toggle button, and from the tool flyout, choose the 2D Snaps Toggle button ().

3. Right-click the Snaps Toggle button to bring up the Grid and Snap Settings dialog box.

4. Uncheck Grid Points and check Vertex, as shown in Figure 3.6.

5. Close the dialog box.

   This will make it possible to snap from the vertices in the AutoCAD drawing.

FIGURE 3.6 The Grid and Snap Settings dialog box

6. Go to the Create panel and from the Create Panel drop-down menu, choose AEC Extended and click the Wall button.

7. You should see the wall parameters:

   a. Set Width to 0'5.0" unless it is already set to this value. This will define the thickness of the wall.

   b. Set Height to 8'0.0" unless it is already set to this value. This will define the height of the wall.

   c. Change Justification to Left, as shown in Figure 3.7.

FIGURE 3.7
The Parameters rollout
for the Wall object

8. In the Top viewport, click and release on an outside corner of the
AutoCAD drawing, then move in a clockwise direction to a connected
corner, and click to set the position of that corner.

This will create a wall 0′5.0″ thick and 8′0.0″ tall between the two
corners you clicked.

9. Continue around the room, clicking on the outside wall corners,
making sure you snap to the vertex of the lines at each corner.

Disregard the doors and windows in the drawing and put your
walls right over them.

10. When you have made it all the way around the room, click on the
corner where you started.

11. A Spline pop-up warning will ask, "Close spline?" Click Yes and right-
click to release the wall primitive.

12. Use Alt+W to return to the four-viewport layout and look at the walls
in the Perspective viewport.

The finished wall is shown in Figure 3.8.

13. With the wall selected, go to the Modify panel and look at the parameters.

14. In the modifier stack, click the black box with the plus sign.

The wall has three components: Vertex, Segment, and Profile. You
can edit a wall primitive in a way that's similar to how you edit splines.

15. To edit the walls—say, to straighten out a wall or extend a wall to
make a space bigger—select the Vertex component in the Modify
panel.

If you mistakenly
click, you can select
Backspace, which will
undo the last click.

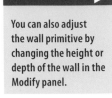

You can also adjust the wall primitive by changing the height or depth of the wall in the Modify panel.

16. At the corners of the room, you should see small plus signs. Select one of the vertices and move it to adjust the wall section it is connected to.

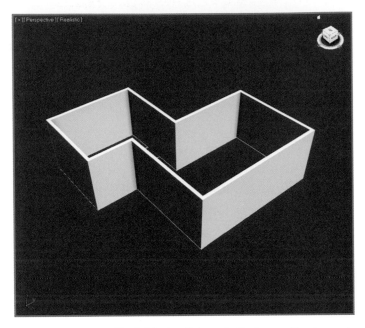

FIGURE 3.8 The finished wall shown in the Perspective viewport

17. Click the Segment component, and then click on a wall in your scene.

18. You can use the Parameters section at the bottom of the rollout to change the settings for the wall, as shown in Figure 3.9.

FIGURE 3.9
Wall parameters

Now that the walls are laid out, we'll move on to the doors.

Creating the Doors

The 3ds Max Door objects that are available allow you to control the look of the door—not just the size, but the frame and glass inserts as well. They also let you determine whether the door is open or closed. The types of door are

Pivot (which is the most common), BiFold, and Sliding. To perform this exercise, you can use your last file from the ArchModel exercise, or you can load `ArchModel_01.max` from the `Scenes` folder of the ArchModel project on the book's companion web page at www.sybex.com/go/3dsmax2014essentials.

1. Select the walls if they aren't already selected.

   The walls will appear slightly transparent with a gray cast, but you will be able to see the AutoCAD drawing underneath.

2. Go to the Create panel. From the drop-down menu, choose Doors. Choose Pivot under Object Type.

3. Return to the four views (Alt+W). Make sure the Top viewport is active and zoom in on the door in the horizontal wall on the left in the AutoCAD drawing.

4. The 2D Snaps Toggle button should still be active. If it's not active, go to the main toolbar and click the 2D Snaps Toggle button, or use the keyboard shortcut (S).

5. Starting at the left of the door opening on the outside of the wall, click and drag to the right side of the opening in the AutoCAD drawing underneath, until it snaps. Then move the cursor and click on the opposite side of the wall to set the door thickness.

6. After that, move the cursor toward the top of the viewport to adjust the door height.

   You won't be able to see the adjustment in the Top viewport, so you should look in another viewport as you drag to set the height.

7. Click again to set any height. Don't try to get the exact height; you will set the correct height in the next step.

8. Go to the Modify panel and enter the correct height parameter for the door: 6′8.0″. Check Flip Hinge, as shown in Figure 3.10. Flip Hinge sets on which edge the door swings.

   When door primitives are created using snaps, you can insert a door in a Wall object, automatically linking the two and creating a cutout for the door. This doesn't always work; many factors can affect the outcome. If the door fails to create the cutout, you can move on to the next step. If it does create the cutout, skip step 9.

9. In the main toolbar, click the Select and Link tool (🔗) and click and drag from the door to the wall, as shown in Figure 3.11. This will make a doorway opening in the wall.

FIGURE 3.10
The Door object parameters

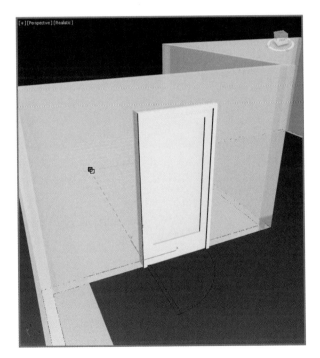

FIGURE 3.11 Use the Select and Link tool to create
an opening in the wall for the door.

The next type of door to be added is the sliding glass door, as shown
in Figure 3.3 (middle image).

10. In the Top viewport, zoom into the sliding door in the AutoCAD
drawing.

11. In the Create panel, choose Sliding under Object Type.

12. Start by clicking and dragging from the right outside of the door to the left outside of the door, making sure to snap to the vertices where the door lines meet the wall lines. This will establish the width of the sliding door.

13. Then move your cursor to the inside of the door and click when your cursor snaps to the vertex.

14. Next, drag the cursor to set any height, and click to finish.

15. Don't worry if you can't get the height correct; just type 6′8.0″ in the Height type-in field, as you did for the first door.

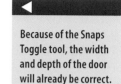

Because of the Snaps Toggle tool, the width and depth of the door will already be correct.

16. Switch to the Perspective viewport and check to see if the sliding door looks correct.

The automatic linking should create a cutout for the door. If it failed to work, move on to the next step. If it does create the cutout, skip to step 18.

17. Use the Select and Link tool ( ) and click and drag from the door to the wall to create the opening in the wall.

The finished sliding door is shown in Figure 3.12.

18. Add the remaining door using the previous steps.

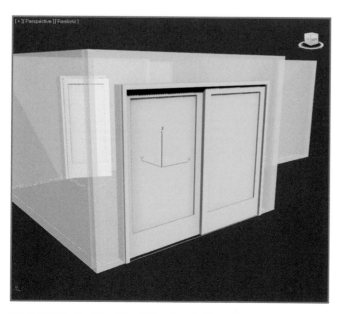

FIGURE 3.12   The sliding door in the wall

This is a good time to save your file. You will create the window in the room in the next exercise.

Creating the Window

AEC Window objects work in a way that is similar to the way the Wall and Door objects work. There are six window types: Awning, Fixed, Projected, Casement, Pivoted, and Sliding. You will be using the Fixed window for this section. You can use your last file from the ArchModel exercise, or you can load ArchModel_02.max from the Scenes folder of the ArchModel project on the companion web page to continue.

1. Go to the Create panel, and from the drop-down menu, choose Windows. Choose Fixed under Object Type.

2. In the main toolbar, click and hold the Snaps button. This will bring up the Snaps flyout. Choose the 2 Snaps button.

3. Create the Window object as you did the Door objects: Use the snaps to click/drag from left to right, following along the drawing; then drag to create the depth and then the height.

4. In the Modify panel, go to the Fixed Window parameters and change Height to 6′0.0″.
   If the automatic linking failed to work, move on to the next step. If it does create the cutout, skip to step 6.

5. Use the Select and Link tool and click from the window to the wall to create the opening in the wall, just as with the doors.

6. Press S to turn off Snaps.

7. Switch to a Perspective viewport so you can see the newly created window; then select and move the window up so it is centered on the wall, as shown in Figure 3.13.

8. Select the wall and press Alt+X to turn off See-Through mode.

The model to this point is shown in Figure 3.14.

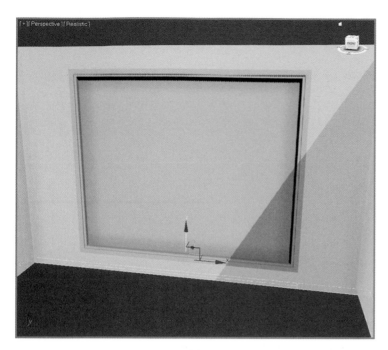

FIGURE 3.13 The window is centered on the wall.

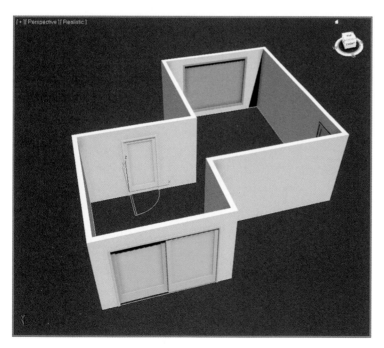

FIGURE 3.14 Walls with doors and a window

Adding a Floor and Ceiling

You can use your last file from the ArchModel exercise, or you can load `ArchModel_03` `.max` from the `Scenes` folder of the ArchModel project on the companion web page. What's a room without a floor and ceiling? Not any room we want to walk into. To create the floor and ceiling for your room, you will use the Line tool to create a shape:

1. Go to the Create panel and click the Shapes button (); then click the Line tool, as shown in Figure 3.15.

FIGURE 3.15
Select the Line tool.

2. Press S on your keyboard to turn on the Snaps Toggle tool.
The Snap tool should still be set to the 2D Snaps Toggle button. Keep it that way. This will ensure that the line stays at the ground plane of the scene.

3. In the Top viewport, click on the outside corner of the room, then click the other corners around the room in a clockwise direction, and then click again on the corner where you started.

4. The Spline dialog box will appear. Click Yes.
This closes the line to form a closed shape.

5. Choose the Select Object tool (Q), and select the line you just created, if it is not already selected.

6. Go to the Modify panel (<!-- icon -->), and from the Modifier List drop-down menu, choose Extrude, as shown in Figure 3.16.

7. Now look at the Extrude parameters, and change the Amount value to 0'0.1". You just need a small amount of thickness to give to the floor's shape.

FIGURE 3.16
From the Modifier List
drop-down menu, choose
Extrude.

8. Switch to the Front viewport and move the new Floor object down so the top of the floor lines up with the bottom of the walls.

9. Name the new object **Floor**.

   To create the ceiling, you are going to make a clone of the floor.

10. Select the floor, and while holding the Shift key, move the Floor object up toward the top of the wall.

11. Let go of the mouse; a Clone Options dialog box will appear, as shown in Figure 3.17.

FIGURE 3.17   The Clone
Options dialog box

12. Choose Copy from the Object section, rename the object **Ceiling**, and click OK.

   For now, you don't need to have the Ceiling object visible; you will be using it in a later chapter. You can hide the Ceiling object.

13. Center your cursor over the Ceiling object and right-click.

14. From the quad menu, select Hide Selection, as shown in Figure 3.18.

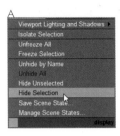

FIGURE 3.18
Use the right-click menu
to access the quad menu
and choose Hide Selection.

You can also choose
Unhide by Name to
bring up a dialog box
with which you can
choose a specific item
from a list to unhide.

When you are ready to have the ceiling back in your scene, you can right-click anywhere in your scene and select Unhide All.

Creating Baseboard Moldings

In architectural terminology, a *baseboard* is a board covering the area where the wall meets the floor. Baseboards are used to cover the gap between the wall and the floor as well as add a sense of style to a room. An example of the baseboard we will be creating is shown in Figure 3.19.

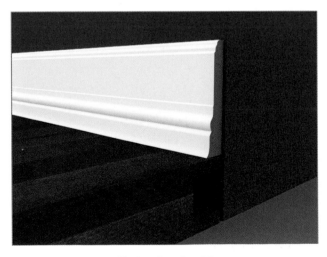

FIGURE 3.19   The baseboard molding

This room does not have a baseboard, so it would be a great way to add some pizzazz to the room. Also, feel free to modify the baseboard to meet your skill level with the Line tool.

You can use your last file from the ArchModel exercise, or you can load ArchModel_04.max from the Scenes folder of the ArchModel project on the book's companion web page at www.sybex.com/go/3dsmax2014essentials. To begin creating the baseboard, we will use a spline that has already been created, the floor:

1. In the Perspective viewport, select the Floor object.

2. Select and maximize the Top viewport (Alt+W), and in the Edit menu, choose Duplicate ➤ Clone.

3. In the Clone Options dialog box, choose Copy and change the name to **Baseboard Path**.

4. In the Modify panel, remove the Extrude modifier by right-clicking the modifier in the modifier stack and choosing Delete when the pop-up menu appears, as shown in figure 3.20.

FIGURE 3.20
Deleting the Extrude modifier
in the modifier stack

5. In the modifier stack, select the plus sign in the black box to expand the line to display the sub-object of the line, and select the sub-object of the line.

6. Select the baseboard line.
   It will turn red when selected. You may not be able to see it because the walls are on top of the line.

7. In the Geometry rollout, scroll down to Outline.

8. In the Outline Type-In, which is to the right of the Outline button, change the amount to –0′6.0″, as shown in Figure 3.21.

Outline clones the spline and offsets it on all sides as specified by the amount in the Outline Type-In.

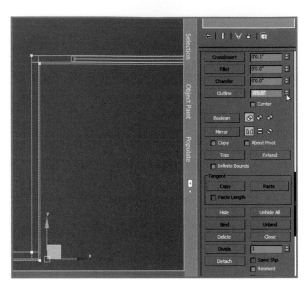

FIGURE 3.21   Change the Outline amount to –0′6.0″
to offset the spline.

9. Select the original spline and delete it. Click Line to exit Spline mode.
Because we are using the newly created spline for the baseboards,
we don't need the original line.

Now we'll create the shape of the molding, shown in Figure 3.22.

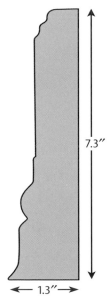

7.3″

← 1.3″ →

FIGURE 3.22
Profile of the
baseboard molding

10. Switch from the Top viewport to the Front viewport.

11. From the Application button, choose Import ➤ Merge. From the `Scenes` folder of the ArchModel project folder, choose the `Baseboard Image Plane.max` file.

12. Select the Baseboard Image Plane object. Click OK in the Merge dialog box.

    The image plane shows a cross section of the intended baseboard.

13. Enter Isolate Selection mode ( ) by selecting the icon at the bottom of the interface below the timeline. Switch to the Front viewport and change the viewport shading to Realistic (F3).

    This will hide everything in the scene except the image plane.

You can use the keyboard shortcut (F) to switch from the Top viewport to the Front viewport.

14. Go to Create ➤ Shapes ➤ Line, and at the top-right corner of the baseboard, click and release the left mouse button. This will create a corner point.

15. Move the mouse to the left, over where the baseboard begins to curve down, and click and drag to create a Bezier vertex.

    This is a vertex type that has handles, which allow for greater control over the curve in the lines segments.

16. Drag until the curve is following the curve of the baseboard.

17. Now continue around the baseboard cross section until you are back at the first vertex that was created. Click the first vertex and select Yes from the dialog box to close the spline.

18. Right-click to release from the Line tool.

19. To edit the line, go to the Modify panel and select Vertex mode. In Vertex mode, you can edit the path to match the image on the image plane.

    If you don't want to create your own baseboard, you can merge in one that is already created. Refer to step 11 and select the `Baseboard Path.max` file.

20. Select the baseboard path. Go to the Modify panel, and from the Modifier List, choose Sweep.

21. In the Section Type rollout, choose Use Custom Section, and in the Custom Section Types area, select Pick. Then select the baseboard path in the scene.

22. In the Sweep modifier, pick the baseboard shape to create the baseboard, as shown in Figure 3.23.

The Sweep modifier extrudes a cross section along a path, creating a 3D version of the baseboard cross section.

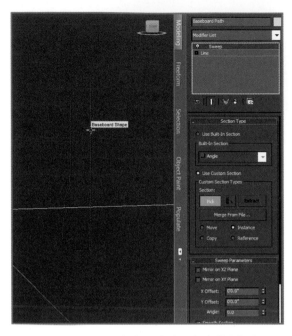

FIGURE 3.23   Picking the baseboard in the Sweep modifier

Some parameters need to be adjusted.

23. In the Sweep Parameters rollout, check the box next to Mirror on XZ Plane. This will flip the baseboard shape so it is facing in toward the room.

    The baseboard molding should run along the floor except at the door openings. Right now, the molding is going straight through, as shown in Figure 3.24. It isn't difficult to fix; just edit the path.

24. Switch to a Perspective viewport (Alt+W) to exit Maximize Viewport and then Ctrl+click the floor plan and the baseboard to select them both.

25. Enter Isolate Selection mode (Alt+Q), and then select just the baseboard.

26. Zoom in on the door on the right of the Top viewport.

27. Go to the Modify panel, and in the modifier stack, enter Vertex mode.

28. Go to the Geometry rollout and select the Refine button.

29. Move to the baseboard spline and click directly on the spline on both sides of the door to add new vertices. Right-click to exit Refine.

30. Switch to Segment mode; select the segment in between the two new vertices and delete it, as shown in Figure 3.25.

If the floor plan is hidden, unhide it by right-clicking in the viewport and choosing Unhide by Name from the Display quad menu. Choose the floor plan from the list and click OK to close the dialog box.

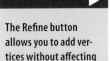

The Refine button allows you to add vertices without affecting the spline curve.

FIGURE 3.24   The baseboard molding is going through the door opening.

FIGURE 3.25   Use Refine to add two new vertices on either side of the door; then delete the segment.

31. Repeat the same process for the remaining pivot door and sliding door.

32. When you finish, select the Sweep modifier in the Modify Stack to exit edit mode in the Sweep modifier. Exit Isolate Selection mode. The finished results of the Sweep modifier are shown in Figure 3.26.

FIGURE 3.26   The baseboard with proper gaps at doors

THE ESSENTIALS AND BEYOND

In this chapter, you learned how to use some of the 3ds Max architectural tools. You started by importing an AutoCAD drawing and using it to create the walls, doors, and window of a room.

ADDITIONAL EXERCISES

▶ Try importing different AutoCAD drawings and creating your own space. You can find free AutoCAD drawing on many websites.

▶ Try adding trim around the doors and windows.

▶ Try creating a different profile for the molding. Go to websites that show molding profiles or just make up your own.

▶ Use some of the other AEC primitives; add a different type of window or door.

▶ The Sweep modifier can be used to create items like picture frames, using the same technique used to create the moldings. Try creating different styles of picture frames for your space.

CHAPTER 4

Modeling in 3ds Max: Architectural Model Part II

In this chapter, you will continue working with the interior space from the previous chapter by modeling and adding some furniture—specifically, a couch and chair.

This chapter includes the following topics:

▶ **Modeling the couch**

▶ **Modeling the lounge chair**

Modeling the Couch

For this book we are using the Enhanced Menu workspace to switch to the Quick Access toolbar. It is located at the top of the interface, and in the Workspaces drop-down list, choose the Enhanced Menus workspace. For more information refer to the beginning of Chapter 1.

When you are starting a modeling project, make sure you have plenty of measurements, as shown in Figure 4.1, the photo of the couch you'll model in this chapter. Always remember: reference, reference, reference. Modeling this couch is a very straightforward process. If you break it down into separate components, it is just 16 different-sized boxes. The boxes are soft and cushy; they have various details, but nonetheless they are still just boxes. With the exception of the lounge end of the couch, the top cushion is the only piece on the couch that isn't a box shape.

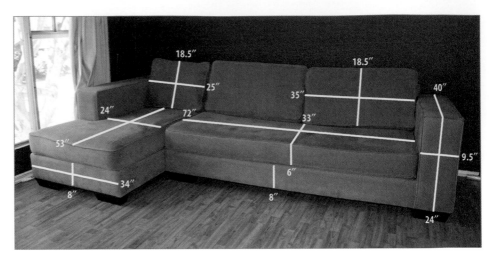

FIGURE 4.1   Couch with measurements

Blocking Out the Couch Model

Blocking out the model means creating a simpler version of the model starting
with whatever primitives fit the bill—in this case, boxes. Using the measurements shown in Figure 4.1, you will create a series of boxes and then orient
them to mimic the couch. The first piece you'll create is the bottom (the part
between the seat cushions and the feet). It is 8 inches high by 72 inches wide by
33 inches deep. In the previous chapter, you used standard units of measurement (feet and inches); but for this chapter, you will use the default generic
units. If your units are still set to feet and inches, refer to the section "Units
Setup" in Chapter 3, "Modeling in 3ds Max: Architectural Model Part I" to
review how to change the setting to generic units. Then follow these steps:

1. Open a new file in Autodesk® 3ds Max® software, and select the
   Perspective viewport. Then go to the command panel and choose
   Create ➢ Geometry and click Box.

2. In the Keyboard Entry rollout, enter 33 for Length, 72 for Width, and
   8 for Height, but don't change the XYZ Type-In boxes.

3. Click the Create button.

4. The box should be in the center of the scene. Rename the box **Seat Base**.

5. Next, create the cushion above this box: Select the box with the Move
   tool, and then hold Shift and move the box up in the Z-axis to create
   a new box so that it is on top of the old box.

This is a quick method you can use to clone an object. The Clone Options dialog box will appear (Figure 4.2).

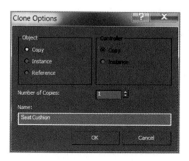

FIGURE 4.2 In the Clone Options dialog box, select Copy and click OK.

6. In the Clone Options dialog, select Copy. Change the name from Box to **Seat Cushion** and click OK.

7. Go to the Modify panel and change the height of the new cushion box to **6.0**.

8. As in step 1, create another box, but change the parameters to **40** for Length, **9.5** for Width, and **24** for Height. Rename the box **Side Armrest**.

9. Move the box so it sits on the right side of the two stacked boxes.

10. Create a clone for the left side of the couch using the same Shift and Move technique you used in steps 5 and 6.

    Now for the back piece: this is the part the back cushions sit on. You don't see it in the picture in Figure 4.1, but it is there.

11. Create a box with Length set to **6**, Width set to **96**, and Height set to **27**. Move it behind the seat-cushion boxes to form the backrest, as shown in Figure 4.3 (left).

◄

Don't worry if the boxes don't fit together like a puzzle; just get them close.

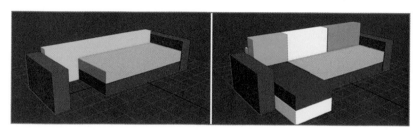

FIGURE 4.3 The first few pieces to start the couch (left); the blocked-out couch (right)

Creating the chaise part of the couch is a bit more challenging. You'll create a box now, and later you can alter it with the wing on the side.

12. Select the Perspective viewport. Choose the Create Panel ➤ Geometry and select Box, and in the Keyboard Entry rollout, input 53 for Length, 24 for Width, and 8 for Height. Click the Create button.

13. Move the new box to the left of the seat cushions: Hold Shift and move the new box up so it is sitting on the old box. Choose Copy from the dialog box, and then change the box's height to 6.0 inches.

14. Create another box with the following measurements: Length = 8, Width = 35, and Height = 18.5. Click the Create button to create a box for the back pillows.

15. Move the box so that it is sitting on the top of the seat cushions and against the right armrest.

16. Make a clone of this box and move it to the left, so it is next to the other pillow.

17. Make one more clone, and move it to the left so it sits on top of the chaise seat cushions. This box is too big. With the box selected, go to the Modify panel and change Width to 24.0.

   The completed blocked-out couch is shown in Figure 4.3 (right). This process is getting a bit tedious, but you still need to create the backrest cushions.

18. Create three backrest cushions (two the same size and one that is smaller). As you are creating the couch pieces, name them. Use descriptive names to help you keep the project organized. Refer to Figure 4.1 for the measurements.

19. Once the cushions are created, move them into place on the couch to finish blocking out the couch, as shown in Figure 4.3 (right).

20. Once you begin adding more detail to the couch pieces, make some adjustments to them by resizing and repositioning them.

Using NURMS to Add Softness

Non-Uniform Rational Mesh Smooth (NURMS) is a subdivision surface technique that allows you to take a low-poly model and smooth the surface into a high-poly model. This isn't a lighting trick; you are actually changing the geometry of the model. When you apply NURMS to your model, you will see a control cage in the shape of the low-poly model; this is the mesh you actually model.

Subdivision increases the poly count of your model; every level of subdivision increases the number of polygons by a factor of four. At a subdivision level (or iteration) of 1, 1 polygon in the control cage will become 4 polygons in the subdivided model. At an iteration level of 2, that 1 polygon becomes 16 polygons, and so on. When you're working on a model with NURMS, it is best to work with a lower iteration level and then render with a higher level of iterations.

Polygons are flat between the vertices, but when NURMS is turned on, a flat polygon starts to curve and smooth out as it subdivides. When you use NURMS smoothing, the more distance there is between the edges on a mesh, the smoother the result will be. When you want sharp corners, just place the edges close together. When you turning on NURMS, those close edges will retain their sharpness better. If you want a smoother, more rounded surface, then place the edges farther apart.

The best way to model with smooth surfaces is to use quad polygons in a grid formation; two edges will cross each vertex—and because each edge flows from vertex to vertex uninterrupted, the edges will continue and the 3D form will be smoothed predictably. If you have a vertex with no more than four edges coming out of it, the splines will end and the mesh may not smooth the way you expect it to.

All of the couch cushions will receive the same treatment, so let's go over the next technique using only the side armrest of the couch and the chaise lounge section. After you're finished with that, you can practice the techniques on the remaining couch boxes yourself. Continue with the project from the previous exercise or open the Couch_01.max file from the Scenes folder of the ArchModel project on the companion web page at www.sybex.com/go/3dsmax2014essentials. Then follow these steps:

Be cautious: Poly counts rise very quickly and an iteration count needlessly high can slow you down.

If you want to fully understand how edges flow and end across a 3D surface as a result of subdivision leads, spend some time studying topology, which is key to creating good 3D models that subdivide well when animated.

1. Select the Right Armrest object. Click the Isolate Selection Toggle button ( ).
   This turns off the view of the other objects in the scene to allow you to focus on this one piece.

2. In the Perspective viewport, set the rendering type to Edge Faces (F4).

3. In the Graphite Modeling Tools tab, select Polygon Modeling ➤ Convert To Poly.

4. Then choose the Edit tab and click Use NURMS ( ).

You will see a box that looks like the air was let out of it, as shown in Figure 4.4.

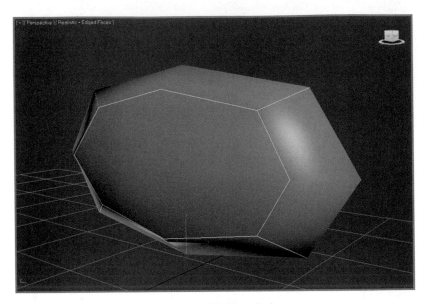

FIGURE 4.4   Couch armrest with NURMS applied

If you refer to the picture of the couch from Figure 4.1, you'll see that the arm is much more structured and closer to the shape of a box than this deflated balloon. You still need to sharpen the corners by adding more edges to the base model.

5. Back in the modeling ribbon, select the Edit panel and click the Use NURMS button again to turn it off.

6. In the Edit tab, click the SwiftLoop tool ( ) and hover your cursor over the box to reveal a loop of edges on the box.

7. Place one of the lines shown in Figure 4.5 by clicking where you want the loop to be added on the box, and then place the other three loops shown in Figure 4.5.

8. Turn on Use NURMS again to see the difference after using the SwiftLoop tool. Then turn Use NURMS off again to prepare for the next section.

If you refer to the picture in Figure 4.1, you can see that the couch arm is even more squared off than the current mesh. In the next section, you will learn how to add more detail.

> ▶
>
> **Editing the box is easier at this stage while it is still in box form.**

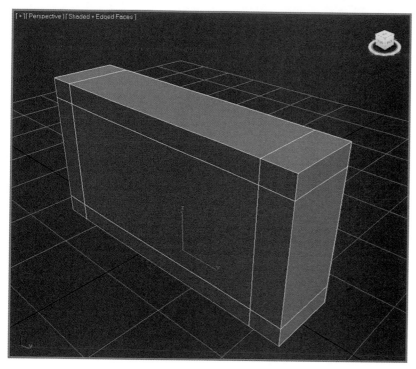

FIGURE 4.5   Use the SwiftLoop tool to add edge loops to the box.

Adding Details to the Couch

The next step in the process of creating the couch is to add the piping, which is the round decorative trim along the seam of the pillows, as shown in Figure 4.6.

FIGURE 4.6   Decorative piping runs along the seams of the couch.

1. In the modeling ribbon, select Polygon Modeling and click the Edge mode button; then select the edges on the box that are identified in Figure 4.7.

Select these edges on both sides of the box.

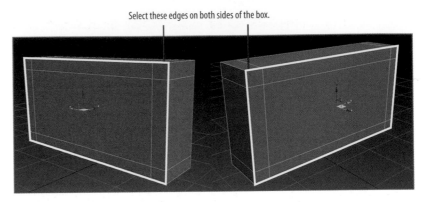

FIGURE 4.7   **Select the highlighted edges.**

2. Go to the Edges tab, and open the Chamfer Settings caddy. Change Edge Chamfer Amount to **0.15** and click OK.

3. Switch to Polygon mode and select the polygons that were created with the Chamfer.

4. In the Graphite Modeling Tools tab, go to the Polygons panel and open the Extrude caddy.

5. Change the Extrusion type to Local Normal, as shown in Figure 4.8.

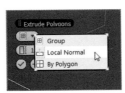

FIGURE 4.8
Set the Extrusion Type
to Local Normal.

6. Set the Height to –0.2 and click the Apply and Continue button (⊕). This will keep the caddy open and allow you to perform another extrusion.

7. Change the height to 0.3, and click the OK button (⊘) in the caddy.

8. Go to the Edit panel and select Use NURMS.

   The couch looks pretty good, but if you look closely, you can see that it is still very choppy around the corners. The NURMS iterations need to be turned up.

9. Turn on Use NURMS; a Use NURMS tab appears in the modeling ribbon (sometimes a floating window will appear instead).

10. In the Use NURMS tab, turn the iterations up to 2.

The finished product looks pretty good, as shown in Figure 4.9.

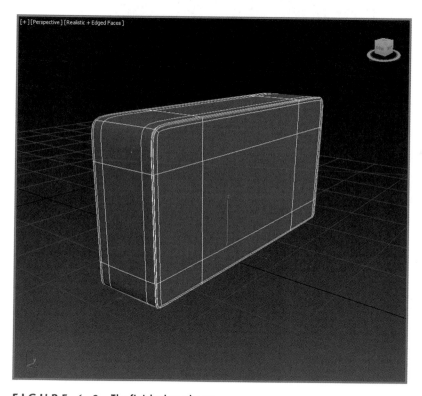

FIGURE 4.9 The finished couch arm

Now it is time to perform the same piping detail on the seat and back cushions of the couch.

1. The seat cushion and three back cushions need to have piping just like the couch arm, so repeat steps 1 through 8 of the preceding set of steps for the cushions.

2. The seat base and couch back don't have any piping, so smooth them using NURMS.

3. Add edge loops at the corners to create the right amount of smoothing and detail. Play around with the settings to match the reference model as much as possible.

4. Select vertices and polygons and move them around to give the surfaces a more random and organic or "lived-in" appearance.

In Figure 4.10, everything but the chaise lounge part of the couch was finished using NURMS with an Iterations level of 2. All the finished pieces were selected, and in the Name and Color rollout the color was changed so the finished pieces would be a consistent color. This is not required to continue with the exercise.

FIGURE 4.10   Finished pieces of the couch

The Chaise Lounge

The chaise lounge isn't that much different from the rest of the couch. It just has a wing section that comes out from the side, as shown in Figure 4.11. Continue with your own couch file or load Couch_02.max from the Scenes folder of the ArchModel project on the companion web page.

FIGURE 4.11 The chaise lounge section of the couch

Follow these steps:

   1. Select the chaise cushion box (the one on top), and in the Graphite Modeling Tools tab ➤ Modeling, select Polygon Modeling ➤ Convert To Poly.

2. In the Edit panel, select SwiftLoop and place a new edge loop on the box, as shown in Figure 4.12 (left). Right-click to release the SwiftLoop tool.

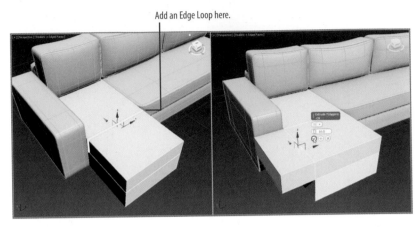

FIGURE 4.12 Use SwiftLoop to add an edge loop on the chaise cushion box (left). Extrude the new polygon that was created from adding the new loop (right).

3. Swing your view around to see the left side of the couch. Enter Polygon mode and select the polygon on the left side where you placed the edge loop.

4. In the Polygons panel, select Extrude Settings, set the height to 10.0, and click OK, as shown in Figure 4.12 (right).

5. Repeat steps 1 through 4 for the base of the chaise section of the couch. You can select the chaise parts and change the colors to match the rest of the couch.

Now that you have completed the chaise lounge section of the couch, you just have to add the finishing touches. Repeat the same steps you performed to smooth out the meshes using NURMS, add the piping detail at the edges, and move some vertices around to give the cushion a lived-in look.

Creating the Couch Feet

The final pieces you need to create for the couch are the feet. The feet are all the same, so you just need to create one foot and copy it for the other three. In Figure 4.13, look at the feet and note that they are a box shape that is thinner on the bottom. Continue with your own couch file or load the `Couch_03.max` from the `Scenes` folder of the ArchModel project on the companion web page.

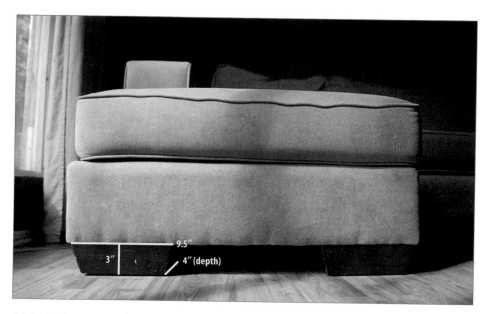

FIGURE 4.13 The couch feet with measurements

Follow these steps:

1. Go to the command panel's Create panel, select Geometry, and click Box.

2. Click and drag in the Perspective viewport to create a box that will be the first foot.

3. Then go to the command panel's Modify panel, and enter **4.0** for Length, **9.5** for Width, and **3.0** for Height.

4. In the Modify panel, click the Modifier List to expand an alphabetical list of modifiers and choose Taper.
    When the Taper modifier is applied, nothing will happen to your model until you change the Taper parameters.

5. Change Amount to **0.15**, as shown in Figure 4.14. Press Enter on the keyboard to set the amount.

A *modifier* changes the geometric structure of a model, and a Taper modifier will move the vertices near the top or bottom closer together. Using a Taper modifier is an easy way to make simple changes to your model.

FIGURE 4.14
The Taper parameters

6. Now move the couch foot into place under one of the corners of the couch. Use the clone operation (hold down the Shift key while you move the foot) to make duplicates of the foot and place them around the bottom of the couch at the remaining corners.

7. Take the time to select each couch foot box and rename it; use a simple naming convention such as Couch Foot01, 02, 03, and so on.

8. Save your project.

Now that the couch is finished, as shown in Figure 4.15, it should resemble the original couch but perhaps without the lived-in look and feel the real couch has. You can create some of that look by moving vertices and polygons around so that it does not look quite so perfect.

FIGURE 4.15 The final couch

Modeling the Lounge Chair

To model the chair, you'll be taking a different approach. You'll use a spline technique that the software is particularly good at. If you are used to Maya CV curves, the Bezier will seem a bit awkward, but if you are used to Photoshop's Pen tool, then the 3ds Max Line tools' way of making lines should be pretty easy. It isn't just the way you make the lines that makes the 3ds Max tools so nice, it's also the tools you use to make the lines into 3D objects.

Figure 4.16 shows the chair that will be modeled in this section. Click the Application button and choose Reset from the list that appears. This will set your interface and file back to a startup state.

FIGURE 4.16   The chair for the spline modeling exercise

Creating Image Planes

This exercise begins with creating planes and applying reference images to them. Set your project to the ArchModel project downloaded to your system. The image with measurements is shown in Figure 4.17.

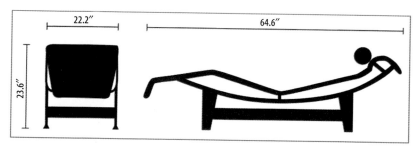

FIGURE 4.17   The lounge chair with measurements

Follow these steps:

1. In the new scene, go to the Left viewport and create a plane.

2. In the Parameters rollout of the Command panel, set Length to 23.6 and Width to 64.6.

3. Rename this box **Lounger_Side** View.

4. With the plane still selected, go to the Modify tab, and in the Parameters rollout, set Length and Width Segs to 1.

The units are in generic units (which is a system unit of inches), which is the 3ds Max default.

5. Then select the Move tool (W) in the main toolbar, and in the Transform Type-In areas at the bottom of the user interface, input 0.0 for X , 0.0 for Y, and 0.0 for Z to place the image at the center of the scene, known as the origin point.

6. Repeat steps 1 through 4 with the Front viewport active. The plane parameters are 23.6 for Length and 22.2 for Width.

7. Move the plane to these coordinates using the Transform Type-In area: X = –11.0, Y = 32.3, Z - 1.5.

8. Rename the plane **Lounger_Front** View.

Adding the Materials

At this point, the reference materials are texture-mapped onto the planes to provide a reference inside the scene itself while you model the character. Therefore, it's critical to ensure that the features of the chair that appear in both reference images (the front and the side) are at the same height. For instance, the top of the chair should be at the same height in both the front and side views to make the modeling process easier.

1. Make sure the Front and Side viewports are set to Shaded.

2. Open Windows Explorer and navigate to the `ArchModel/sceneassets/ images` folder on your hard drive from the ArchModel project you downloaded from the book's web page.

3. Drag `Lounger_Side View.tif` from the Explorer window to the image plane in the Left viewport.

4. Drag `Lounger_Front View.tif` onto the image plane in the Front viewport.

The image planes should have the two images mapped on them, as shown in Figure 4.18.

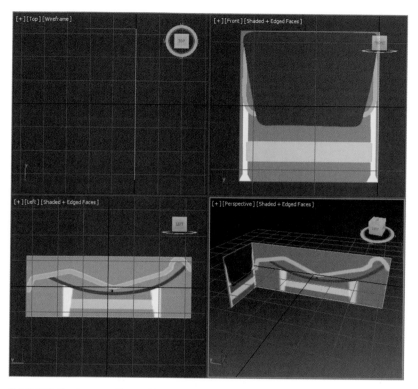

FIGURE 4.18 Mapped image planes in viewports

Building the Splines for the Chair Frame

Now it's time to create the splines for the lounge chair. Continue with your own couch file or load LoungeChair_01.max from the Scenes folder of the ArchModel project from the book's web page. The colors added to the images that we used on the planes are to help us build the splines for the lounge chair. To begin, we will build a spline using the green line as a reference.

1. Select the Left viewport and then maximize the viewport (Alt+W).

2. Click on the command panel and select Create ➢ Shapes ( ), and then select the Line tool.

You will use the Line tool to create a spline that follows the side view of the chair. Refer to Figure 4.19; it shows where the vertices should go (corresponding to the numbers in parentheses in the following steps).

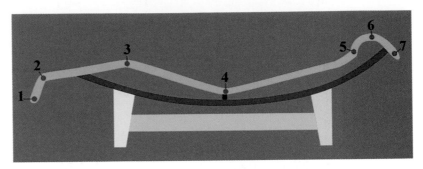

FIGURE 4.19   Create vertex points by following the numbers.

3. Starting at the bottom left of the green line in Figure 4.19, click and release the mouse button to create a corner vertex (1).

4. Move your mouse up and to the right; click and release for a corner vertex (2).

5. Move to the right; click and release for a corner vertex (3).

6. Continue right; click and release for a corner vertex (4).

7. Continue right; click and release for a corner vertex (5).

8. Drag to make a Bezier curve on the green line (6).

9. Right-click and release to create another corner vertex (7), and then right-click to release the Line tool.

10. In the Modify panel, select Modifier Stack and enter Vertex mode.

11. Select vertex (2) shown in Figure 4.19. In the Geometry rollout, click the Fillet button and drag on the vertex until the curve matches the curve in Figure 4.20, an approximate amount of 0.8.

   Fillet will split the vertex into two separate vertices and curve the segment in between them.

12. Repeat the process on vertices 3, 4, and 5. The completed spline is shown in Figure 4.21. Use whatever Fillet value is appropriate for the part of the lounge chair you are working on.

13. When you're finished, exit Vertex mode.

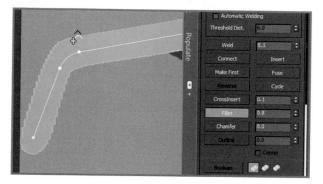

FIGURE 4.20 A vertex fillet creates two vertices from one and curves the segment between.

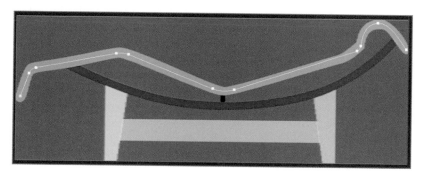

FIGURE 4.21 The competed spline for the side of the lounge

14. Switch to the Move tool (W) and select the spline. Move the spline to align it with the edge of the image plane.

15. Then, in the Front viewport, Shift+Move and align the spline to the frame of the chair on the left side, as shown in Figure 4.22.

16. When the Clone Options dialog pops up, select Copy and then click OK.

Shift+Move to clone the lounge chair spine

FIGURE 4.22 Shift+Move to clone the chair spline so it lines up with the chair frame on the left.

Now, these two splines need to be attached to form a single spline. This will allow you to create the bridge piece that runs along the two ends of the frame. Let's get the image planes out of the way.

17. Select both image planes and then right-click to bring up the quad menu. Choose Hide Selection from the Display menu.

18. With either spline selected, go to the Geometry rollout, click the Attach button, and then click on the other spline, as shown in Figure 4.23.

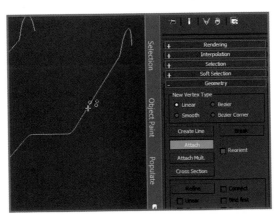

FIGURE 4.23 Attach both sides of the chair frame.

19. Enter Vertex mode. In the Geometry rollout, click the Connect button (below the Weld button).

20. Rotate the Perspective viewport so you can see both splines.

21. Click and drag from one vertex to the other, as shown in Figure 4.24. Do the same for the other end of the frame.

22. Right-click to exit from Connect.

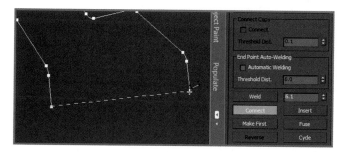

FIGURE 4.24 Use Connect to create a segment between the two separate splines.

23. Select the four vertices at the ends of the frame, and in the Geometry rollout, click the Fillet button and move to one of the selected vertices. Drag on the vertex until the curve looks appropriate, an amount of about 1.8.

   The 3ds Max software has a very cool function you can use to create a shape along a path. The splines you just created are the paths. In the parameters of the editable spline, there is a rollout called Rendering. The controls let you turn on and off the renderability of the spline and specify its thickness. Once you enable the function, the mesh can be seen in the viewport and will show when rendered. The default 3D mesh that is enabled is a radial mesh, which would make a pipe of sorts, but there is also a rectangular mesh, and both shapes have parameters that can be edited.

24. With the spline selected, go to the Rendering rollout and check the boxes for Enable In Viewport and Enable In Renderer.

25. Select Radial and change Thickness to 0.8, as shown in Figure 4.25.

FIGURE 4.25
The Rendering parameters
for the chair frame

26. Click the Render button in the main toolbar ( ) to see the results of the spline rendering, shown in Figure 4.26.

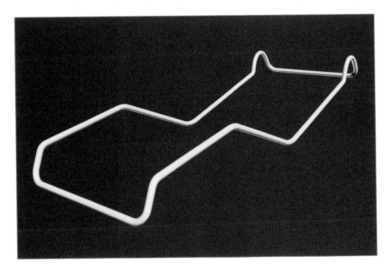

FIGURE 4.26   The radial mesh enabled

You can create the remaining parts of the frame, the arc shape, using the same technique. Continue with your chair file or load the LoungeChair_02.max from the Scenes folder of the ArchModel project from the companion web page. This file has the completed seat/back frame, as shown in Figure 4.27.

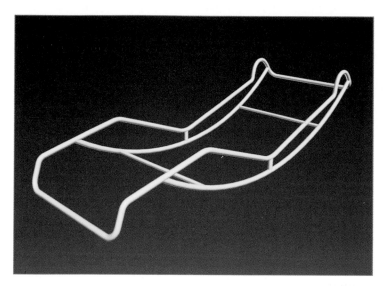

FIGURE 4.27 The arc frames are attached and connected at the base and top.

Creating the Chair Cushion

For the lounge chair cushion, you can't use the same spline technique you used on the frame. To create it, you have to return to the same technique you used for the couch: create a simple box representation and then use NURMS to soften it up. Here's how:

1. Go to the command panel, select Create ➢ Geometry, and click Box.

2. In the Perspective viewport, create a box, and then in the Modify panel, change Length to 64.0, Width to 22.0, and Height to 3.0. Change Length Segs to 4. Move the box so it is over the lounge chair frame.

3. In the modeling ribbon, select Polygon Modeling ➢ Convert To Poly.

4. In the modeling ribbon, choose Edit ➢ SwiftLoop, and add two edge loops close to the ends. These will help you rough out the shape of the lounge cushion.

5. Switch to Vertex mode (1); select and move the vertices where the segments are and line them up to follow the chair frame, as shown in Figure 4.28.

6. Use SwiftLoop again, and place edge loops along the left and right edges as well as along the sides. This will keep the outer edges from curving in too much to keep the box shape.

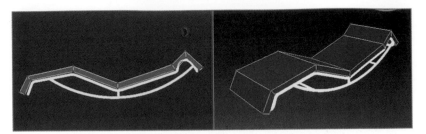

FIGURE 4.28   Arrange the vertices on the box so they follow the lounge chair frame.

7. Go to the Graphite Modeling Tools tab ➢ Edit ➢ Use NURMS. In the Use NURMS panel, set Iterations to 2, as shown in Figure 4.29. NURMS has smoothed out the model and molded the lounge-chair cushion to the frame, but it still needs some work.

8. Use SwiftLoop to add edge loops as shown in Figure 4.29. This will help to mold the cushion to the frame.

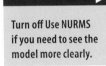

Turn off Use NURMS if you need to see the model more clearly.

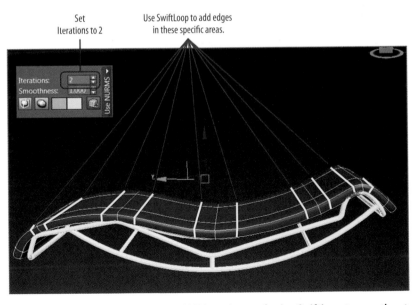

FIGURE 4.29   Turning up NURMS iterations and using SwiftLoop to smooth out the model

To finish the cushion, continue adjusting the edges/vertices to create the perfect shape. Also, look at the original reference image in Figure 4.16. There are straps that connect the cushion to the frame. Using the same spline techniques, create the straps to add realism to the overall look. Use the Line tool to create

an oval shape that surrounds the frame, and in the Rendering rollout, choose
Rectangular (see Figure 4.30).

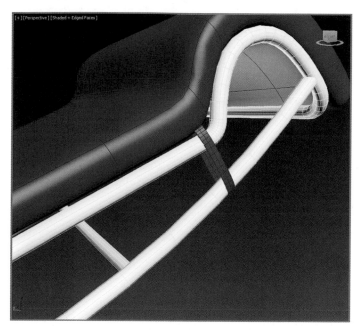

FIGURE 4.30   Create straps using splines and the Rendering rollout.

Creating the Lounge Chair's Base

The base is made up of the objects on which the frame of the lounge chair sits.
There are nine different objects that make up the base: the four legs, four blocks
that sit between the legs, and a block that connects the legs together, as shown
in Figure 4.31.

FIGURE 4.31
The lounge base

Follow these steps to create the lounge base:

1. Continue with your chair file or load LoungeChair_03.max from the Scenes folder of the ArchModel project on the companion web page.

2. Start by unhiding the side image plane. Maximize the Left viewport and zoom in so you can see one of the base legs, which are the yellow box shapes.

3. Create a box that is the general size of the base leg. The parameters are as follows: Length = 13.2, Width = 4.0, Height = 0.35, Length Segs = 1, Width = 1, and Height= 1.

4. Activate See-Through mode (Alt+X) so you can see the image plane through the box primitive, and move the box so it is aligned with the lounge chair frame, as shown in Figure 4.32.

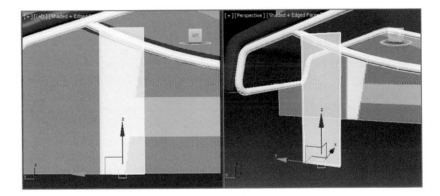

FIGURE 4.32   Create a box the size of the base leg in the image plane.

5. Choose the modeling ribbon ≻ Polygon Modeling ≻ Convert To Poly, and enter Vertex mode.

6. In the Left viewport, move the vertices so they line up with the yellow box in the image plane, as shown in Figure 4.33.

7. Choose the modeling ribbon ≻ Edit ≻ SwiftLoop, and add a loop at the bottom. This will set up for the foot. Right-click to exit SwiftLoop.

8. Switch to a Perspective viewport and rotate the viewport so you can see an angled view.

9. Enter Polygon mode, and select the polygons between the new edge loop and the bottom of the leg object. Exit See-Through mode (Alt + X).

FIGURE 4.33 Move the vertices so they line up with the image plane.

10. Choose the modeling ribbon ➢ Polygons ➢ Extrude ➢ Extrude
    Settings. In the caddy, change the extrusion type to Local Normal
    and change the height to **1.6**. Press Enter to set the input, then click
    the OK button in the caddy, as shown in Figure 4.34.

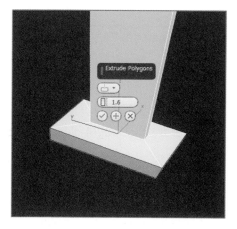

FIGURE 4.34 Use Extrude to begin
the creation of the foot.

11. Choose the modeling ribbon ➢ Edit ➢ SwiftLoop, and add edge loops, Shown in Figure 4.35 with edged faces turned on for better visibility.

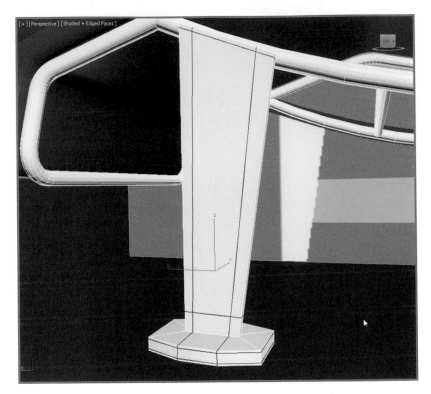

FIGURE 4.35 Add edge loops using SwiftLoop in designated areas.

12. Choose the modeling ribbon ➢ Edit and turn on Use NURMS.
This will round out the sharp corners and give the leg an overall smooth look, as shown in Figure 4.36.

13. This looks very good, but move vertices/edges to refine the shape of the object to match the leg shown in Figure 4.31.

14. With the leg finished, copy it three times and position the copies so they are aligned with the frame (use Figure 4.16 as a reference for the position of the legs).

15. Create the remaining pieces using the same techniques you used to create the leg.

16. Save the file.

The final result is shown with appropriate colors applied (default colors) in Figure 4.37.

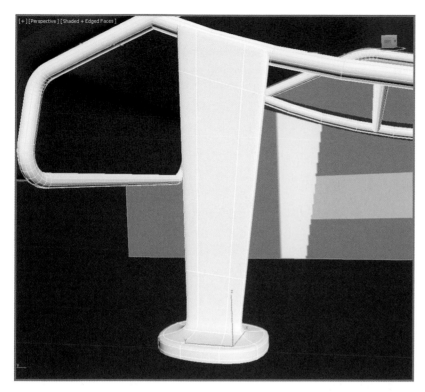

FIGURE 4.36 The leg with Use NURMS turned on, giving a smooth look to the model

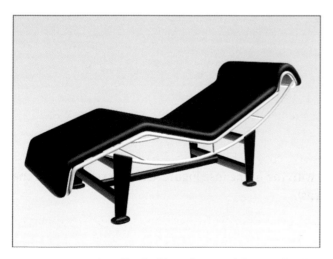

FIGURE 4.37 The final base shown with frame and cushion

Bringing It All Together

Now that the furniture is built, it's time to furnish the room you built in Chapter 3. You can do this by merging the furniture 3ds Max files into the room file. Merge allows you to load objects from one MAX file into your current file. From the `Scenes` folder of the `ArchModel` project folder on the companion web page, open the `ArchModel_Final.max` file. This is the file that you completed in Chapter 3. Then follow these steps:

1. In the `ArchModel_Final.max` project file, click the Application button ( ) and select Import ➤ Merge.

2. When the Merge File dialog box opens, navigate to the `ArchModel` project folder, and find the spline lounge chair and couch that were built earlier in this chapter. Select the `Couch_04.max` file or use your own file, and click Open.

   The Merge dialog box will open, and you will see a list of objects available to merge from that file.

3. At the bottom of the dialog box, select All, as shown in Figure 4.38, and click OK. If you use your own files, the name may be different than in the figure.

> Merged objects come into a scene already selected. They always merge into a scene at the same X-, Y-, Z-coordinates as in their original file.

FIGURE 4.38   In the Merge dialog box, select the All button at the bottom of the dialog.

4. Click the Zoom Extends All Selected button located at the lower-right corner of the interface; it is a flyout, which means there are more buttons under Zoom Extends All; this will zoom in on the already selected couch objects.

5. Go to the Edit ➤ Group menu and select Group. Name the group **Couch** and click OK.

Grouping lets you combine objects into a group. A group uses something like an invisible carrying case, called a *dummy object*, to hold your objects. Select the group and move it around, and the objects will move along with it. A group has its own pivot point. You can transform and modify a group as if it were a single object. If you want to modify an individual object in the group, do the following:

a. Select the group and then go to the Edit ➤ Group menu and choose Open. A pink bracket will appear. The objects can be individually selected.

b. Select and modify an individual object inside the group, as needed.

c. When you are finished and want to close the group, choose Edit ➤ Group ➤ Close.

d. When you want to dissolve a group, just select the group, and in the Edit ➤ Group menu, choose Ungroup.

6. Position the couch in the room.

7. Check the images of the room for couch location (see reference Figure 4.1 from the beginning of the chapter). Check the Front and Left viewports to make sure the couch is level with the floor.

8. Repeat the steps 1 through 7 to merge in and place the spline chair using the file `LoungeChair_06.max`.

Groups can also be nested, meaning you can have a group within a group.

These two pieces of furniture look great, but they don't fill up the room very much. To help furnish your newly built room, you can merge some prebuilt items into the space. Repeat steps 1 through 7 for the extra furniture pieces, which can be found in the `Chapter 04 Extra Furniture` folder in the `Scenes` folder of the ArchModel project. The room will look better after you merge the objects, as shown in Figure 4.39. The next phase for you may be to create some of your own objects to populate the room.

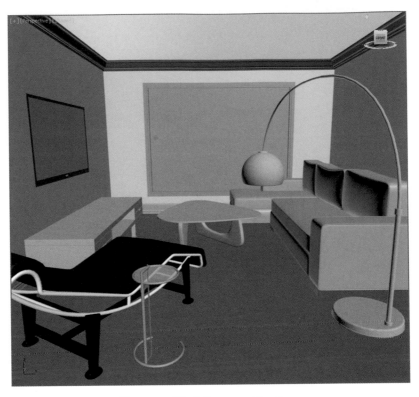

FIGURE 4.39   The room with all the merged furniture

THE ESSENTIALS AND BEYOND

In this chapter, you took a closer look at many of the modeling tools you had already used in Chapter 2 when you made the clock. The modeling ribbon is a staple in the model-building arsenal. The two new main tools you looked at in this chapter were the Use NURMS tool and the Line tool. Both are very powerful tools that can give you a lot of flexibility when modeling complex pieces.

ADDITIONAL EXERCISES

▶ Create more furniture. To start, choose a piece that resembles the ones you've already created. Create another chair or table with a frame similar to the chair you completed in the chapter. Create some tables and chairs that feature chrome or stainless steel tube frames or create any style of cushy chair.

▶ Try to use some of the other Spline tools from previous chapters to create baseboard molding as in Chapter 3, lamps and vases, and maybe a side table or more chairs.

CHAPTER 5

Introduction to Animation

Animation is the process of changing values of an object over time by setting keyframes and controlling those values. *Keyframing* is the process— borrowed from traditional animation—of setting positions and values at particular frames of the animation. The computer interpolates between these keyframes to fill in the other frames to complete a smooth animation.

Animation puts your scene into action and adds life to your characters. It is change over time. Anything in a scene that needs to change from one second to another will need to be animated to do so.

Everyone has their own reflexive sense of how things move. This knowledge is gleaned through years of perception and observation. Therefore, your audience can be more critical of a CG scene's motion than its lighting, coloring, or anything else. You know when something doesn't look right. So will your audience.

It's thrilling to see your hard work on a scene come to life with animation. On the flip side, it can be extremely aggravating to see your creation working improperly. Making mistakes is how you learn things, and your frustrations will ease over time. The results of your first several attempts at animating a scene will not look like Pixar films, but that should not dissuade you from working on more animations and scenes. You will get better with more practice.

The best way to learn how to animate is to jump right in and start animating. By doing so, you'll get a good look at the Autodesk® 3ds Max® software animation tools so you can start editing animation and developing your timing skills.

This chapter includes the following topics:

▶ **Animating the ball**

▶ **Refining the animation**

Animating the Ball

A classic exercise for all animators is to create a bouncing ball. It is a straight-forward exercise, but there is much you can do with a bouncing ball to show character. Animating a bouncing ball is a good exercise in physics as well as cartoon movement. You'll first create a rubber ball, and then you'll add cartoonish movement to accentuate some principles of the animation. Aspiring animators can use this exercise for years and always find something new to learn about bouncing a ball.

In preparation, download the Bouncing Ball project from the companion web page at www.sybex.com/go/3dsmax2014essentials to your hard drive. Set your current project by clicking the Application button, choosing Manage ➢ Set Project Folder, and selecting the Bouncing Ball project that you downloaded.

Your first step is to keyframe the positions of the ball.

Open the Animation_Ball_00.max scene file from the Scenes folder of the Bouncing Ball project you downloaded. If you receive a Gamma & LUT Settings Mismatch warning, click OK.

Start with the *gross animation,* or the overall movements. This is also called *blocking.* First, move the ball up and down to begin its choreography.

Follow these steps to animate the ball:

1. Move the pivot point from the center of the ball to the bottom of the ball.

2. Select the ball, and then go to the Hierarchy panel ( ).

3. Choose Pivot, and under the Adjust Pivot rollout, click the Affect Pivot Only button.

4. Zoom in on the ball in the Front viewport and with the Select And Move tool, drag on the Y-axis of the pivot to move to the bottom of the ball.

5. Click the Affect Pivot Only button again to deactivate.

6. Move the time slider to frame 10.

   The time slider is at the bottom of the screen below the viewports, as shown in Figure 5.1. It's used to change your position in time, counted in *frames.*

FIGURE 5.1 The time slider is used to change your position in time, counted in frames.

You can click and drag the horizontal time slider bar to change the frame in your animation on the fly; this is called *scrubbing*. The bar displays the current frame/end frame. By default, your 3ds Max window shows a start frame of 0 and an end frame of 100. When you move the time slider, the movement is reflected in the viewports.

7. Click the Auto Key button below the time slider.

    Both the Auto Key button and the time slider turn red, as shown in Figure 5.2. This means that any movement in the objects in your scene will be recorded as animation.

FIGURE 5.2   The Auto Key button records your animations.

8. Using the Perspective viewport, select the ball and move it down along the Z-axis to the ground plane, so it is 0 units in the Z-axis Transform Type-In box at the bottom of the interface. You can also just enter the value in the Z-axis Transform Type-In box and press Enter. This will work the same as moving the ball.

This exercise has created two keyframes, one at frame 0 for the original position of the ball, and one at frame 10 for the position to which you just moved the ball.

Copying Keyframes

Now you want to move the ball up to the same position in the air as it was at frame 0. Instead of trying to estimate where that was, you can just copy the keyframe at frame 0 to frame 20.

You can see the keyframes you created in the timeline; they appear as red boxes. Red keys represent Position keyframes, green keys represent Rotation, and blue keys represent Scale. When a keyframe in the timeline is selected, it turns white. Now let's copy a keyframe:

1. Select the keyframe at frame 0; it should turn white when it is selected.

2. Hold down the Shift key (this is a shortcut for the Clone tool), and click and drag the selected keyframe to copy it to frame 20.

   This will create a keyframe with the same animation parameters as the keyframe at frame 0, as shown in Figure 5.3.

FIGURE 5.3 Press Shift and drag the keyframe to copy it to frame 20.

3. Click and drag the time slider to scrub through the keyframes.

   You should see the ball start in the up position and then move down and then back up.

4. Turn off Auto Key.

Using the Track View–Curve Editor

Right now the ball is going down and then back up. To continue the animation for the length of the timeline, you could continue to copy and paste keyframes as you did earlier—but that would be very time-consuming, and you still need to do your other homework and clean your room. A better way is to loop, or *cycle,* through the keyframes you already have. An *animation cycle* is a segment of animation that is repeatable in a loop. The end state of the animation matches up to the beginning state, so there is no hiccup at the loop point.

In 3ds Max, you use the Parameter Curve Out-Of-Range Types feature to cycle animation. This is a fancy way to create loops and cycles with your animations and specify how your object will behave outside the range of the keys you have created. This will bring us to the Track View, which is an animator's best friend. You will learn the underlying concepts of the Curve Editor as well as its basic interface throughout this exercise.

Track View is a function of two animation editors, the Curve Editor and the Dope Sheet. The Curve Editor allows you to work with animation depicted as curves on a graph that sets the value of a parameter against time. The Dope Sheet displays keyframes over time on a horizontal graph, without any curves. This graphical display simplifies the process of adjusting animation timing because you can see all the keys at once in a spreadsheet-like format. The Dope Sheet is similar to traditional animation exposure sheets, or X-sheets.

You will use the Track View–Curve Editor (or just the Curve Editor for short) to loop your animation in the following steps:

Navigation inside the Track View–Curve Editor is pretty much the same as navigation in a viewport; the same keyboard/mouse combinations work for panning and zooming.

1. With the ball selected, in the menu bar choose Animation ➢ Motion Editors ➢ Track View–Curve Editor.

   In Figure 5.4, the Curve Editor displays the animation curves of the ball so far.

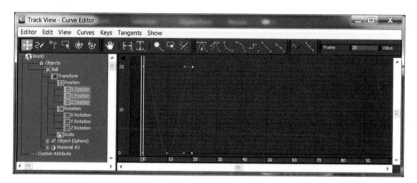

FIGURE 5.4 The Curve Editor shows the animation curves of the ball.

2. A menu bar runs across the top of the Curve Editor. In the Edit menu, choose Controller ➢ Out Of Range Types, as shown in Figure 5.5.

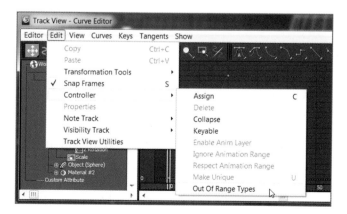

FIGURE 5.5 Selecting Out Of Range Types

Doing so opens the Parameter Curve Out-of-Range Types dialog box, shown in Figure 5.6.

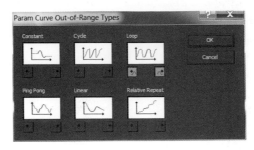

FIGURE 5.6 Choosing to loop your animation

3. Select Loop in this dialog box by clicking its thumbnail. The two little boxes with arrows beneath it will highlight (see Figure 5.6). Click OK.

Once you set the curve to Loop, the Curve Editor displays your animation, as shown in Figure 5.7. The out-of-range animation is shown as a dashed line.

FIGURE 5.7 The Curve Editor now shows the looped animation curve.

4. Scrub your animation in a viewport and see how the ball bounces up and down throughout the timeline range.

Reading Animation Curves

As you can see, the Curve Editor gives you control over the animation in a graph setting. The Curve Editor's graph is a representation of an object's parameter, such as position (values shown vertically) over time (time shown horizontally). Curves allow you to visualize the interpolation of the motion. Once you are used to reading animation curves, you can judge an object's direction, speed, acceleration, and timing at a mere glance.

Here is a quick primer on how to read a curve in the Curve Editor.

In Figure 5.8, an object's Z Position parameter is being animated. At the beginning, the curve quickly begins to move positively (that is, to the right) on the Z-axis. The object shoots up and comes to an *ease-in*, where it decelerates to a stop, reaching its top height. The ease-in stop is signified by the curving beginning to flatten out at around frame 95.

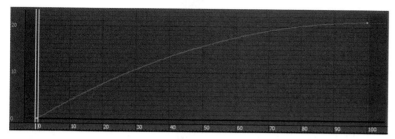

FIGURE 5.8   The object quickly accelerates to an ease-in stop.

In Figure 5.9, the object slowly accelerates in an *ease-out* in the positive Z direction until it hits frame 100, where it suddenly stops.

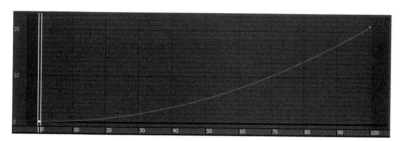

FIGURE 5.9   The object eases out to acceleration and suddenly stops at its fastest velocity.

In Figure 5.10, the object eases out and travels to an ease-in where it decelerates, starting at around frame 69, to where it slowly stops, at frame 100.

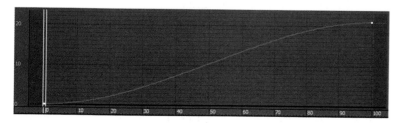

FIGURE 5.10   Ease-out and ease-in

Finally, in Figure 5.11, to showcase another tangent type, step interpolation holds its position from frame 0 to frame 20 and then makes the object jump from its Z position in frame 20 to its new position in frame 21.

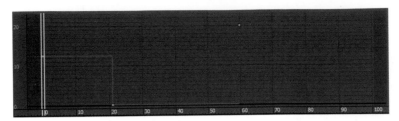

FIGURE 5.11 Step interpolation makes the object "jump" suddenly from one value to the next.

Figure 5.12 shows the Curve Editor, with its major aspects called out for your information.

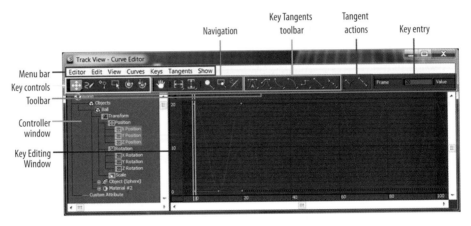

FIGURE 5.12 The Curve Editor

Refining the Animation

Certification
Objective

Let's play the animation now. In the bottom right of the interface, you will see an animation player with the sideways triangle to signify Play Animation. Select the Camera01 viewport and click the Play Animation button. The framework of the movement is getting there. Notice how the speed of the ball is moving in a consistent way. If this were a real ball, it would be dealing with gravity; the ball would speed up as it got closer to the ground and there would be "hang time" when the ball was in the air on its way up as gravity took over to pull it back down.

This means you have to edit the movement that happens between the keyframes. This is done by adjusting *how* the keyframes shape the curve itself, using tangents. When you select a keyframe, a handle will appear in the user interface (UI), as shown in Figure 5.13.

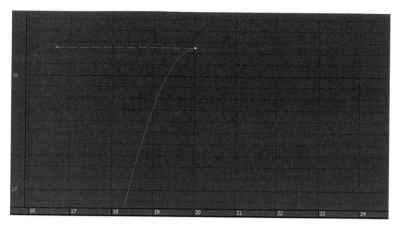

FIGURE 5.13   The keyframe's handle

This handle adjusts the tangency of the keyframe to change the curvature of the animation curve, which in turn changes the animation. There are various types of tangents, depending on how you want to edit the motion. By default the Auto tangent is applied to all new keyframes. This is not what you want for the ball, although it is a perfect default tangent type to have.

ANIMATION CONTROLLERS

Certification
Objective

Anything you animate is handled by a controller. Controllers store animation and interpolate between values. There are three default controllers:

Position   Position XYZ

Rotation   Euler XYZ

Scale   Bezier Scale

Editing Animation Curves

Let's edit some tangents to better suit your animation. The intent is to speed up the curve as it hits the floor and slow it down as it crests its apex. Instead of opening the Curve Editor through the menu bar, this time you are going to use the shortcut:

Certification
Objective

1. Close the large Curve Editor dialog box.

2. At the bottom-left corner of the interface, click the Open Mini Curve Editor button shown in Figure 5.14.

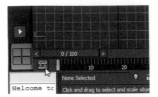

FIGURE 5.14 Click the
Open Mini Curve Editor button.

The Mini Curve Editor is almost exactly the same as the one you launch through the main menu. A few tools are not included in the Mini Curve Editor toolbars, but you can find them in the menu bar of the Mini Curve Editor.

To edit the curves, follow these steps:

1. With the ball selected, scroll down the Controller window on the left of the Mini Curve Editor by dragging the Pan tool (the hand cursor) to find the Ball object's position.

2. Click on the Z Position track.

   This will bring to the Key Editing window only the curves that you want to edit. The Z Position curve is blue, as is almost everything relating to the Z-axis. The little gray boxes on the curves are keyframes.

3. Select the keyframe at frame 10.

   You may need to scrub the time slider, which in the Curve Editor appears as double yellow vertical lines, out of the way if you are on frame 10. The key will turn white when selected. Remember, if you need to zoom or pan in the Curve Editor's Key Editing window, you can use the same shortcuts you would use to navigate in the viewports. You will change this key's tangency to make the ball fall faster as it hits and bounces off the ground.

4. In the Mini Curve Editor toolbars, change the tangent type for the selected keyframe from the Auto default to Fast by clicking the Set Tangents To Fast icon (⬛).

   When you do this, you will see the animation curve change shape, as shown in Figure 5.15.

FIGURE 5.15 The effect of the new tangent type

5. Select the Camera01 viewport and play the animation.

You can easily correlate how the animation works with the curve's shape as you see the Time slider travel through the Mini Curve Editor as the animation plays.

FINESSING THE ANIMATIONS

Although the animation has improved, the ball has a distinct lack of weight. It still seems too simple and without any character. In situations such as this, animators can go wild and try several different things as they see fit. Here is where creativity helps hone your animation skills, whether you are new to animation or have been doing it for 50 years.

Animation shows change over time. Good animation conveys the *intent,* the motivation for that change between the frames.

Squash and Stretch

The concept of *squash and stretch* has been an animation staple for as long as there has been animation. It is a way to convey the weight of an object by deforming it to react (usually in an exaggerated way) to gravity, impact, and motion.

You can give your ball a lot of flair by adding squash and stretch to give the object some personality. Follow along with these steps:

1. Press the N key to activate Auto Key.

2. In the Mini Curve Editor, drag the yellow double-line time slider (called the track bar time slider) to frame 10.

3. Click and hold the Scale tool to access the flyout.

4. Choose the Select And Squash tool (▣).

5. Center the cursor over the Z-axis of the Scale Transform gizmo in the Camera viewport.

6. Click and drag down to squash down about 20 percent.

Doing so will scale down on the Z-axis and scale up on the X- and Y-axes to compensate and maintain a constant volume, as shown in Figure 5.16.

FIGURE 5.16 Use the Select And Squash tool to squash down the ball on impact.

7. Move to frame 0, and click and drag up to stretch the ball up about 20 percent (so that the ball's scale in Z is about 120).

    When you scrub through the animation, you will see that the ball is stretched at frame 0; then the ball squashes and stays squashed for the rest of the time. You'll fix that in the next step.

    You need to copy the Scale key from frame 0 to frame 20 first and then apply a loop for the parameter curve out-of-range type. Because the Mini Curve Editor is open, it obstructs the timeline; therefore, you should copy the keys in the Mini Curve Editor. You can just as easily do so in the regular Curve Editor in the same way.

8. In the Mini Curve Editor, scroll in the Controller window until you find the Scale track for the ball.

9. Highlight it to see the keyframes and animation curves.

10. Click and hold the Move Keys tool in the Mini Curve Editor toolbar to roll out and access the Move Keys Horizontal tool ( )

11. Click and drag a selection marquee around the two keyframes at frame 0 in the Scale track to select them.

12. Hold the Shift key and then click and drag the keyframes at frame 0 to frame 20.

13. In the Mini Curve Editor's menu bar, choose Edit ➤ Controller ➤ Out Of Range Types. Choose Loop, and then click OK.

14. Play the animation.
The curves are shown in Figure 5.17.

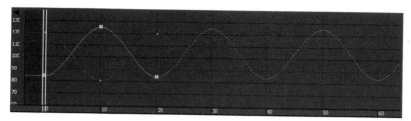

FIGURE 5.17   **The final curves**

Setting the Timing

Well, you squashed and stretched the ball, but it still doesn't look right. That is because the ball should not squash before it hits the ground. It needs to return to 100 percent scale and stay there for a few frames. Immediately before the ball hits the ground, it can squash into the ground plane to heighten the sense of impact. The following steps are easier to perform in the regular Curve Editor than in the Mini Curve Editor. So close the Mini Curve Editor by clicking the Close button on the left side of its toolbar.

Open the Curve Editor to fix the timing, and follow these steps as if they were law:

1. Move the time slider to frame 8; Auto Key should still be active.

2. In the Curve Editor, in the Controller window, select the ball's Scale track so that only the scale curves appear in the Editing window.

3. In the Curve Editor's toolbar, click the Add Keys icon ( ).
Your cursor will change to an arrow with a white circle at its lower right.

4. Click on one of the Scale curves to add a keyframe on all the Scale curves at frame 8.
Because scales X and Y are the same value, you will see only two curves instead of three.
Because they are selected, the keys will be white. In the Key Entry toolbar, you will find two text type-in boxes. The box on the left is the frame number, and the box on the right is the selected key's (or

keys') value. Because more than one key with a different value is selected, there is no number in that type-in box.

5. Enter **100** (for 100 percent scale) in the right type-in box, for the scale in X, Y, and Z for the ball at frame 8, as shown in Figure 5.18.

FIGURE 5.18   Enter a value of 100.

6. Move the time slider to frame 12, and do the same thing in the Curve Editor.

   These settings are bracketing the squash so that the squash happens only a couple frames before and a couple frames after the ball hits the ground.

7. Press the N key to deactivate Auto Key. Save your work.

Once you play back the animation, the ball will begin to look a lot more like a nice cartoonish one, with a little character. Experiment by changing some of the scale amounts to have the ball squash a little more or less, or stretch it more or less to see how that affects the animation. See if it adds a different personality to the ball. If you can master a bouncing ball and evoke all sorts of emotions from your audience, you will be a great animator indeed.

Moving the Ball Forward

You can load the `Animation_Ball_01.max` scene file from the Bouncing Ball project on your hard drive (or from the companion web page) to catch up to this point or to check your work.

Now that you have worked out the bounce, it's time to add movement to the ball so that it moves across the screen as it bounces. Layering animation in this fashion, where you settle on one movement before moving on to another, is common. That's not to say you won't need to go back and forth and make adjustments through the whole process, but it's generally nicer to work out one layer of the animation before adding another. The following steps will show you how:

1. Move the time slider to frame 0.

2. Select the ball with the Select And Move tool, and move the ball in the Camera01 viewport to the left so it is still within the camera's view. That's about –30 units on the X-axis.

3. Move the time slider to frame 100.

4. Press the N key to activate Auto Key again.

5. Move the ball to the right about 60 units so that the ball's X Position value is about 30.

   Don't play the animation yet; it isn't going to look right.

6. Go to the Curve Editor, scroll down in the Controller window, and select the X Position track for the ball, as shown in Figure 5.19.

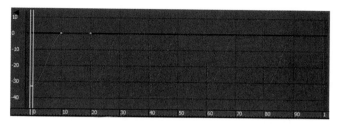

FIGURE 5.19   The X Position track of the ball does not look right.

There is no keyframe at frame 100; this is because of the loop that you set on the ball earlier; it will be addressed in the following steps.

When you created the keyframes for the up-and-down movement of the ball (which was along the Z-axis), 3ds Max automatically created keyframes for the X and Y Position tracks, both with essentially no value. To fix it, keep following these steps.

7. Select the keyframes on the X Position track at frame 10 and frame 20 by dragging a selection box around them, and delete them by pressing the Delete key on your keyboard.

8. In the Parameter Curve Out-Of-Range Types dialog (Edit ➤ Controller), select Constant.

   This removes the loop from the X Position track but won't affect the Z Position track for the ball's bounce.

9. Move the ball to the right so that its X Position value is about 30.

10. Play the animation. You can use the / (slash) button as a shortcut to play the animation.

    There is still a little problem. Watch the horizontal movement. The ball is slow at the beginning, speeds up in the middle, and then slows again at the end. It eases out and eases in. This is caused by the default tangent, which automatically adds a slowdown as the object goes in and out of the keyframes.

11. In the Curve Editor, select both keys for the X Position curve and click the Set Tangents To Linear icon (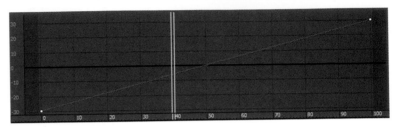) to create a straight line of movement so there is no speed change in the ball's movement left to right. Figure 5.20 shows the proper curve.

FIGURE 5.20   The X Position curve for the ball's movement now has no ease-out or ease-in.

You need to add some rotation, but there are several problems with this. One, you moved the pivot point to the bottom of the ball in the very first step of the exercise. You did that so the squashing would work correctly—that is, it would be at the point of contact with the ground. If you were to rotate the ball with the pivot at the bottom, it would look like Figure 5.21.

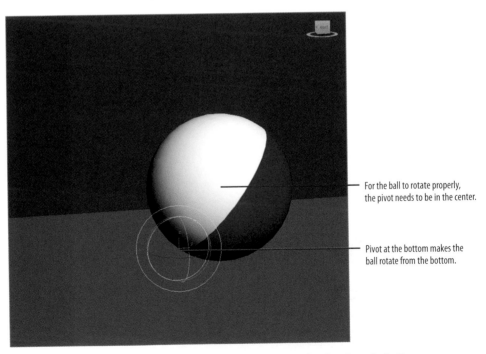

For the ball to rotate properly, the pivot needs to be in the center.

Pivot at the bottom makes the ball rotate from the bottom.

FIGURE 5.21   The ball will not rotate properly because the pivot is at the bottom.

Using the XForm Modifier

You need a pivot point at the center of the ball, but you can't just move the existing pivot from the bottom to the middle—it would throw off all the squash and stretch animation. Unfortunately, an object can have only one pivot point. To solve the issue, you are going to use a modifier called *XForm*. This modifier has many uses. You're going to use it to add another pivot to the ball in the following steps:

1. Select the ball, and then from the menu bar, select Modifiers ➢ Geometry (Parametric) ➢ XForm.

   You may also select this option from the modifier list in the command panel's Modify tab. XForm will be added to the ball in the modifier stack, and an orange bounding box will appear over the ball in the viewport. XForm has no parameters, but it does have sub-objects.

2. Expand the modifier stack by clicking the black box with the plus sign next to XForm, and then click Center.

   In the next step, you will use the Align tool to center the XForm's center point on the ball.

3. Click the Align tool (), and then click on the ball.

4. In the resulting dialog box, make sure the check boxes for X, Y, and Z Position are checked, which means those axes are active.

5. Now click Center under Target Object, and then click OK, as shown in Figure 5.22. The XForm's center will move.

FIGURE 5.22 Align
Sub-Object Selection dialog box

Now to be clear, this *isn't* a pivot point. This is the *center point* on the XForm modifier. If you go to the modifier stack and click Sphere, the pivot point will still be at the bottom.

The XForm modifier allows the ball to rotate without its squashing and stretching getting in the way of the rotation. When the rotation animation for the ball's roll is separated into the modifier, the animation on the Sphere object is preserved.

Animating the XForm Modifier

To add the ball's roll to the XForm modifier, follow along with these steps:

1. Turn on Auto Key and choose the Select And Rotate tool.

2. In the modifier stack, click the Gizmo sub-object of XForm.
   This is a very important step because it tells the modifier to use the XForm's center instead of using the pivot point of the ball.

3. In the Camera01 viewport, move the time slider to frame 100 and rotate the ball 360 degrees on the Y-axis; you can use Angle Snap Toggle (⚠), found in the main toolbar, to make it easier to rotate exactly 360 degrees.

4. Click the XForm modifier to deactivate the sub-object mode.

5. Play the animation.

THE BALL DOESN'T ROTATE 360 DEGREES!

If you rotate the ball in the third step 360 degrees but the ball does not animate, 3ds Max could be interpreting 360 degrees to be 0 degrees in the Curve Editor, thereby creating a flat curve. If this is the case, you can try rotating the ball 359 degrees instead to force the animation to work. You could also manually change the value in the Curve Editor for the keyframe at frame 100 to a value of 360.

The ball should be a rubbery cartoon ball at this point in the animation. Just for practice, let's say you need to go back and edit the keyframes because you rotated in the wrong direction and the ball's rotation is going backward. Fixing this issue requires you to go back into the Curve Editor as follows:

1. Open the Curve Editor (mini or regular) and scroll down in the Controller window until you see the Ball tracks.
   Below the ball's transform track is a new track called Modified Object.

2. Expand the track by clicking the plus sign in the circle next to the name.

3. Also expand the XForm track, and then go to the Gizmo track and select the Y Rotation track.
   You will see the function curve in the Key Editing window.

4. Select the keyframe at frame 0; it has a value of 0 and the keyframe at frame 100 has a value of 360.

5. Select both keyframes and change the tangents to Linear ( ), as shown in Figure 5.23.

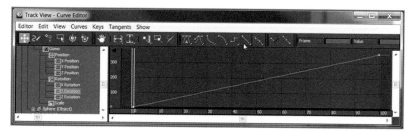

FIGURE 5.23 The Gizmo track's Y-axis rotation is selected in the Controller window and Linear tangents are set.

6. Close the Curve Editor and play the animation.

7. Play the `Bounce Ball.avi` movie file located in the `renderoutput` folder of the Bouncing Ball project to see a render of the animation.
   You can also load the `Animation_Ball_02.max` scene file from the Bouncing Ball project to check your work.

THE ESSENTIALS AND BEYOND

Working with the bouncing ball gave you quite a bit of experience with the 3ds Max animation toolset. There are several ways to animate a bouncing ball using the 3ds Max software. It is definitely a good idea to try this exercise a few times at first and then to come back to it later—after you have learned other 3ds Max techniques.

Animation can be a lot of fun, but it is also tedious and sometimes aggravating. A lot of time, patience, and practice are required to become good at animation. It all boils down to how the animation makes you think. Is there enough weight to the subjects in the animation? Do the movements make sense? How does nuance enhance the animation? These are all questions you will begin to discover for yourself. This chapter merely introduced you to how to make things move using the 3ds Max toolset. It gave you some basic animation techniques to help you develop your eye for motion. Don't stop here.

ADDITIONAL EXERCISES

Try variations on the same themes:

▶ Bounce the ball on the floor and then off a wall. Try bouncing the ball off a table, onto a chair, and then onto the floor.

▶ Animate three different types of balls bouncing next to one another, such as a bowling ball, a Ping-Pong ball, and a tennis ball.

Most important, keep working at it!

CHAPTER 6

Animation Principles

This chapter is a continuation of the animation work you began in Chapter 5, "Introduction to Animation." It introduces you to some new animation fundamentals—this time by animating a clock that you built in Chapter 2, "Your First 3ds Max Project." Then we will look at using some animation principles by completing a knife throwing project.

This chapter includes the following topic:

▶ **Anticipation and momentum in knife throwing**

Anticipation and Momentum in Knife Throwing

This exercise will give you more experience with Autodesk 3ds Max software animation techniques. You will edit more in the Curve Editor (yeah!) and be introduced to some animation principles and concepts, anticipation, momentum, and secondary movement. First, download the Knife project from this book's companion web page (`www.sybex.com/go/3dsmax2014essentials`). Set your 3ds Max project folder by choosing Application ➢ Manage ➢ Set Project Folder and selecting the Knife project that you downloaded.

Blocking Out the Animation

To begin this exercise, open the `Animation_Knife_00.max` file in the Knife project. When you open the file, you might see a Gamma & LUT Mismatch error dialog; click OK and then follow these steps.

1. Move the time slider to frame 30 and activate the Auto Key button.

2. Move the knife to the Target object, as shown in Figure 6.1.

FIGURE 6.1   Move the knife to the target at frame 30.

3. Move the time slider to frame 15, where the knife is halfway between its start and the target, and in the Camera001 viewport, move the knife slightly up on the Z-axis, as shown in Figure 6.2, so that the knife moves with a slight arc.

FIGURE 6.2   Move the knife up slightly at frame 15.

4. Click the Time Configuration icon at the bottom of the UI next to the navigation controls.

Figure 6.3 shows the Time Configuration dialog box.

5. In the Animation section, change End Time to 30 from 100 and click OK. The time slider will reflect this change immediately.

6. Play your animation, and you should see the knife move with a slight ease-out and ease-in toward the target, with a slight arc up in the middle.

You are going to move the keyframes from frame 0 to frame 10 so there is a pause before the knife moves toward the target.

7. Open the Curve Editor and scroll down in the Controller window until you see the Knife X, Y, and Z Position tracks.

8. Hold the Ctrl key and select all three tracks to display their curves (if they are not already selected), shown in Figure 6.4.

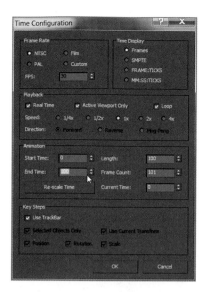

FIGURE 6.3 Change the frame range in the Time Configuration dialog box.

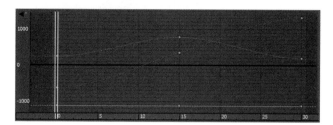

FIGURE 6.4 The initial curves for the knife

9. Drag a selection marquee around the three keyframes at frame 0.

10. In the Key Controls toolbar, select and hold the Move Keys tool ( ) to access the flyout icons, and select the Move Keys Horizontal tool in the flyout ( ). Use this tool to move the keyframes to frame 10.

11. Doing so compacts the curve, so you need to move the keyframes at frame 15 to the new middle, frame 20.

12. Repeat what you did in steps 9 and 10. Now you can turn off the Auto Key button (N).

   The finished curve is shown in Figure 6.5.

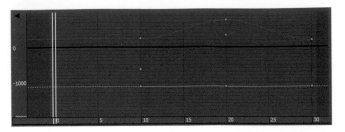

FIGURE 6.5   Finished curves with the position of the knife starting at frame 10

That's it for the gross animation (or *blocking*) of the shot. Did you have fun?

Trajectories

When it comes to animation, it is very helpful to be able to see an object's *trajectory* (the path the object is taking over time):

1. Select the THROW KNIFE object.

2. In the command panel, click the Motion icon ( ).

3. Click Trajectories, shown in Figure 6.6.

FIGURE 6.6   Turning on Trajectories for the knife

Your viewports will display a red curve to show you the path of the knife's motion as it arcs toward the target, as shown in Figure 6.7.

FIGURE 6.7   The curve shows the trajectory for the knife's motion.

The large, hollow, square points on the trajectory curve represent the keyframes set on the knife so far. Let's adjust the height of the arc using the trajectory curve:

1. Select the Sub-Object button at the top of the Motion panel.
     Keys is your only sub-object choice in the pull-down menu to the right of the button.

2. Select the middle keyframe and move it up or down to suit your tastes.

3. Once you settle on a nice arc for the path of the knife, turn off Trajectories mode by clicking the Parameters button in the Motion panel.

As you can imagine, the Trajectories option can be useful in many situations. It not only gives you a view of your object's path: it also allows you to edit that path easily and in a visual context, which can be very important.

Adding Rotation

Throwing knives in real life is usually a bad idea, but you can throw something else at a target (the inanimate kind) to see how to animate your knife. You'll find that the object will rotate once or twice before it hits its target. To add rotation to your knife, follow these steps:

1. Auto Key should still be active. Move to frame 30, and press the E key for the Select And Rotate tool.

2. In the Camera001 viewport, rotate on the Y-axis about 443 degrees.

3. With the knife selected, open the Curve Editor.

4. Scroll down to find the X, Y, and Z Rotation tracks.

5. Select the keys at frame 0, and then use the Move Keys Horizontal tool to move the keyframes to frame 10.

Figure 6.8 shows the Curve Editor graph for the knife.

FIGURE 6.8   The Curve Editor graph for the knife

6. Press N to deactivate Auto Key.

7. Play the animation, and you will see that the knife's position and rotation ease in and out.

   The rotations or movement would not ease in or out with a real knife. Its speed would be roughly consistent throughout the animation.

8. Go back to the Curve Editor; change Move Keys Horizontal back to Move Keys.

9. Then select both X Position track keyframes and change them to Linear.

10. Now select the Z Position track; you'll need to finesse this one a bit more than you did the X Position track.

    You are going to use the handles on the tangents that appear when you select a key. These handles can be adjusted.

11. Just center your cursor over the end on the tangent handle and drag using the Move Keys tool. Pull it up so it is even with the curve. Then repeat the same with the keyframe at frame 30.

    Figure 6.9 illustrates how you want the Z Position animation curve to look. This will give the trajectory a nice arc and a good rate of travel.

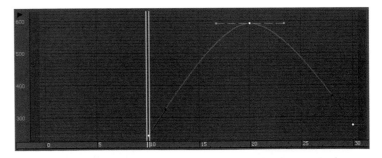

FIGURE 6.9   Adjust the curve for the knife's arc through the air.

Now it is time to edit the Rotation keys.

12. In the Curve Editor, scroll to find the X, Y, and Z Rotation tracks.
The first thing you can do is add a bit of drama to the knife to make the action more exciting. To this end, you can see that the rotation of the knife is too slow.

13. Choose the X Rotation track and select its key at frame 30.

14. In the Key Entry type-in, change the value to about **–660**.
If the total value of the rotation is more than 360 degrees, it will increase the speed of the rotation. This will add one full revolution to the animation and some more excitement to the action.

15. Adjust the tangent handles to resemble the curve shown in Figure 6.10.
The knife will speed up just a bit as it leaves the first rotation keyframe. The speed will be even as it goes into the last keyframe.

FIGURE 6.10 Match your curve to this one.

With just a little bit of fast rotation as the knife leaves frame 10, you give the animation more spice. The knife should now have a slightly weightier look than before, when it rotated with an ease-in and ease-out.

Adding Anticipation

Now let's animate the knife to create *anticipation,* as if an invisible hand holding the knife pulled back just before throwing it to get more strength in the throw. This anticipation, although it's a small detail, adds a level of nuance to the animation that enhances the total effect. Follow these steps:

1. Move the time slider to frame 0.

2. Go to the Curve Editor, scroll in the Controller window, and select the X Rotation track for the knife.

3. In the Curve Editor toolbar, click the Add Keys icon (), bring your cursor to frame 0 of the curve, and click to create a keyframe.

   Doing so creates a key at frame 0 with the same parameters as the next key, as shown in Figure 6.11.

FIGURE 6.11   Add a key to the beginning to create anticipation for the knife throw.

4. Using the Move Keys tool, select the keyframe at frame 10.

5. In the Key Entry type-in box, change the value of the key at frame 10 to 240.

   If you play back the animation, it will look weird. The knife will cock back really fast and spin a bit. This is due to the big hump between frames 0 and 10.

6. Keep the tangent at frame 0 set to the default, but change the tangent on the key at frame 10 to Linear ( ). Play the animation.

   You'll have a slight bit of anticipation, but the spice will be lost and the knife will look less active and too mechanical.

7. To regain the weight you had in the knife, press Ctrl+Z to undo your change to the tangency on frame 10 and set it back to what you had. You may have to undo more than once.

8. Now, select the Move Keys Vertical tool ( ) and select the In tangent handle for keyframe 10.

   This is the tangent handle on the left of the key.

9. Press Shift and drag the tangent handle down to create a curve that is similar to the one shown in Figure 6.12.

   By pressing Shift as you dragged the tangent handle, you broke the continuity between the In and Out handles so that only the In handle was affected.

10. Play back the animation. It should look much better now.

It's common to try something and rely on Undo—even several times—to get back to the starting point. You can also save multiple versions of your file to revert to an earlier one.

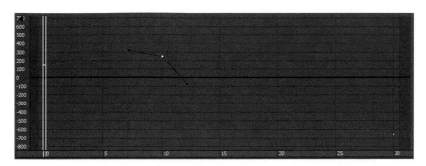

FIGURE 6.12 To create a believable anticipation for the knife throw, set your curve to resemble this one.

Following Through

The knife needs more weight. A great way to show that in animation is by adding follow-through; have the knife sink into the target a little bit. To add follow-through to your animation, use these steps:

1. Click the Time Configuration icon and change End Time to **45** to add 15 frames to your frame range.

2. Click OK. Doing so will not affect the animation; it will merely append 15 frames to the current frame range.

3. Select the knife and go to frame 30, where it completes its hit on the target.

4. In the Curve Editor, select the X Position track of the knife.

5. Add a keyframe with the Add Keys tool at frame 35.
   Note the value of the key in the type-in boxes at the top right of the Curve Editor (*not* the type-in boxes at the bottom of the main UI). In this case, the value in this scene is about 1290. You will want to set the value for the key at frame 35 to about **1300** to sink it farther into the target. If your values are different, adjust accordingly so you don't add too much movement. Also make sure the movement flows *into* the target and not back out of the target as if the knife were bouncing out. Keep the tangent for this new key set to Auto.

6. With these relative values, scrub the animation between frames 30 and 35. You should see the knife's slight move into the target.
   The end of your curve should look like the curve in Figure 6.13.
   You still need to add a little bit of follow-through to the rotation of the knife to make it sink into the target better.

7. In the Curve Editor, select the X Rotation track to display its curve.

8. Add a key to the curve at frame 35. The value of the key at frame 30 should already be about –660.

FIGURE 6.13 Your animation should end like this.

9. Set the value of the keyframe at frame 35 to be about –655. Keep the tangent set at Auto.

10. If your values are different, adjust according to what works best in your scene.

Be careful about how much the knife sinks into the target. Although it is important to show the weight of the knife, it is also important to show the weight of the target; you do not want the target to look too insubstantial.

Transferring Momentum to the Target

To make the momentum work even better for the knife animation, you will have to push back the target as the knife hits it. The trouble is, if you animate the target moving back, the knife will stay in place, floating in the air. You have to animate the knife *with* the target.

Parent and Child Objects

To animate the knife and target together, the knife has to be linked to the target so that when the target is animated to push back upon impact, the knife will follow precisely because it is stuck in the target. Doing this won't mess up the existing animation of the knife because the knife will be the child in the hierarchy and will retain its own animation separate from the target. Just follow these steps:

1. Go to frame 35, about when the knife impacts.

2. On the far left of the main toolbar, choose the Select And Link tool ( ).

3. Select the knife and drag it to the target, as shown in Figure 6.14 (left).

Nothing should change until you animate the target object.

FIGURE 6.14 Link the knife to the target (left), and then rotate the target in the X axis (right).

4. Move the time slider to frame 34 and press the N key to activate the Auto Key tool.

5. With the Select And Rotate tool, select the Target object and rotate it back about 5 degrees, as shown in Figure 6.14 (right).
   The pivot of the target has already been placed properly, at the bottom back edge.

6. Go to the Curve Editor, scroll to find the Y Rotation track for the target object, select the keyframe at frame 0, and move it to frame 30.

7. Then hold the Shift key, and click and drag the keyframe (which will make a copy of it) to frame 37.

8. Change the tangent for the key at frame 30 to Fast and leave the other key tangents alone.

9. Add a little wobble to the target to make the animation even more interesting. This can be done easily in the Curve Editor. Use Add Keys to add keys at frames 40 and 44.

10. Using the Move Keys Vertical tool, give the key at frame 40 a value of about 1.7.
    Your curve should resemble the one in Figure 6.15.

11. Finally, add a little slide to the target. Using the Select And Move tool, move the time slider to frame 37, and move the target just a bit along the X-axis.

12. Go to the Curve Editor, scroll to the X position of the Target object, select the keyframe at frame 0, and move it to frame 30 so the move starts when the knife hits the target.

13. Change the tangent for frame 30 to Fast and leave the other tangent at Auto.

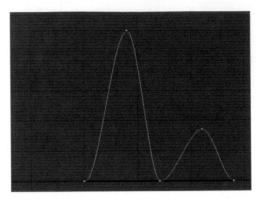

FIGURE 6.15   The target animation curve

Done! Play your animation. Experiment and change some of the final timings and values of the target's reaction to the impact to see different weights of the knife and target and how the weight looks to the viewer.

You can see a sample render of the scene in the `knife_animation.mov` QuickTime file in the `Render Output` folder of the Knife project. You can also open the `Animation_Knife_01.max` scene file from the `Scenes` folder of the Knife project to check your work.

THE ESSENTIALS AND BEYOND

In this second chapter on animation, you further expanded your knowledge of creating and editing animation. You learned about hierarchies and how to link objects together to create a hierarchy useful for the knife animation, as well as how pivot points are used. You also learned some key animation concepts (such as anticipation, follow-through, and momentum) and how they apply to an animation.

ADDITIONAL EXERCISES

▶ Use the Clock file to play around with animating the clock hands to have different speeds.

▶ If you built the bell hammer in Chapter 2, animate it.

▶ Try animating simple objects like boxes and just play around with anticipation, follow-through, and momentum.

▶ Again using simple primitives create hierarchies and play around with anticipation, follow-through, and momentum.

CHAPTER 7

Character Poly Modeling: Part I

In games, characters are designed and created cleverly to achieve the best look with the lowest amount of mesh detail to keep the polygon count low. With that in mind, this and the next two chapters introduce you to character modeling, focusing on using the Editable Poly toolset to create a relatively low-polygon-count soldier model suitable for character animation and for use in a game engine (though that topic is not covered in this book). This chapter begins with the basic form of the character first.

This chapter includes the following topics:

▶ **Setting up the scene**

▶ **Beginning the Soldier Model**

Setting Up the Scene

You can import and use sketches of the character's front and side as background images as you create the character using the Autodesk® 3ds Max® software toolset. Additional sketches of your character from several points of view can be used as quick references to help you target your goal.

HIGH- AND LOW-POLY MODELING

High-polygon-count models are used when a model's level of detail needs to be impeccable, such as when the model is used in close-ups. High-polygon models are also used to generate displacement and normal maps to use on lower-resolution models. This technique is used to add needed detail without the issues that come with large model sizes.

(Continues)

HIGH- AND LOW-POLY MODELING *(Continued)*

Low-polygon-count modeling, also called *low-poly modeling,* refers to a style of modeling that sacrifices some detail in favor of efficient geometry and places a very low load on the system on which it is being created or rendered. The number of triangles needed to consider something low-poly is based on the rendering platform, and increases as the technology improves.

Creating Image Planes

You'll begin this exercise by creating crossed boxes and applying reference images to them. Set your project to the Soldier project you downloaded from the book's web page at www.sybex.com/go/3dsmax2014essentials:

1. In a new scene, go to the Front viewport and create a plane.

2. In the Parameters rollout of the command panel, set Length to **163** and Width to **160**.

   The units are in inches, which is the 3ds Max default. The size of the image planes in units is the same size as the reference images in pixels. Therefore, when you apply the image to the plane, it will be proportional, maintaining its width and length with no stretching or squeezing of the images.

3. Rename this plane **Image_Plane_Front**.

4. With the plane still selected, go to the Modify tab, and in the Parameters rollout, set Length Segs and Width Segs to **1**.

5. Then select the Select And Move tool (W) in the main toolbar, and in the Transform Type-In areas at the bottom of the user interface, move the plane to these coordinates: **0.0, 80, –5**.

6. Click in a blank space in the user interface (UI), and then press Ctrl+Shift+Z on your keyboard to initiate the shortcut for Zoom Extents All.

7. In the main toolbar, turn on Angle Snap Toggle (![icon] or press A on your keyboard).

   Doing so will snap your rotation to every 5 degrees.

8. Select the Select And Rotate tool (E) and select the Image_Plane_Front object. Hold down the Shift key on the keyboard and, in the Front viewport, rotate the image plane along the Y-axis 90 degrees.

9. Using the Shift key activates the Clone Options dialog box, shown in Figure 7.1.

FIGURE 7.1 The Clone Options dialog box

10. In the Clone Options dialog box, under Object select Copy; name the copy **Image_Plane_Side** and click OK.

11. Switch to the Select And Move tool and move the plane to these coordinates: –82, 0, –5.

Adding the Material to the Image Plane

At this point, the reference materials are texture-mapped onto the planes to provide a reference inside the scene itself while you model the character. Therefore, it's critical to ensure that the features of the character that appear in both reference images (the front and the side) are at the same height. For instance, the top of the head and the shoulders should be at the same height in both the front and side views to make the modeling process easier. Follow these steps:

1. In the Left viewport, press the V key on your keyboard and select Right View from the list.

2. Change the shading in the Right viewport to Shaded if it isn't already set to Shaded.

3. Open an Explorer window and navigate to the `Soldier/ sceneassets/images` folder on your hard drive from the Soldier project you downloaded from the book's web page.

4. Drag `ImagePlane_Front.jpg` from the Explorer window to the image plane in the Front viewport.

5. Drag `ImagePlane_Side.jpg` onto the image plane in the Right viewport.

6. Change the Left viewport to a Right viewport, set the all the viewports to Shaded, and turn on Edged Faces.

   The image planes should have the two images mapped on them, as shown in Figure 7.2.

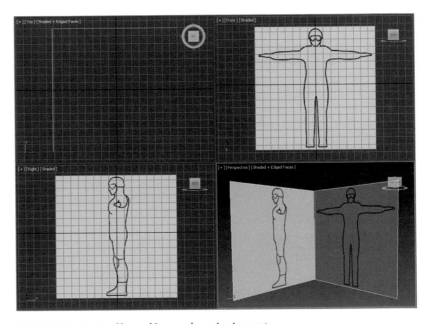

FIGURE 7.2   Mapped image planes in viewports

Beginning the Soldier Model

A good practice is to block out the basic form of the character and focus on the size and crucial shapes of the major elements, and then add detail for the finer features. The following exercises describe the steps required to block out a soldier's major features. Go wild!

Forming the Torso

The basic structure for the torso will begin with a simple box primitive. After converting the box into an editable poly, you will use the Mirror tool on the object so that any manipulations performed on one side are also performed on the other. You will begin forming the basic shape of the torso by moving the editable poly's vertices and extruding its polygons in the following steps.

Continue with the previous exercise's scene file, or open the `Soldier_V01.max` scene file in the `Scenes` folder of the Soldier project downloaded from this book's web page. Then follow these steps:

1. In the Perspective viewport, go to the Shading viewport label menu and choose Shaded, and then select F4.

    This will turn on Edged Faces; do this if it isn't already set that way.

2. Start by creating a box primitive in the Perspective viewport with these parameters: Length: **25**, Width: **16**, Height: **53**, Height Segs: **8**.

    Leave Length Segs and Width Segs at **1**, as shown in Figure 7.3. This is a starting point for the detail needed to create the form of the body. Press Alt+X to make the box see-through, and change the box's name to **Soldier**.

FIGURE 7.3
Box parameters

3. Position the box as shown in Figure 7.4.

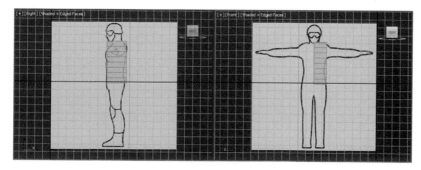

FIGURE 7.4 Box position from the front and side views

4. In the Graphite Modeling Tools tab ➤ Polygon Modeling panel, click Convert To Poly.

5. In the Polygon Modeling panel, enter the Vertex sub-object level.

6. In the Right viewport, position the vertices on the right side of the box to match the side outline of the character on the image plane, as shown in Figure 7.5. Use a selection box to select the vertices. This will ensure that you are selecting both the backface vertex and the vertex that can be seen in the viewport.

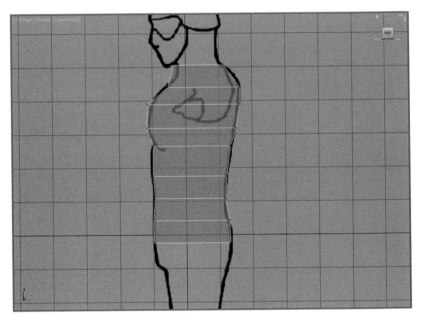

FIGURE 7.5   Move the vertices to match the soldier image in the Right viewport.

7. Select the Graphite Modeling Tools tab ➤ Edit panel and click SwiftLoop. Switch to Edge mode, and then use the SwiftLoop tool to create two new edge loops that run vertically from the front of the model to the back, as shown in Figure 7.6.

   The dashed lines show the loop running in the back and bottom of the model.

8. Using SwiftLoop again, create a single new edge on the side of the model running from the left side to the right side, as shown in Figure 7.7.

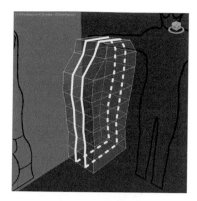

F I G U R E   7 . 6   Create two new
edge loops using SwiftLoop.

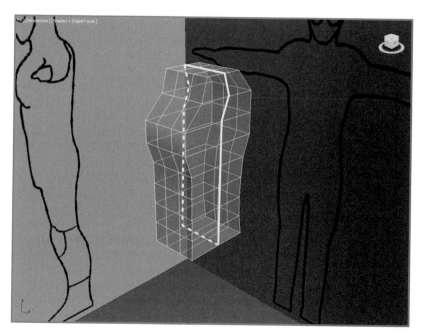

F I G U R E   7 . 7   Create a single new edge on the side of the model using SwiftLoop.

The dashed yellow line shows the loop running across the bottom
and back of the model

9. Right-click to exit the SwiftLoop tool.

10. Now round the side of the torso. You should still be in Edge mode. Double-click on one of the edges running vertically on the side of the torso box; this is a shortcut to the Loop tool on the Modify Selection panel in the modeling ribbon. Move the loop of edges toward the back of the model to begin rounding the torso. Refer to Figure 7.8.

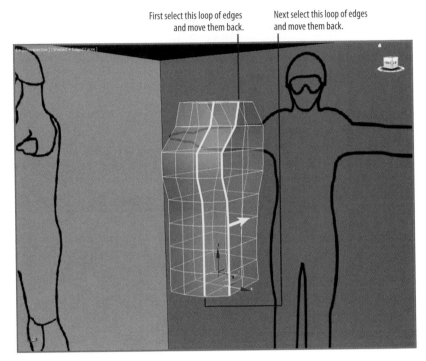

First select this loop of edges and move them back.

Next select this loop of edges and move them back.

FIGURE 7.8   Select and move edges toward the back of the model.

11. Then select the loop of edges to the left of the previous one and move them back to form a more rounded front to the torso, as shown in Figure 7.8.

12. While still in Edge mode, Ctrl+click to select the three edges on the front of the torso (the line of edges one down from the top edge) and move them out, as shown in Figure 7.9.

13. Exit See-Through mode (Alt+X), switch to Vertex mode, and select the vertex on the left side below the top edge, as shown in Figure 7.10, (left image).

Select edges and move out

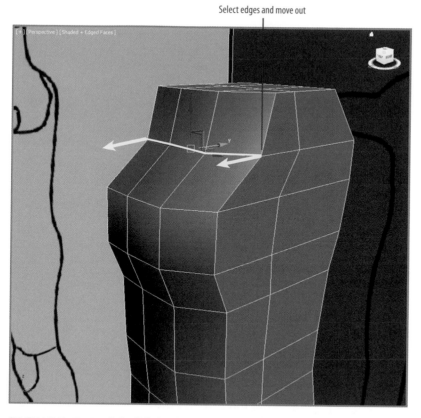

FIGURE 7.9 Ctrl+click the three edges on the front of the torso and move them out.

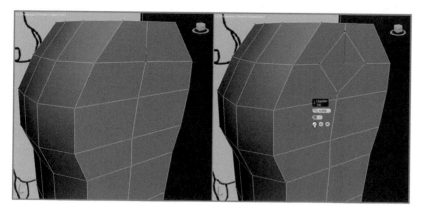

FIGURE 7.10 Select the vertex (left image). Use Chamfer to create a new polygon where the arm will be positioned (right image).

14. On the Graphite Modeling Tools tab ➤ Polygon Modeling panel, click the Vertex sub-object level. This should open the Vertices panel; click the arrow on the right of the Chamfer button, which reveals Chamfer settings. Doing so opens the Chamfer caddy.

15. Use a Vertex Chamfer Amount value of 4.808, and click OK (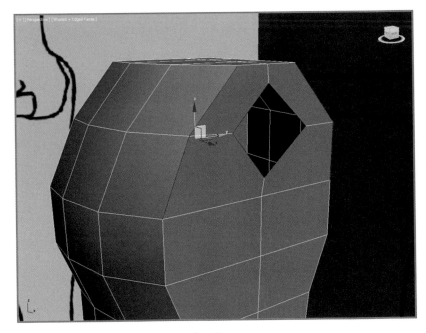) in the caddy to commit the action, as shown in Figure 7.10 (right image). This is where the arm will be positioned.

16. Switch to Polygon mode (keyboard shortcut 4), select the new diamond-shaped polygon in the middle, and press Delete to delete the polygon. A hole appears where the arm will be positioned.

17. Also, while in Polygon mode, select all the polygons on the inside surface of the torso model (the side opposite the new armhole) and delete.

18. Switch to Edge mode (keyboard shortcut 2) and select the four diagonal edges of the diamond-shaped armhole and the four edges shown in Figure 7.11.

FIGURE 7.11 Select these eight edges.

19. On the Graphite Modeling Tools tab ➤ Modify Selection panel, click Ring to select the ring of edges running across the top of the torso.

20. Select the Graphite Modeling Tools tab ➤ Loops ➤ Flow Connect to create more horizontal divisions for the upper chest.

    The newly created edges are illustrated in Figure 7.12. The diamond-shaped hole in the shoulder is now more rounded (the hole is now an octagon) as well because more edges were created at the hole. The dashed lines show the loops running behind the model.

Flow Connect connects selected edges across one or more edge rings and adjusts the new loop position to fit the shape of the surrounding mesh.

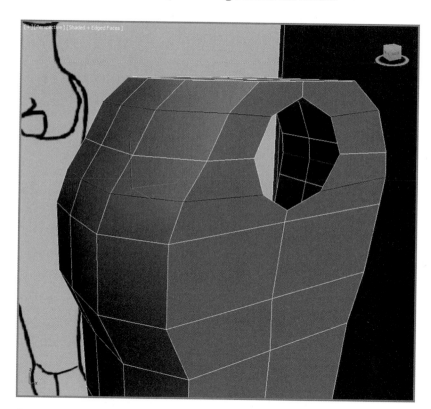

FIGURE 7.12 Use Flow Connect to create two new edges around the model.

21. Enter See-Through mode (Alt+X), and select the two horizontal edges under the armhole, as shown in Figure 7.13 (left). On the Graphite Modeling Tools tab ➤ Modify Selection panel, click Ring.

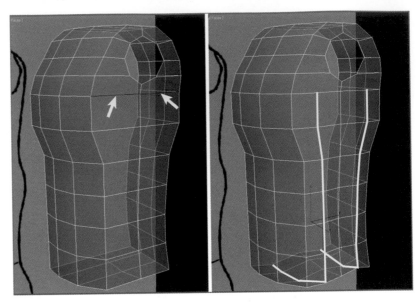

FIGURE 7.13 Select the two horizontal edges under the armhole (left) and use Flow Connect to create more edges (right).

22. Again, select Graphite Modeling Tools tab ➤ Loops ➤ Flow Connect to create two new loops of edges, as shown on the right in Figure 7.13.

    The new edge rings do not reach all the way up to the octagon armhole. You will need to cut an edge from the top of the new edges you just made to the bottom of the armhole.

23. Exit See-Through mode, and then in the Graphite Modeling Tools tab ➤ Edit panel, click Cut (⬛). Click on the first vertex under the armhole, and then click on the second vertex to create the first new edge; right-click to commit the edge.

24. The Cut tool will still be active, so click on the third vertex and create the second new edge down to the fourth vertex, shown in Figure 7.14; right-click to commit the second edge.

    The armhole is not a good shape right now; it will be easier to start the arm of the soldier from a circular shape rather than the uneven octagon form you have now.

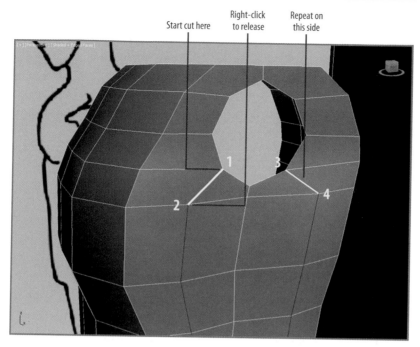

FIGURE 7.14   Use the Cut tool to add two edges under the armhole.

25. Enter Border mode (〔 〕), select the armhole border, and on the Graphite Modeling Tools tab ➢ Geometry (All) panel, click the Cap Poly tool to create a polygon cap to fill the hole.

This is not a four-sided polygon; it's an eight-sided polygon sometimes known as an n-gon, a polygon with more than four sides.

ABOUT POLYGONS

A polygon is traditionally a plane that is bounded by a closed path, composed of sequences of straight line segments. These segments are called its *edges* or *sides*. The preferred number of sides for a polygon in 3D modeling is four, but polygons can have three sides (triangle, or tri-polygon) or more than four sides (n-gon).

26. Enter Polygon mode and select the new polygon.

GeoPoly untangles a polygon and organizes the vertices to form a perfect geometric shape. This will make it easier for you when you create the arm later.

27. In the Graphite Modeling Tools tab ➢ Polygons, click the GeoPoly tool to create a symmetrical polygon from the previous shape, as shown in Figure 7.15.

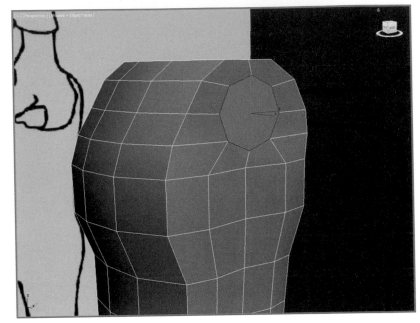

FIGURE 7.15　Use GeoPoly to create a symmetrical shape for the armhole.

28. Select the new n-gon cap and press Delete.

29. Also select and delete the top and bottom polygons on the model, as shown in Figure 7.16. Your torso should now have only a front, side, and back.

30. In the Graphite Modeling Tools tab ➢ Polygon Modeling panel, turn on Ignore Backfacing ( ).

31. Select Edge mode, and then select the edge loops on the right of the model and move them in toward the center of the model, as shown in Figure 7.17.

Delete
top polygons

Delete
armhole polygons

Delete
bottom polygons

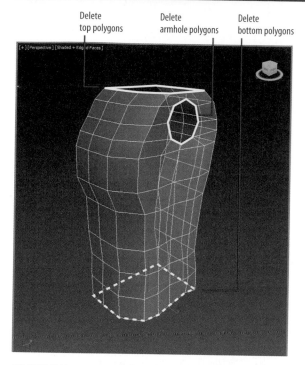

FIGURE 7.16   Delete the armhole polygons as well
as the topmost and bottommost polygons of the model.

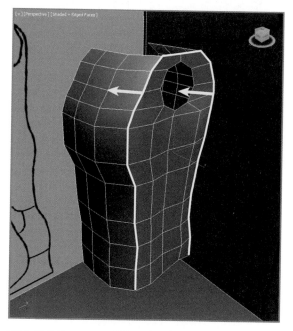

FIGURE 7.17   Select the edge loops and move them
to create a more rounded look to the model.

32. Go into Edge mode and select the edge running vertically on the right side of the model's back, as shown in Figure 7.18, and move it toward the armhole. This action will make the back rounder.

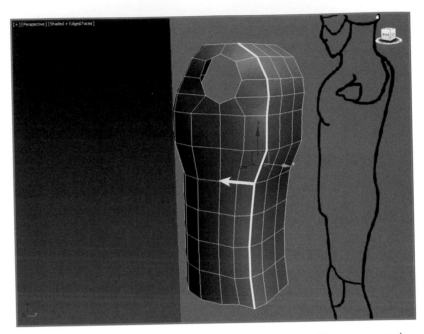

FIGURE 7.18 Move the selected edge toward the front of the torso to round out the back.

Now we are starting to see some shape in the torso. Let's move on to the arms.

Creating the Arms

Continue with the previous exercise's scene file, or open the `Soldier_V02.max` scene file in the `Scenes` folder of the Soldier project on this book's companion web page. If you are starting with a newly opened file, you will need to select the model. Then follow these steps:

1. In the Front viewport, enter Border mode and select the armhole.

2. Hold down the Shift key, and with the Select And Move tool, drag out from the body on the X-axis, extruding new polygons as you drag. When you get to where the elbow is, release the mouse button.

3. Hold down the Shift key, and with the Select And Move tool, drag out from the last extrude to the wrist and release the mouse button.

> ▶
>
> This method is a form of Border Extrude. It gives you more control over the extrude process because you can more easily choose the axis along which to extrude.

4. In the Graphite Modeling Tools tab ➤ Edit panel, click SwiftLoop. Create two edge loops on the arm, one on either side of the elbow edge; then right-click to release the SwiftLoop tool.

5. Enter Edge mode (keyboard shortcut 2), double-click to select the horizontal edges running around the body under the arm, and move the edges down.

6. Repeat the process with the loop of edges under and above the previous loop, as shown in Figure 7.19. Continue until the edges are evenly spaced along the torso.

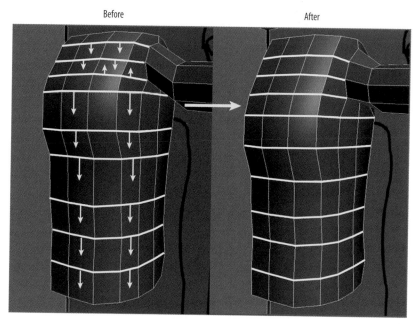

FIGURE 7.19   Move these looped edges down to evenly space the edges along the torso.

7. Enter See-Through mode (Alt+X). In the Front viewport, double-click to select the middle elbow edge.

8. In the Graphite Modeling Tools tab ➤ Edges ➤ Chamfer, select Chamfer Settings to open the caddy. Enter an Edge Chamfer Amount value of 2 and a Connect Edge Segments value of 2 and click OK to close the dialog box, as shown in Figure 7.20.

    Because this is the area where the elbow bends, it is a good idea to include more detail there for deformations at the elbow.

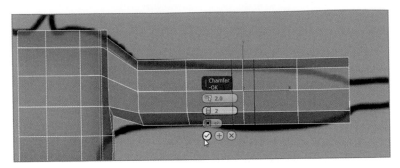

FIGURE 7.20 Chamfer edge at the middle of the arm

9. Then chamfer the edges to the right and left of the newly chamfered middle edge, using an Edge Chamfer Amount value of 3 and a Connect Edge Segments value of 1, as shown in Figure 7.21.

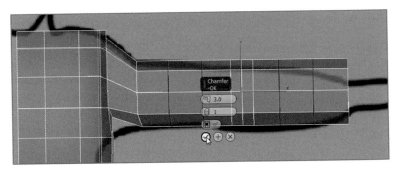

FIGURE 7.21 Chamfer the arm to add more edges for detail.

10. Select the edge at the wrist and, using the Select And Scale tool, scale down the wrist until it matches the image plane.

11. Move your way up the arm, selecting and scaling edges to match the image plane, as shown in Figure 7.22.

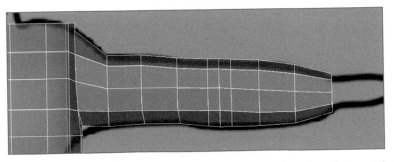

FIGURE 7.22 Scale down the edges along the arm from the wrist to match the image plane.

12. In Border mode, select the end of the arm (wrist) and, while holding down the Shift key, use the Select And Scale tool to scale the wrist border down, as shown in Figure 7.23 (left image).

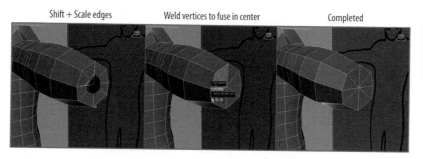

Shift + Scale edges · Weld vertices to fuse in center · Completed

FIGURE 7.23 Select the wrist's border and Shift+Scale down to center of wrist (left image). Weld the vertices (middle image), and the wrist cap is complete (right image).

13. Switch to Vertex mode, select the vertices of the smaller wrist hole, and select the Graphite Modeling Tools tab ➢ Vertices ➢ Weld ➢ Weld Settings to open the Weld Vertices caddy, as shown in Figure 7.23 (middle image). Click OK to close the dialog box.

This creates a completed cap at the end of the arm, as shown in Figure 7.23 (right). You will continue with the hand in a later section.

Creating the Legs

Continue with the previous exercise's scene file, or open the `Soldier_V03.max` scene file in the `Scenes` folder of the Soldier project downloaded from the book's companion web page. If you are starting with a new file, you will need to select the object before continuing. Then follow these steps:

1. In Edge mode, select the bottommost loop of edges on the model's torso.

2. Now Shift+Move the loop down on the Y-axis to create a new extrusion all the way down to the groin in the reference illustration, as shown in Figure 7.24.

You are starting to prepare the model for the legs and groin area.

3. Go to the top level by exiting the Edge tool. Use the Cut tool (Graphite Modeling Tools tab ➢ Edit panel ➢ Cut), and cut an edge starting at the top corner of the polygon closest to the groin. Cut about halfway to the right from the corner of the model's bottommost edge. See Figure 7.25 (left).

Using Shift while performing a Scale operation clones the selected objects much as with an extrusion using the Shift+Move method.

Shift + Move this edge loop down.

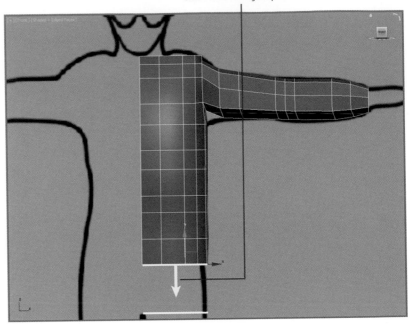

F I G U R E 7 . 2 4   **Select the edge loop at the bottom of the model and Shift+Move it down.**

Use the Cut tool to cut from here . . .   . . . to here.   In Vertex mode, select and move this vertex up.

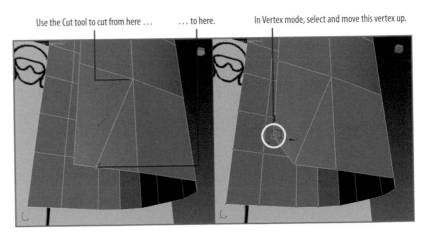

F I G U R E 7 . 2 5   **Cut the polygon at an angle to raise the corners (left). Select the corner vertex and move it up (right).**

4. Do the same for the polygon at the back of the model in the corresponding corner.

5. In Vertex mode, select the lowest inside vertices and move them up a bit to create a diagonal edge, as in Figure 7.25 (right). Do this for both the front and back of the model.

6. In Edge mode, select both of the new diagonal edges (front and back), and then in the Graphite Modeling Tools tab ➢ Edges panel, select Bridge ➢ Bridge Settings.

7. Use four segments to create a bridge, as shown in Figure 7.26. Doing so creates a bridge between the front and back.

   With the bridge in place, the border edge on the bottom of the torso resembles a capital letter *D*, as shown in Figure 7.26. If you extrude the leg down from here, the inner thigh will be flat. For a better starting point to form the leg, you need to cap the hole as you did with the arm previously.

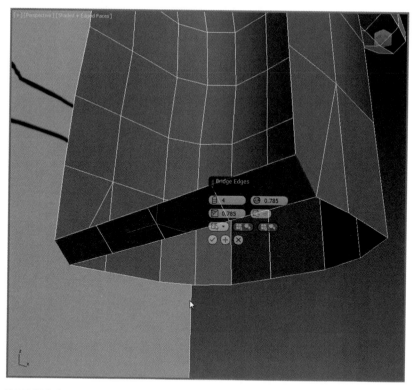

FIGURE 7.26 Bridge between two edges to create the groin area.

To begin the upper-thigh extrusion, continue with the following steps to cap the D shape.

8. Enter Border mode, select the D-shaped border edge, and Shift+Move down on the Z-axis to extrude the upper thigh downward to the middle of the thigh, as shown in Figure 7.27 (left).

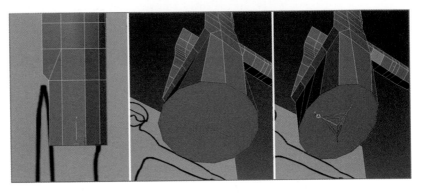

FIGURE 7.27   Creating the upper thigh

9. With the D-shaped border still selected, on the Graphite Modeling Tools tab ➢ Geometry (All) panel, click Cap Poly to cap the end of the thigh stump.

10. Enter Polygon mode and select the new poly. In the Graphite Modeling Tools tab ➢ Polygons, select the GeoPoly tool to make the end of the thigh a more even shape, as shown in Figure 7.27 (middle).

11. Select the thigh's end polygon and scale on the X-axis, as shown in Figure 7.27 (right) to create a more oval shape.

12. Delete the cap so the bottom of the leg is open once again.

13. Switch to See-Through mode, and then in the Front viewport, switch to Vertex mode and scale and move the vertices on the leg to match the image plane.

14. Check the Right viewport and shape the thigh as needed.

Notice that the bottom of the geometry should be located at about the top of the where the knee will be located. Use the Perspective viewport often to make sure some of the vertices are not being accidentally moved.

15. On the inside of the groin area where you created the four-segment bridge in steps 6 and 7, move the edges to make sure the segments are evenly spaced.

16. Switch to Border mode and select the border opening at the bottom of the leg.

17. Then use the Extrude Border method (Shift+Move) to extrude the leg down to the ankle, as shown in Figure 7.28 (left).

Step 15 should be repeated throughout the exercise to keep edges evenly spaced and ensure that the model is organized and clean.

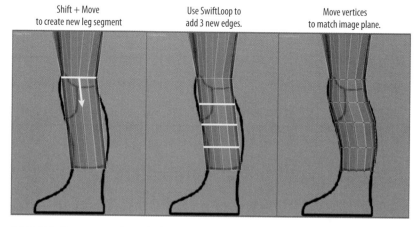

Shift + Move to create new leg segment — Use SwiftLoop to add 3 new edges. — Move vertices to match image plane.

F I G U R E 7 . 2 8 Extrude down to the ankle (left), use the SwiftLoop tool to create three new loops (middle), and fit the new edges to the image plane (right).

18. In the Graphite Modeling Tools tab ➣ Edit panel, click SwiftLoop, and create three new horizontal segments around the leg, as shown in Figure 7.28 (middle).

19. Then fit the vertices to the shape of the soldier's leg in the side image plane in the Right viewport, as shown in Figure 7.28 (right).

20. Go into the Front viewport and do the same to shape the leg properly.

21. In Border mode, select the ankle border, as shown in Figure 7.29 (left) and Shift+Scale the border down on the Z- and Y-axis and in toward the center of the ankle, leaving a small hole, as shown in Figure 7.29 (middle).

22. Then switch to Vertex mode, select the vertices around the resulting small hole, and use Weld (Graphite Modeling Tools tab ➣ Vertices ➣ Weld ➣ Weld Settings) to bring the vertices together, as shown in Figure 7.29 (right).

Select the border.   Shift + Scale into   Weld the vertices.
                         the center of the ankle.

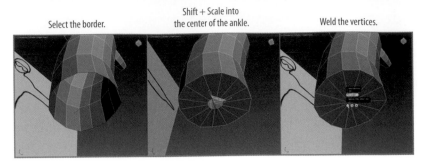

FIGURE 7.29   Closing the ankle's hole

23. Adjust the Weld Threshold setting as needed to weld these vertices together.

Fixing Up the Body

Continue with the previous exercise's scene file, or open the `Soldier_V04.max` scene file in the `Scenes` folder of the Soldier project from the book's companion web page. If you are starting with a newly opened file, you will need to select the soldier.

The pelvis looks a bit funky. You need to streamline the mesh by combining some edges:

1. Select the vertical edges at the waist (select a single vertical edge and then on the Graphite Modeling Tools tab ➤ Modify Selection panel, click Ring), as shown in Figure 7.30.

Select the ring of vertical edges.

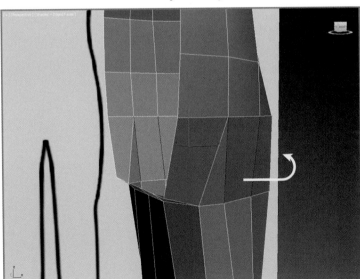

FIGURE 7.30   Select a single edge at the pelvis area and use Ring to prepare for Collapse.

2. Right-click to bring up the quad menu.

3. In the upper-left quad, in the tools 1 section, choose Collapse.
   Doing so brings the two horizontal edge loops at the top and bottom of the selected vertical edges together into one edge loop.

4. In the Perspective viewport, use Orbit (or the ViewCube®) to adjust the view to see under the groin area.

5. In Edge mode, select and move the segments up (left) to round out the groin section (right), as shown in Figure 7.31.

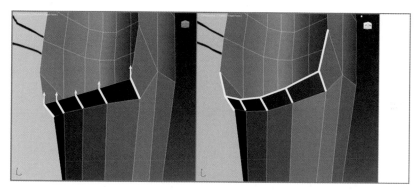

FIGURE 7.31 Select the edges in the groin area (left) and move them up to round them (right).

6. In the Perspective viewport, use Orbit again around the leg and look for any spikes or pinches that may have occurred in the model.
   The goal is to split the difference between edges so that they're as close to midway between adjacent edges as possible.

7. Save your work!

Keep in mind that joint edges, such as the edges that make up the knee and elbow, need to stay where they are. Figure 7.32 shows the leg with good edge spacing. Take a moment to go back through the model and tweak the rest of it until you feel it is right. When you're modeling for animation, the mesh flow is an important factor.

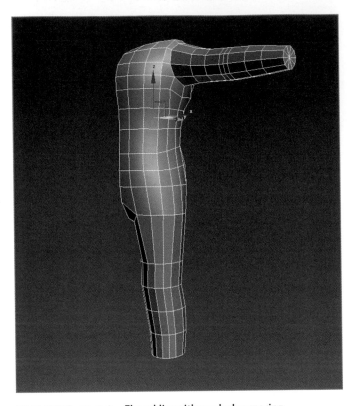

FIGURE 7.32 The soldier with good edge spacing

THE ESSENTIALS AND BEYOND

This chapter explored and explained several tools used in modeling, organic and otherwise, to begin the basic form of the soldier character. Reference planes of the soldier design were used at first. Then from a simple box, a torso was formed to match the general shapes shown in the reference images. The arms and legs were extruded and shaped to match as well. As you can see, the more that you model, the easier the process becomes and the more detailed and finessed your models will turn out.

ADDITIONAL EXERCISE

▶ Try creating a character of your own—a female character or something more edgy like an alien. Get reference images or draw out what you want the character to look like, scan the drawings, and use them for reference. Use and expand on the techniques used in this chapter and Chapters 8 and 9.

CHAPTER 8

Character Poly Modeling: Part II

Realistic computer-generated (CG) characters are common in television and films; they appear as stunt doubles, as members of vast crowds, and as primary characters. Sometimes using a CG character works better than using a real person. Using a CG stunt double is safer and sometimes cheaper than using a live stunt person, and weird creatures can be created with better clarity by using CG rather than puppetry or special makeup effects.

In this chapter, you will continue with the model of a soldier, focusing on using the Editable Poly toolset to create a relatively low-polygon-count soldier model suitable for character animation and for use in a game engine.

This chapter includes the following topics:

▶ **Completing the main body**

▶ **Creating the accessories**

▶ **Putting on the boots**

▶ **Creating the hands**

Completing the Main Body

Continue with the previous chapter's exercise scene file, or open the `Soldier_V05.max` scene file in the `Scenes` folder of the Soldier project from this book's companion web page at `www.sybex.com/go/3dsmax2014essentials`.

To create the other half of the model you have so far, as shown in Figure 8.1, you are going to use the Symmetry modifier, which works by mirroring and then automatically welding the vertices along a seam. When the Symmetry modifier is applied to a mesh, any edits you make to the original half of the mesh also occur interactively to the other half of the mesh. This saves time and keeps the two halves of the model consistent.

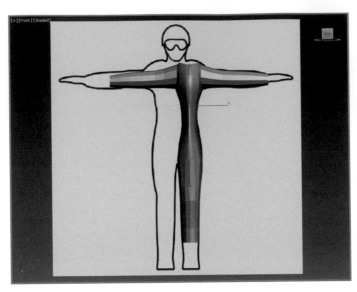

FIGURE 8.1 The results of the Symmetry modifier added when the pivot point is not in the center of the model

This mirror technique gives the same results but does not weld separate halves of the model together. You will mirror the soldier's body in the following steps:

1. In the Front viewport, select the model.

2. Go to the command panel to the right of the interface, and in the Modify panel, go to the Modifier List.

3. From the list, choose Symmetry.
   Depending on where the pivot point is on your mesh, the results of the modifier may look a bit strange, as shown in Figure 8.1.

4. In the Symmetry Parameters rollout, set Mirror Axis to X.

5. In the modifier stack, click the plus-sign icon (▣) to expand the Symmetry modifier hierarchy and then select Mirror.
   This will release the mirror plane in the modifier and allow you to edit where the mirroring takes place.

6. In the Front viewport, select the X-axis arrow of the Transform gizmo and move the mirror plane to the left until you get a whole soldier, as shown in Figure 8.2.
   When you begin to edit the mesh, the first thing you will do is go back down the modifier stack to the editable poly. It will appear that the symmetry side of the mesh has disappeared. This is not the case. In fact, the Autodesk 3ds Max software evaluates the modifiers in the stack

from the bottom up, and when you are below a modifier in the stack, the software doesn't calculate the modifiers above it. It is easy enough to fix. In a line of icons below the modifier stack, select Show End Result On/Off Toggle (**I**). This will allow you to see the end result of the Symmetry modifier regardless of where you are in the stack.

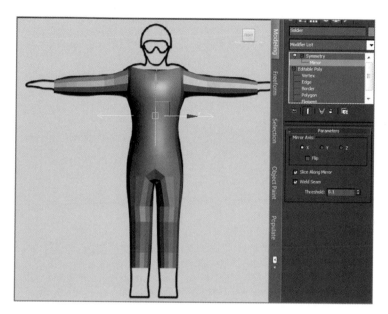

FIGURE 8.2 Using the Symmetry modifier, move the mirror plane so the main body shape is whole.

7. Enter Edge mode, and select the edges at the top of the right side of the torso geometry, as shown in Figure 8.3 (left image).

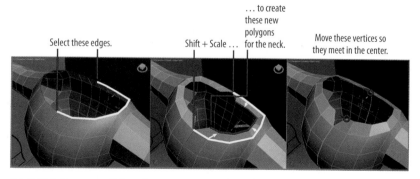

Select these edges.   Shift + Scale ...   ... to create these new polygons for the neck.   Move these vertices so they meet in the center.

FIGURE 8.3 Select the edges around the neck area (left). Shift+Scale to extrude the edges (middle). Move the vertices so they meet in the middle, and adjust the remaining vertices (right image).

8. Shift+Scale them on the X- and Y-axes to extrude the top of the shoulders toward the neck as shown in Figure 8.3 (middle image).

9. Switch to Vertex mode and move the vertices to better match the shape shown in Figure 8.3 (right image).

10. Select all the inside edges of the newly created polygons.

11. Use Shift+Move and extrude the edges down along the Z-axis (if you are working in the Perspective viewport) to create a lip.

12. Switch to Border mode () and select the edge at the bottom of the newly created lip. A border is a sequence of edges with polygons on only one side.

13. On the Graphite Modeling Tools tab ➢ Geometry (All) panel, click Cap Poly. A Cap Poly caps an entire border loop with a single polygon (see Figure 8.4).

When you're ready, you are going to combine the two parts of the model.

FIGURE 8.4   The soldier model shown with the newly created lip and Cap Poly

14. To combine the Symmetry side of the model with the original side, go to the Graphite Modeling Tools tab, choose the Polygon Modeling panel, and click Collapse Stack.

The Symmetry modifier automatically welds the mesh together at the seam, when the edges are within the Threshold value of the modifier and Weld is checked. Collapse Stack makes two sides one object.

Creating the Accessories

Continue with the previous exercise's scene file, or open the `Soldier_V06.max` scene file in the `Scenes` folder of the Soldier project from this book's companion web page. Most of the smaller detail in the model will be added through textures; however, adding detail such as pouches, a vest, and a holster into the actual geometry helps tremendously. This creates a better silhouette for your character.

Utility Belt

To create the belt, you're going to chamfer and extrude an edge loop that's located closest to the belt line on the model.

> You can also use the shortcut by double-clicking one of the edges.
>
>

1. Select the Soldier and enter Edge mode. Choose an edge in the middle of the soldier's waistline, and on the Graphite Modeling Tools tab ➢ Modify Selection panel, click Loop.

2. With the edge loop selected, select the Graphite Modeling Tools tab, enter Edges mode, and then select Chamfer ➢ Chamfer Settings.

3. Set Edge Chamfer Amount to **1.5** and click OK.

4. With the two edges from the chamfer still selected, hold Shift and select the modeling ribbon ➢ Polygon Modeling and then select the Polygon icon.
   Doing so selects the polygons associated with the two selected edges. If that doesn't work, hold down the Ctrl key and click on the remaining polygons that need to be selected.

5. Next, select the modeling ribbon ➢ Polygons ➢ Extrude ➢ Extrude Settings, and make sure you extrude by Local Normal with a Height value of **0.5**, as shown in Figure 8.5.

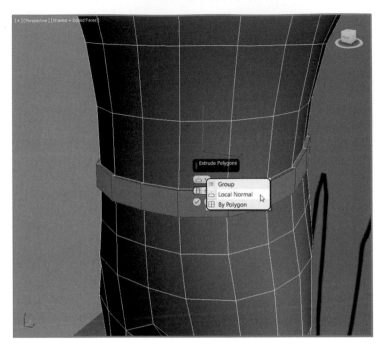

FIGURE 8.5   Extrude polygons for the belt.

Pouch

Next, you're going to block out a pouch on the belt:

1. Delete two polygons of the belt on the body's left, as shown in the left image in Figure 8.6.

2. Then select the four polygons directly above and below the deleted area.

3. Select the modeling ribbon ➢ Polygons ➢ Extrude ➢ Extrude Settings, set an amount of 0.5, and then click Apply And Continue (⊞) to apply one extrusion.

4. Then click OK (☑) for a second extrusion and to exit the caddy. The pouch is now extruded twice for a total extrusion depth of 1 inch.

5. Select the four polygons on top of the bottom half of the pouch and the four polygons on the bottom of the top half of the pouch, as shown in Figure 8.7, and delete them.

   Figure 8.7 shows the model in See-Through (Alt+X) mode to better reveal the polygons to be deleted.

Delete these two polygons, then ...   ... delete these two polygons, then ...

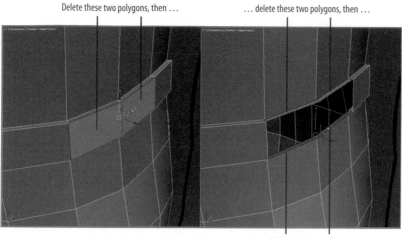

... delete these two polygons.

FIGURE 8.6 Delete the two polygons on the left side of the belt (left image); then select the indicated polygons for the next step (right image).

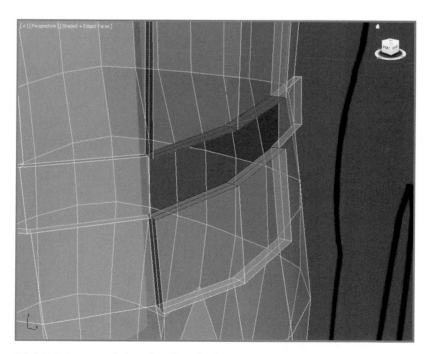

FIGURE 8.7 Delete the selected polygons.

6. Select Edge mode and then select the top and bottom edges around the newly deleted areas, as shown in Figure 8.8.

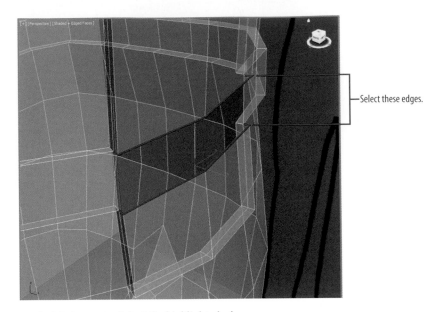

Select these edges.

FIGURE 8.8 Select the highlighted edges.

7. Select Graphite Modeling Tools tab ➤ Edges ➤ Bridge ➤ Bridge Settings to open the Bridge Edges caddy, as shown in Figure 8.9. Accept the default values, and click OK to exit the dialog box.

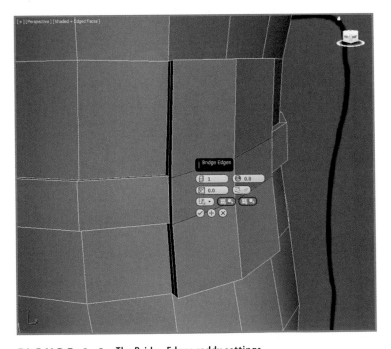

FIGURE 8.9 The Bridge Edges caddy settings

The pouch should look like a box; if it doesn't, move vertices around so it does. Once the pouch has the correct shape, move the side polygons farther out away, from the belt, to give the pouch more depth.

Vest

The vest details will mostly come from images that will be placed on the soldier model later in the book. To add some depth to the vest that the character will be wearing, you will want to cut out a level of clothing under the arms. To do so, follow these steps:

1. Select two columns and three rows of polygons directly underneath the armpit, as shown in Figure 8.10.

2. Select the modeling ribbon ➤ Polygons ➤ Bevel ➤ Bevel Settings, and in the caddy, use a Height value of –0.5 and an Outline value of –1.0. OK the dialog box.

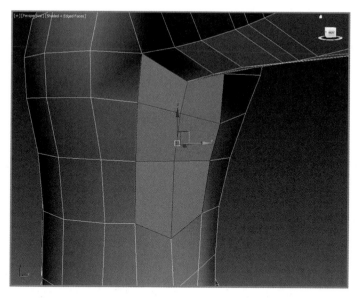

FIGURE 8.10 Select the polygons directly under the armpit.

3. Adjust any vertices as necessary for an even and smooth look. Do the same for the other side of the model.

   The final appearance of the area underneath the armpit is shown in Figure 8.11.

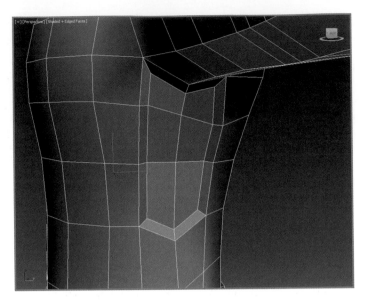

FIGURE 8.11 Final appearance of the area under the arm

Leg Strap

Next, you're going to add a leg strap to hold a gun holster:

1. Select the Graphite Modeling Tools tab ➢ Edit panel and click SwiftLoop. Add a single horizontal loop below the groin area.

    When the loop is created, it is crooked, but you need the new edges to be straight. The SwiftLoop tool should still be active when you're doing this.

2. After you create the edge, hold Ctrl+Alt and click and drag the edge down, and you will see that it straightens.

3. Turn off SwiftLoop. Enter Edge mode and select one edge of the new edge loops you created in the previous step.

4. Select the Graphite Modeling Tools tab ➢ Modify Selection panel and click Loop, and then select Edges ➢ Chamfer ➢ Chamfer Settings.

5. Enter an Edge Chamfer Amount value of **1.5**, and click OK.

    The final results are shown in Figure 8.12.

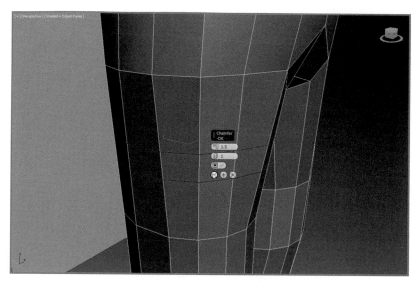

FIGURE 8.12 Edge loop with a 1.5 chamfer amount to create a strap around the leg

6. Select the loop of new polygons by holding Shift and clicking the Polygon icon in the Polygon Modeling panel. This is a shortcut to selecting all the new polygons.

7. Then select the Graphite Modeling Tools tab. Enter Polygon mode ➢ Polygons tab ➢ Extrude ➢ Extrude Settings, change Extrusion Type to Local Normal, and enter a Height value of 0.4, as shown in Figure 8.13. Then click OK.

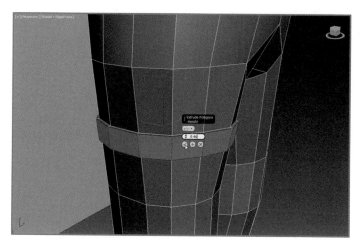

FIGURE 8.13 Extrude polygons to create a strap for the leg.

8. Select a strip of polygons that goes from the top of the leg strap to the bottom of the belt, and delete them, as shown in Figure 8.14.

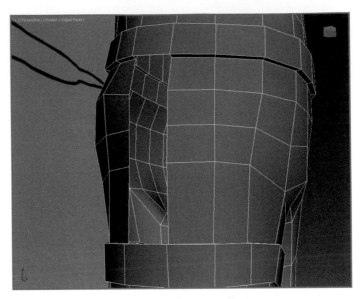

FIGURE 8.14 Select and delete the strip of polygons running from the top of the strap to the bottom of the belt.

9. Use Bridge to create the polygons by selecting the edge at the leg strap and the edge at the belt. The sides of the holster are still open, as shown in Figure 8.15.

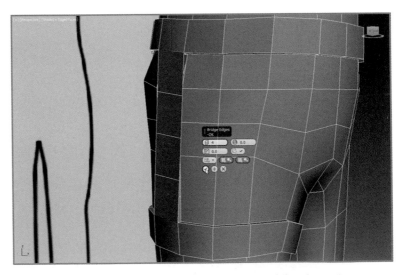

FIGURE 8.15 Select the edge at the leg strap and the edge at the belt, and use Bridge to create the polygons needed to fill out the strap.

10. Select and move the newly created edges so they line up with the contour of the soldier's body, as shown in Figure 8.16.

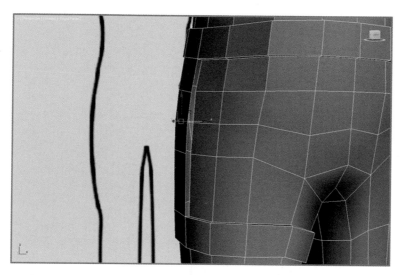

FIGURE 8.16   Select and move the edges from the bridge so they line up with the contour of the soldier's body.

11. Select the edges between the new bridged polygons and the model's hip, and then use Bridge, change segments to 1, and leave all other parameters at the default, as shown in Figure 8.17. Be sure to repeat this on the other side of the holster.

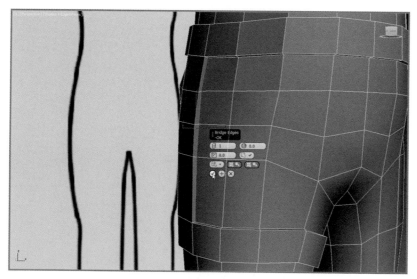

FIGURE 8.17   Use Bridge to fill the gap on the side of the strap.

12. Exit Polygon mode by clicking on the Polygon icon or select 6 on your keyboard and then, with the soldier model still selected, at the bottom of the interface click the Isolate Selection Toggle button (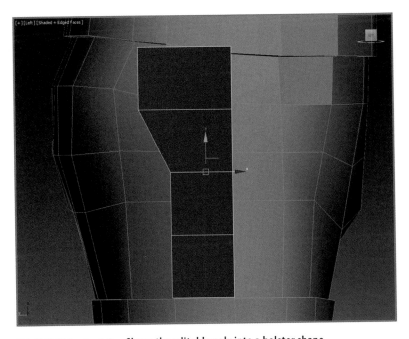) or press Alt+Q.

Gun Holster

Using a simple plane, you will create the gun holster:

1. On the command panel, select Create ➢ Geometry ➢ Plane, and in the Left viewport—in the Point-Of-View (POV) viewport label menu, choose Left—create a plane with these parameters: Length: 20; Width: 7; Length Segs: 4; Width Segs: 1.

2. Then position the plane where the holster will be on the soldier.

3. Convert the plane to an editable poly (Graphite Modeling Tools tab ➢ Polygon Modeling panel ➢ Convert to Poly), and then in Vertex mode, shape it as shown in Figure 8.18.

FIGURE 8.18   Shape the editable poly into a holster shape.

4. In the Modify panel, use the Modifier List to add a Shell modifier to the plane and give it the following parameters: Inner Amount: **1.2**; Outer Amount: **1.2**; Segments: **1**.

5. Select the body, and from the modeling ribbon, select Geometry (All) ➢ Attach and click on the gun holster.

6. Exit Isolate Selection mode by selecting the icon or pressing Alt+Q.

Putting on the Boots

Continue with the previous exercise's scene file, or open the Soldier_V07.max scene file in the Scenes folder of the Soldier project from the book's companion web page. At this point, you are probably feeling comfortable with the tools and interface, so we'll pare down the steps somewhat unless the procedures are new to this chapter. Follow these steps:

1. To create the boots, start by creating a cylinder in the Perspective viewport.

2. In the Create panel, select Geometry ➢ Cylinder, and set the following: Radius: **5.0**; Height: **8.0**; Height Segments: **1**; Cap Segments: **1**; Sides: **8**.

3. Make sure the Smooth option is checked. Create the cylinder.

4. Select the cylinder and choose the modeling ribbon ➢ Polygon Modeling ➢ Convert to Poly.

5. Then position the cylinder under the left leg, below the cuff of the pants.

6. Enter Polygon mode and delete the topmost and bottommost polygons that were created with the cylinder.

7. Using the Right viewport, move vertices on the cylinder so the shape mimics the form of the top of the boot in the image plane.

8. Ignore the two bottom-front edges of the cylinder where the top of the boot would be, and select the bottom U-shaped edges of the cylinder.

9. Extrude-move (Shift+Move) the edges of the back half of the boot top to the bottom of the boot in the image plane, as shown in Figure 8.19.

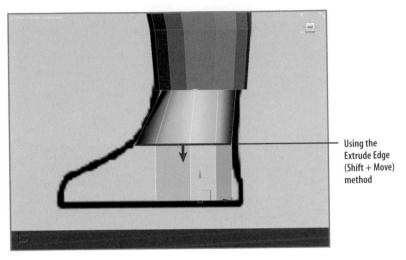

Using the Extrude Edge (Shift + Move) method

FIGURE 8.19   Using the Shift + Move method to create another set of polygons for the U-shaped back and side part of the boot

10. Select the two bottom-front edges that you ignored previously, and extrude-move them four times to form the extruded polygons to the image plane, as shown in Figure 8.20.

FIGURE 8.20   Using Extrude Edge (Shift + Move) method to create four new polygons that form with the image plane for the top of the boot

You will need a total of four rows of polygons for the top and front of the boot. As you extrude, you can release the mouse button after one extrusion, and then Shift+Move again for the next extrusion.

11. Repeat for a total of four new strips of polygons, as Figure 8.20 shows. Form the new polygons as needed to fit the top of the boot.

12. In Edge mode, select the vertical edges on either side of the gap.

13. Then in the Graphite Modeling Tools tab ➤ Edges ➤ Bridge ➤ Bridge Settings, enter three segments, and bridge the gap, as shown in Figure 8.21.

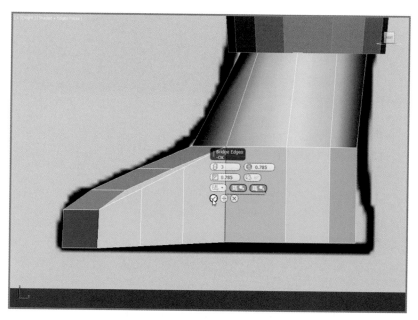

FIGURE 8.21   Use Bridge to fill the gap and connect the two selected edges.

14. Repeat step 13 on the opposite side of the boot.

15. Switch to Vertex mode, and select the vertices on the top/side of the foot and the top vertices from the newly created bridge polygons. From the Graphite Modeling Tools tab ➤ Vertices ➤ Weld, open the caddy, set Weld Threshold to 2.3, and click OK, as shown in Figure 8.22.

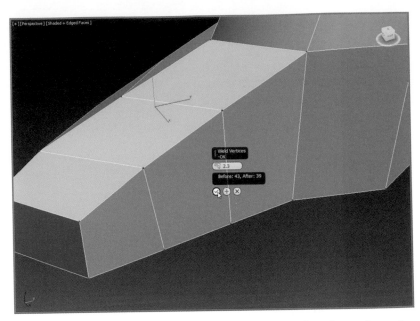

FIGURE 8.22   With the vertices selected, use Weld to close the gap the previous step created.

16. In the Graphite Modeling Tools tab. select ➤ Edit ➤ SwiftLoop.

17. Create a new horizontal edge loop around the boot from heel to toe on the side of the boot and around the ankle, as shown in Figure 8.23.

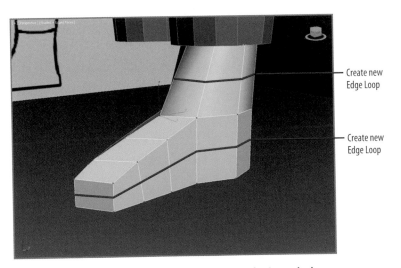

Create new Edge Loop

Create new Edge Loop

FIGURE 8.23   Use SwiftLoop to create new horizontal edges around the side of the lower boot and ankle.

The eight segments you defined on the original boot cylinder are not enough, so you need to create more segments for the cylinder.

18. In Edge mode, select the middle vertical edge of the foot, and select Loop.

19. In the Graphite Modeling Tools tab ➤Edges ➤ Chamfer ➤ Chamfer Settings, enter the caddy parameters:

Edge Chamfer Amount: **1.667**

Connect Edge Segments: **1**

20. Click OK.

21. Follow the same process to chamfer the very back vertical edge on the boot (running just below the calf), and use the added vertices to round out the heel.

The boot is a bit rough still, so edit the vertices and smooth out the foot model as in Figure 8.24.

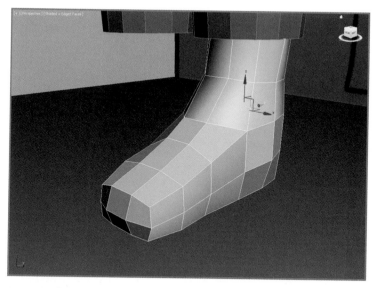

FIGURE 8.24 Smoothing out the sides of the boot

When you are happy with how this looks, follow these steps:

1. Make a clone of the boot (use the Shift+Move method).

2. Orient the boot under the right leg.

3. Attach the boots to the rest of the body, as you did with the gun holster.

Figure 8.25 shows the two completed boots, now attached to the body.

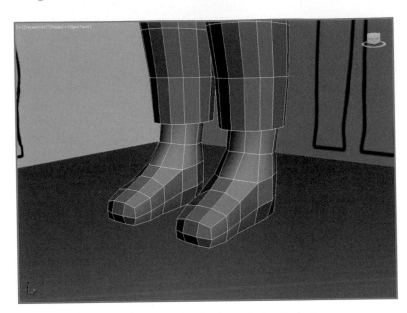

FIGURE 8.25   Boots completed and attached to the body

Creating the Hands

Continue with the previous exercise's scene file, or open the `Soldier_V08.max` scene file in the `Scenes` folder of the Soldier project from the book's companion web page. In this section, you will create simple "mitten hands" for the soldier:

1. To create one of the hands, start with a box: Create a box primitive in the Perspective viewport, and then in the Modify panel, set the following: Length: **7.5**; Width: **16.0**; Height: **5.0**; Length Segs: **3**; Width Segs: **3**; Height Segs: **1**.

2. Position the box in your Top viewport at the wrist.

3. Finish positioning it in the Front viewport and convert it to an editable poly.

4. Then, in Vertex mode, move the vertices to create a mitten arc, as shown in Figure 8.26.

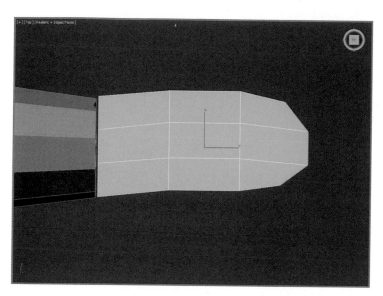

FIGURE 8.26 Reshape vertices to create a mitten shape.

5. With the hand selected, go into Polygon mode and select the polygons on the hand where the wrist and the arm meet; then delete them. The result is a hollow hand.

6. In Edge mode, select the edges running lengthwise along the top and bottom of the hand.

7. Then select the Graphite Modeling Tools tab ➢ Edges ➢ Chamfer ➢ Chamfer Settings, and set Edge Chamfer Amount to 0.7, as shown in Figure 8.27.

Select Edges and Chamfer.

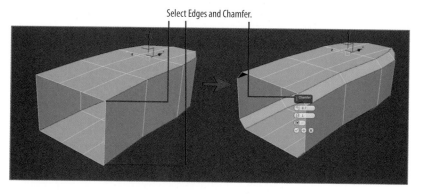

FIGURE 8.27 Select and chamfer the edges running lengthwise along the top and bottom of the hand.

8. Use SwiftLoop to create an edge up from the wrist, as shown in Figure 8.28.

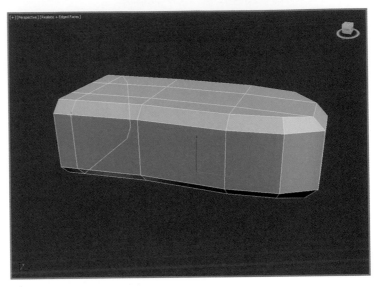

FIGURE 8.28   Use SwiftLoop to create an edge at the wrist.

9. In Polygon mode, select the three polygons on the side of the hand, forward of the newly created edge, as shown in Figure 8.29.

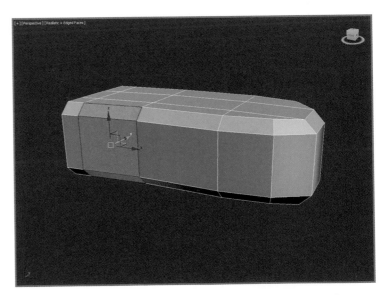

FIGURE 8.29   Select the three polygons to prepare the extrude.

10. Choose Graphite Modeling Tools tab ➤ Polygons ➤ Extrude ➤ Extrude Settings, set Extrusion Type to Group, and enter a Height value of 0.8. Click OK to exit the dialog.

11. Then move the corner edges in to round out the beginning shape of the thumb.

12. Bevel the polygons at the end of the thumb for the knuckle: Choose modeling ribbon ➤ Polygons ➤ Bevel ➤ Bevel Settings.

13. Set Height to 3.0 and Outline to –0.55, and click OK.

14. Bevel again, but change Height to 2.0 and Outline to –0.25, and click OK.

15. Adjust the polygons, vertices, and edges to get the thumb to look like Figure 8.30.

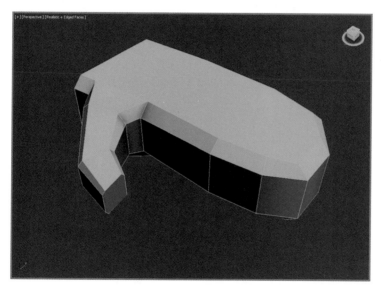

FIGURE 8.30 The thumb with all its joints

16. Select the polygons at the ends of the thumb and fingers.

17. Choose modeling ribbon ➤ Polygon Modeling ➤ Use Soft Selection icon (⬤).

18. In the Front viewport, move the thumb and fingers down to give them a slight slope.

19. In the Perspective viewport, scale the wrist down to fit within the sleeve if necessary.

20. In the main toolbar, select the Mirror tool (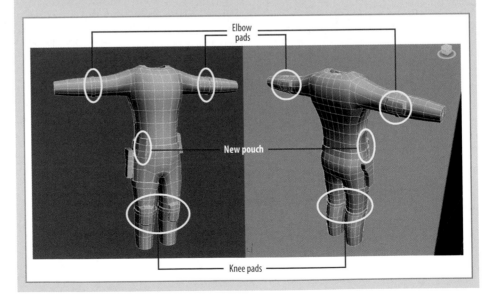). In the Mirror dialog, set Mirror Axis to X and change Offset to –134.5. In Clone Selection, choose Clone. Click OK to close the dialog box.

21. Select the soldier, and in the Graphite Modeling Tools tab ➤ Geometry (All) panel, select Attach, and select the gloves.

THE ESSENTIALS AND BEYOND

In this chapter, you completed the main body for the soldier and continued using edge loops and vertices to shape the accessories and various parts of the character model.

ADDITIONAL EXERCISES

▶ Create additional pouches or straps for your model. (Keep in mind that any changes you make to the design of the book's model will make your model differ from the one you use for texturing in Chapter 11, "Textures and UV Workflow: The Soldier.")

▶ With the tools you used to create the belt and pouches, create geometry for knee pads and elbow pads.

You can see the extra accessories on the soldier model here:

Elbow pads

New pouch

Knee pads

CHAPTER 9

Character Poly Modeling: Part III

Finishing elements are critical to the veracity of a model's design. To make things easier, such elements can be modeled separately and later incorporated into the base model. In this chapter, you will finish the model of the soldier you started in Chapter 7, "Character Poly Modeling: Part I," and continued in Chapter 8, "Character Poly Modeling: Part II." To do that, you will model the head shape, merge the head shape with elements such as goggles and a face mask, and integrate them into the scene.

This chapter includes the following topics:

▶ **Creating the head**

▶ **Merging and attaching the head's accessories**

Creating the Head

Continue with the previous exercise's scene file (from Chapter 8), or open the `Soldier_V09.max` scene file in the `Scenes` folder of the Soldier project on the book's web page at `www.sybex.com/go/3dsmax2014essentials`.

The soldier's head will consist of four parts: a helmet, goggles, a face mask, and a head shape on which they can sit. The easiest way to create and fit these components is to start with the head shape. First, though, you need to adjust the body's neckline so working with it is a bit easier. Right now the neck area is almost a circle shape. You want it to be closer to an oval that follows the contour of the rest of the model. Follow these steps:

1. In Polygon mode, select the front of the neckline, and then, from the Graphite Modeling Tools tab, choose Polygon Modeling ➢ Use Soft Selection (⬤).

2. In the Soft panel, select the tab to reveal the soft parameters. Change the Falloff value to 4.000, as shown in Figure 9.1.

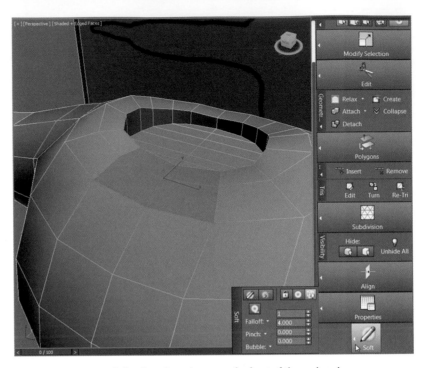

FIGURE 9.1   Soft-select the polygons at the front of the neck and move them down.

3. Move the polygons down on the Y-axis. Do the same for the back of the model.

   These actions will smoothly create a lower neckline, giving more definition to the shoulders as well.

4. Select Create Panel ➤ Geometry ➤ Cylinder. Under the Object Type rollout is an AutoGrid check box.

   When the box is checked, it activates a construction grid that allows you to create objects on the surface of the soldier.

5. Click AutoGrid, and then click and drag within the neck of the soldier model and set these parameters: Radius: **5.0**; Height: **3.0**; Height Segments: **1**; Cap Segments: **1**; Sides: **12**.

6. Convert the cylinder using Polygon Modeling ➤ Convert To Poly.

You'll model half of each part and then use mirroring to save time.

7. In Polygon mode, select and delete the left half, the top, and the bottom of the cylinder, and move the edges and vertices so the new neck geometry is formed better within the neckline, as shown in Figure 9.2.

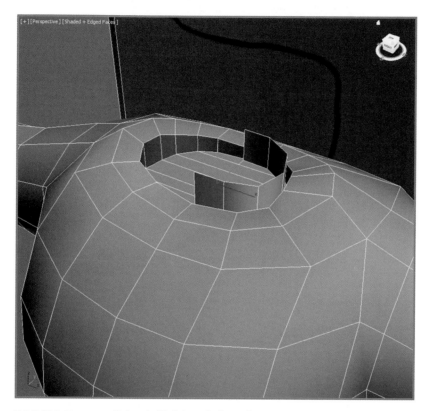

FIGURE 9.2   Delete half of the cylinder and its top and bottom.

8. Select the top edges of the cylinder and extrude-move them (Shift+Move) to create another level of polygons. The neck now has two rows of polygons.

9. Next, select the first edge on the top nearest where the Adam's apple would be, and extrude-move to create a new polygon.

10. Move the edge up along the Z-axis, as shown in Figure 9.3.

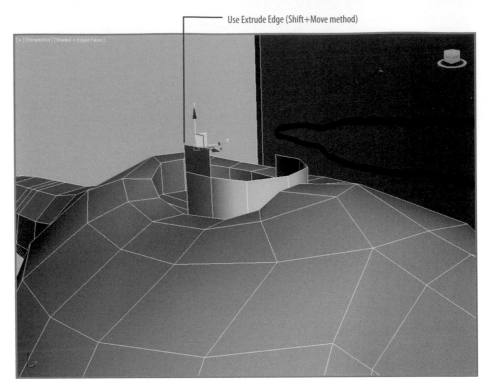

Use Extrude Edge (Shift+Move method)

FIGURE 9.3 Begin the creation of the neck with Extrude.

Outlining the Head

In the following steps, you will create an outline of the head by creating one strip of polygons and then forming them to the side image plane. You will extrude 15 times and move the edges to create the general form of a head. Be sure to keep the outer edge of the head inside the edges of the image plane; that way, you'll have room to fit the head accessories.

You should still have the edge selected from the previous exercise:

1. Use extrude-move again, but when you finish one polygon, release the mouse button; then click again and move the edge to create another extruded polygon.

   You'll do this 14 more times, following the form of the head in the image plane, as shown in Figure 9.4.

2. In the Front viewport, select the edge on the top base of the neck about where the ear might be.

3. Using Shift+Move, position a polygon strip as you did in step 1, but this time for the side of the head. Extrude a total of five segments up from the neck.

4. In Edge mode, use Bridge (Graphite Modeling Tools tab ➢ Edges ➢ Bridge). You will use the Bridge tool with the default settings, which will create a single segment between the two selected edges. This will fill the gap between the side of the head and the nearest edge on the top of the head, as shown in Figure 9.5.

5. To build the front of the face, start by selecting the two edges just under the chin and use Shift+Move to extrude them out to the right, as shown in Figure 9.6.

6. In Vertex mode, go to the Graphite Modeling Tools tab ➢ Vertices ➢ Target Weld.

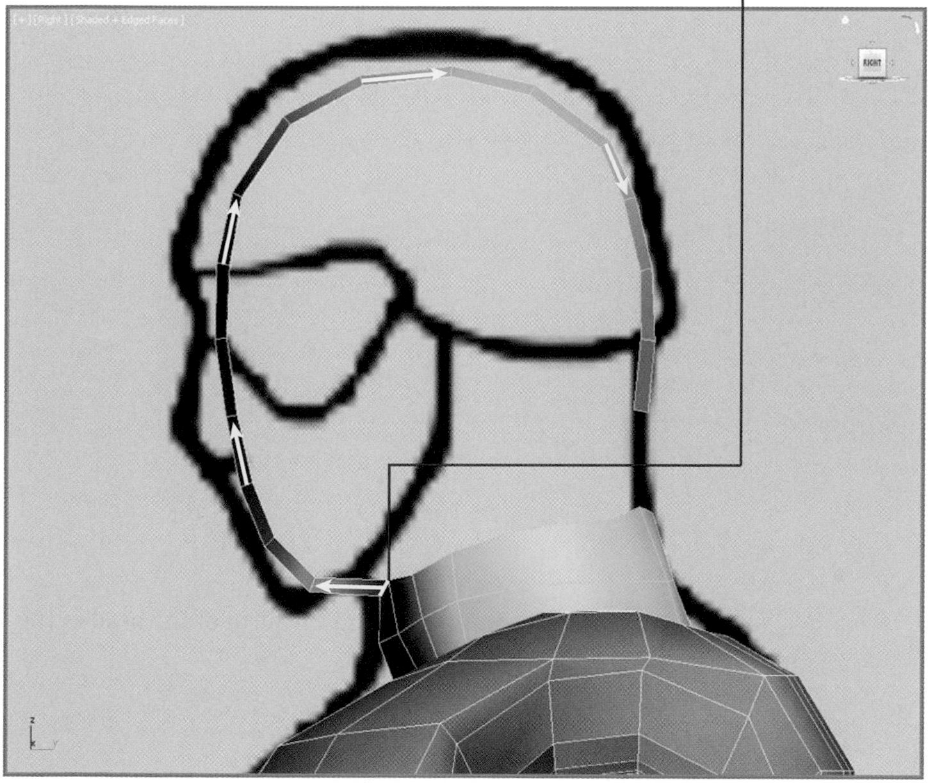

Use Extrude Edge (Shift+Move method). Do this 15 times, following the form of the head in the image plane.

FIGURE 9.4 Following the image plane, create the head outline using the Shift+Move method.

Bridge this gap.   Extrude from here ... to here.

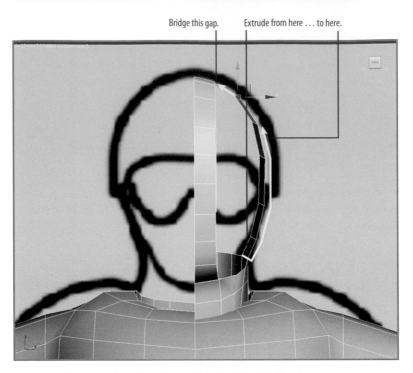

FIGURE 9.5   Creating polygons for the side of the head

Extrude these.   Weld these.

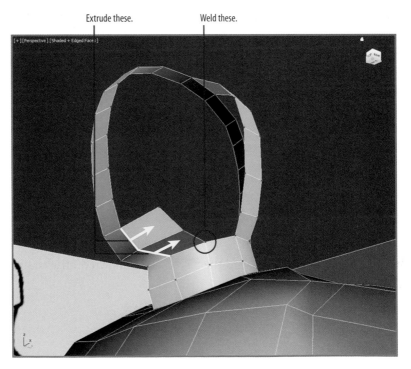

FIGURE 9.6   Extrude edges to the right and weld the neck vertices.

7. Click one vertex and drag a line to the other to fuse the vertices together. First click the vertex on the new polygon closest to the neck, and then click on the neck vertex, shown in Figure 9.6. This will fuse the new polygons for the jowls to the neck.

8. Back in Edge mode, select the two rightmost edges of the polygons you just created for the jowls, and then use Shift+Move to extrude those edges up on the Z-axis.

9. On the side of the head, match the number of segments with the segments on the outer head strip you already created. The result is shown in Figure 9.7.

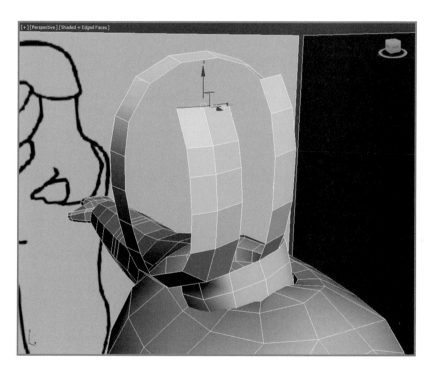

FIGURE 9.7 Extrude a new strip; match the segments.

10. Select the edges shown on the left side of Figure 9.8, and then use Bridge to curve the strip toward the forehead, as shown on the right in Figure 9.8.

11. As you did in step 8, in Edge mode use Shift+Move to extrude another row of polygons in toward the front of the face.

Select these edges and use Bridge.

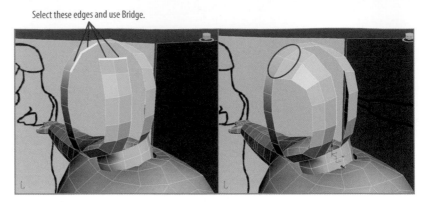

FIGURE 9.8   Use Bridge to close the gap.

12. Then in Vertex mode, use Target Weld on either side of the front face strip, as shown in Figure 9.9.

Looking at the ring of edges from the front of the head to the side of the head, it's clear you don't have enough horizontal edges.

Use Target Weld on the vertices.   Use Extrude Edge (Shift+Move method).

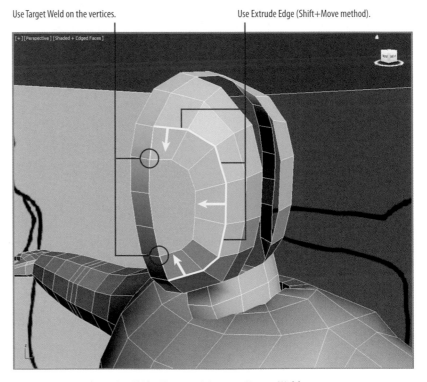

FIGURE 9.9   Use Shift+Move and then use Target Weld.

13. Select the edge closest to where the bridge of the nose would be, and then use Chamfer (from the Graphite Modeling Tools tab, choose Edges ➤ Chamfer ➤ Chamfer Settings) with an Edge Chamfer Amount value of **1.346**, and then click OK. Try to keep the edges equally spaced, as shown in Figure 9.10.

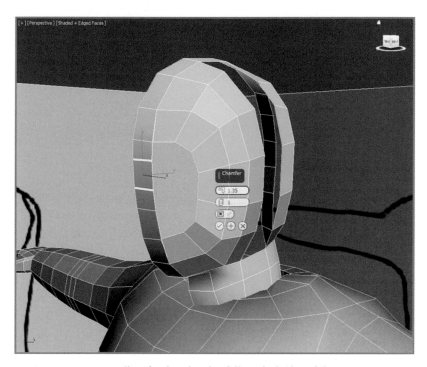

FIGURE 9.10   Chamfer the edge that falls at the bridge of the nose.

14. Select the eight edges on the front of the face and the side of the face, and then use Bridge, as shown in Figure 9.11.

    Notice that there is nowhere to weld to on the vertical edge on the top of the head. You need to create another edge running down the front of the face and then weld the vertices together to close the head.

15. From the Graphite Modeling Tools tab, choose Edit to access the Cut tool, and then cut from the dead-end edge at the top of the face down to the bottom of the neck, as shown in Figure 9.12. Make sure you start and end the cut directly on the vertices.

16. In Vertex mode, select the two vertices at the top of the cut, and then from the Graphite Modeling Tools tab, choose Vertices ➤ Weld ➤ Weld Settings and modify the Weld Threshold setting until the two vertices are welded together.

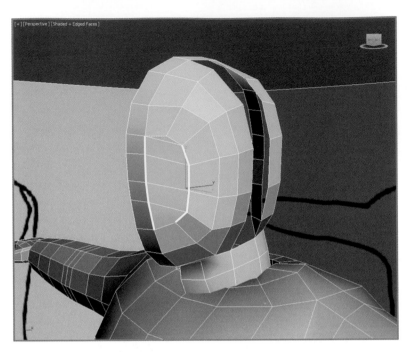

FIGURE 9.11 Select edges and use Bridge.

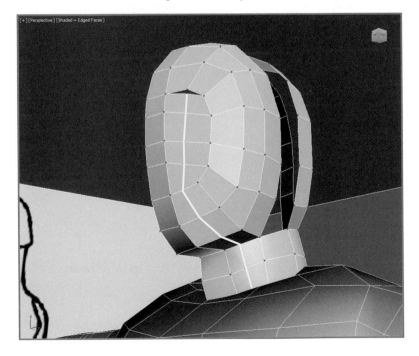

FIGURE 9.12 Use the Cut tool to create a new edge running down the front of the face.

Rounding Out the Face

Now it is time to round out the face a bit. The face doesn't have to be perfectly round, but it will help if it is close to a round shape. The majority of the head mesh you will create will be covered with the goggles, helmet, and face mask. However, you can use the geometry you create to fit and form those accessories:

1. In Edge mode, select the edges around the ear and use Bridge to close the gap, as shown in Figure 9.13.

   Looking at the back of the head, you can see an edge open on the bottom.

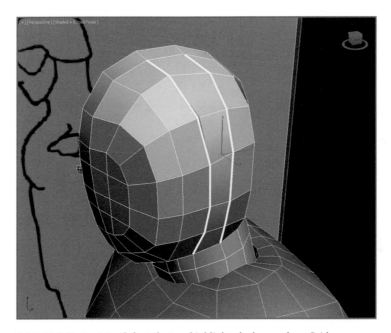

FIGURE 9.13 Select the two highlighted edges and use Bridge.

2. Use the Cut tool to add another vertical edge, as shown in Figure 9.14.

3. Select the edges on the inside of the gap closest to the back of the head and use Shift+Move to extrude more faces toward the front of the head.

4. Switch to Vertex mode and use Target Weld to weld the loose vertices at the top and bottom, as shown in Figure 9.15.

Use the Cut tool to create an edge.   Readjust the spacing here.

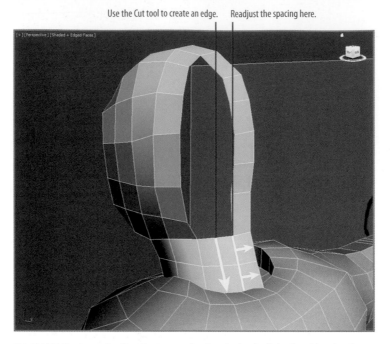

FIGURE 9.14   Create a new edge for the back of the head/neck using the Cut tool.

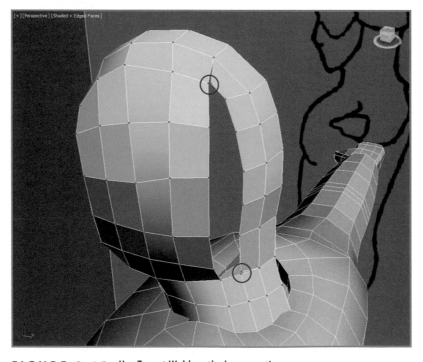

FIGURE 9.15   Use Target Weld on the loose vertices.

Creating the Back of the Head

You have the same problem with the back of the head as you did with the front: There are not enough horizontal edges. Follow these steps:

1. Select and move edges to line up with edges on the other side of the gap, as shown in Figure 9.16.

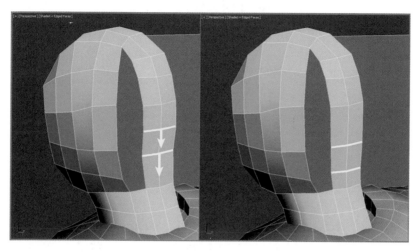

FIGURE 9.16 Select and move edges.

2. Select the edges on either side of the gap and use Bridge to close the gap, as Figure 9.17 shows. This time you have the exact number needed to create a solid head shape.

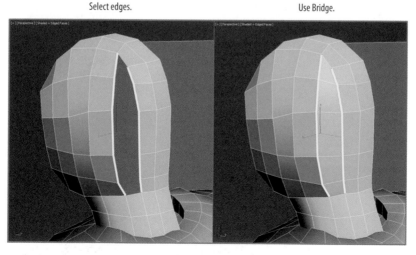

FIGURE 9.17 Bridge the vertical edges to fill the last hole.

3. Now that the head is complete, take the time to move the edges and vertices to more evenly space out and clean up the topography (which is the flow and organization of edges on a given 3D model) of the head, as shown in Figure 9.18.

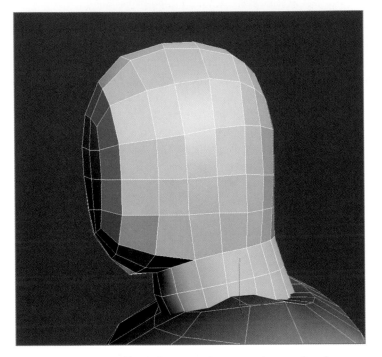

FIGURE 9.18   Move edges or vertices to evenly space the edges.

When you add the Symmetry modifier, the object might appear warped or as if it disappeared, depending on where the pivot point is sitting. The pivot point defines the center from which the Symmetry modifier mirrors.

Mirroring the Head

Now make any necessary adjustments to your mesh to get it just right. Again, it's not terribly vital that this part be perfect because you will cover it up with accessories in the upcoming steps. Once you're satisfied, continue with these steps:

1. With the head selected, go to the Modify panel and from the Modifier List, choose Symmetry.

     This adjusts the symmetry so it appears that the head is whole. If the mesh doesn't appear even when you move the gizmo, click the box next to Flip in the Symmetry parameters.

2. When the head looks correct, choose Modeling ➢ Polygon Modeling ➢ Collapse Stack.

     This integrates the Symmetry modifier into the editable polygon, making the head a whole mesh.

Merging and Attaching the Head's Accessories

The remaining accessories for the soldier are the helmet, goggles, and face mask. To create these objects, you can repeat the methods you've already used, so we'll save a little time and merge the finished pieces.

The finished models for the helmet, goggles, and face mask have been created separately and can be merged into your final model. Keep in mind that if you changed the design of the soldier as you built him in your scene, these premade accessories for the head may not perfectly fit your particular model. If this is the case, you may want to use the scene file of the soldier provided in the following steps or create your own accessories to fit your design.

Continue with the previous exercise's scene file, or open the Soldier_v10.max scene file in the Soldier project's Scenes folder from the book's web page.

1. Click the Application button and select Import ➢ Merge.

2. In the Merge File dialog box, choose the file Soldier_Accessories .max in the Scenes folder of the Soldier project from the web page, and click Open.

3. In the Merge dialog box, select all the objects in the list and click OK.

   You might see a warning about materials, so just click Use Scene Material. The object will appear in the scene, lined up with the model.

   Once the accessories are merged onto the model, there might be some editing to be done. It depends on your soldier's head. The accessories are built for the head in the Soldier_v10.max scene file, so if the accessories don't fit your soldier's head, use vertex editing to adjust them to fit.

   Now you need to attach all the accessories to the main body. This means the entire soldier model will be a single mesh and can be used to create the UVW mapping for the model in Chapter 11, "Textures and UV Workflow: The Soldier."

Using the Attach From List dialog box makes it easier to attach when you have multiple objects.

4. Select the body, and from the Graphite Modeling Tools tab, choose Geometry (All) ➢ Attach (Arrow) ➢ Attach From List to open the Attach List dialog box.

   Because you selected the body when you opened the Attach List dialog box, the window won't show the body as an object that you can select.

5. Select the four objects, but not the image planes, in the list and click Attach.

The soldier is complete—well, at least the model. Now that the head objects are attached to the body, they cannot be selected individually. As a matter of fact, the entire soldier is one object, from the boots to the helmet. You will see this approach in action in Chapter 11 as you lay out texture-mapping UVs for the soldier. Figure 9.19 shows the completed model of the soldier with head and body accessories and elbow and knee pads.

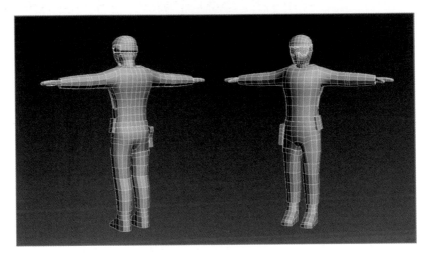

FIGURE 9.19 Completed soldier model

Go grab a frosty beverage; you've earned it!

THE ESSENTIALS AND BEYOND

This chapter explored several tools used in modeling. In Chapter 7, you started with a simple box for the soldier model. Then you formed a torso to match the general shapes shown in the images. The arms and legs were extruded and shaped. Using Mirror required you to model only half of the soldier character at a time, in Chapter 8. The head modeling came next, and then you merged the already completed accessories from another scene file to add detail to the model's head.

ADDITIONAL EXERCISES

Although we used a fairly low-polygon-count soldier character in this chapter, this toolset can be utilized for any type of model. Try some variations on the same themes:

▶ Design and build another soldier to form a team.

▶ Build different accessories for the soldier, such as a rifle.

CHAPTER 10

Introduction to Materials: Interiors and Furniture

A material defines an object's look—its color, tactile texture, transparency, luminescence, glow, and so on. *Mapping* is the term used to describe how the materials are wrapped or projected onto the geometry (for example, adding wood grain to a wooden object). After you create your objects, the Autodesk® 3ds Max® program assigns a simple color to them, as you've already seen.

You define a material by setting values for its parameters or by applying textures or maps. These parameters define the way an object will look when rendered. Much of an object's appearance when rendered also depends on the lighting. In this chapter and in Chapter 14, "Introduction to Lighting: Interior Lighting," you will discover that materials and lights work closely together.

This chapter includes the following topics:

▶ **The Slate Material Editor**

▶ **Material types**

▶ **mental ray material types**

▶ **Shaders**

▶ **Mapping the couch and chair**

▶ **Mapping the windows and doors**

The Slate Material Editor

The Material Editor is the central place where you do all of your material creation and editing. You can assign materials to any number of objects as well as have multiple materials assigned to different parts of the same object.

The 3ds Max 2014 program has two interfaces to the Material Editor: the Slate Material Editor (or Slate) and the Compact Material Editor.

The Slate Material Editor is the interface you will use in this book: it is far superior to the Compact Material Editor and is especially nice when you are first learning mapping, because you can see the material structure, as shown in Figure 10.1.

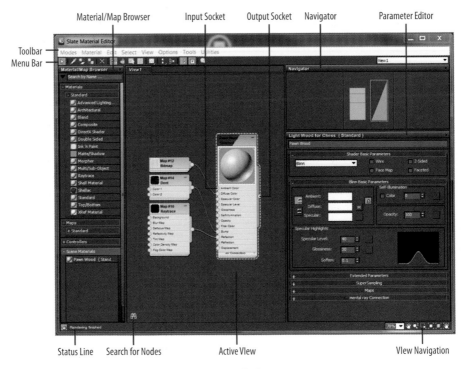

Material/Map Browser   Input Socket   Output Socket   Navigator   Parameter Editor

Toolbar
Menu Bar

Status Line   Search for Nodes   Active View   View Navigation

FIGURE 10.1   The Slate Material Editor

The Slate Material Editor is the default Material Editor, but if it opens as the Compact Material Editor, you can switch it in the menu bar at the top of the Material Editor by selecting Modes ➢ Slate Material Editor.

You can access the Material Editor by choosing from the menu bar Materials ➢ Create/Edit Materials ➢ Slate Material Editor. There is also an icon for it on the main toolbar ( ), and the keyboard shortcut to open the Material Editor is the M key.

The Slate Material Editor has an interface that uses nodes and wiring to display the structure of materials. It has a simple and elegant layout with the Material/Map Browser on the left for choosing material and map types. The center area is the Active View area, where you build materials by connecting maps or controllers to material components. The area on the right is the Parameter Editor; within that area is a Navigator for moving within the Active View area.

Material Types

Different materials have different uses. The Standard material is fine for most uses. However, when you require a more complex material, you can change the material type to one that will fit your needs. To change a material type in the Slate Material Editor, just choose from the list under Materials in the Material/Map Browser. You should see the rollout for Standard. If you are using the mental ray renderer, you will also see a rollout for mental ray and MetaSL. As you can see, the list is extensive; there are not enough pages in this book to cover the multitude of material types, so we will touch on some of the best for an introduction. You will also see some examples using the Slate Material Editor.

Standard Materials

Standard materials typically use a four-color model to simulate a surface of a single color reflecting many colors. The four colors are known as the material's color components. Ambient color appears where the surface is in shadow, diffuse color appears where light falls directly on the surface, specular color appears in highlights, and filter color appears as light shining through an object. Along with the color components, there are parameters that control highlights, transparency, and self-illumination. Some of these parameters are different depending on the shader you are using. With the Standard material, as shown in Figure 10.2, you can imitate just about any surface type you can imagine.

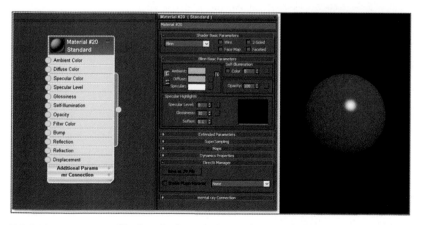

FIGURE 10.2   The Standard material type shown in the Slate Material Editor

mental ray Material Types

The 3ds Max program comes with several materials created specifically for use with the mental ray renderer. These materials are visible in the Material/Map Browser when mental ray is the active renderer. For the sake of time and space, we are going to cover only one here, Arch & Design.

The mental ray Arch (architectural) & Design material improves the image quality of architectural renderings. It improves workflow and performance in general, and performance for glossy surfaces (such as floors) in particular.

Special features of the Arch & Design material include self-illumination, advanced options for reflectivity and transparency, ambient occlusion settings, and the ability to round off sharp corners and edges as a rendering effect. These material types will be explored further in Chapter 16, "mental ray."

Shaders

The way light reflects from a surface defines that surface to your eye. With the 3ds Max program, you can control what kind of surface you work with by changing the shader type for a material. In either the Compact or Slate Material Editor, you will find the shader type in the material parameters in the Shader Basic Parameters rollout. This option will let you mimic different types of surfaces, such as dull wood, shiny paint, or metal. The following descriptions outline the differences in how the shader types react to light, as shown in Figure 10.3:

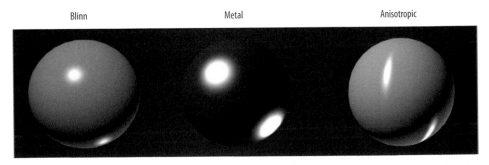

FIGURE 10.3 Shader types shown on a rendered sphere

Anisotropic   Most of the surface types that you will see typically create rounded specular highlights that spread evenly across a surface. By contrast, *anisotropic* surfaces have properties that differ according to direction. This creates a specular highlight that is elliptical in shape and uneven across the surface, changing according to the direction you specify on the surface. The Anisotropic shader is good for surfaces such as foil wrappers or hair. There are extra controls for how the specular highlights will fall across the surface.

Blinn   This is the default shader because it is a general-purpose, flexible shader. The Blinn shader creates a smooth surface with some shininess. If you set the specular color to black, however, this shader will not display a specular highlight and will lose its shininess, making it perfect for regular dull surfaces, such as paper or an interior wall.

Metal   The Metal shader is not too different from the Blinn shader. Metal creates a lustrous metallic effect, with much the same controls as a Blinn shader but without the effect of any specular highlights.

When you are first starting, it's best to create most of your material looks with the Blinn shader until you're at a point where Blinn simply cannot do what you need.

Mapping the Couch and Chair

Now let's dive into creating material for the couch we modeled in Chapter 4, "Modeling in 3ds Max: Architectural Model Part II," to get it ready for lighting and rendering in later chapters.

Study the full-color image of the couch shown in Chapter 4 in Figure 4.1. That will give you an idea of how the couch is to be textured. The couch's material is basically all the same; once you create the material, it can be added to all the couch pieces.

Creating a Standard Material

Start by opening your final couch model from your work in Chapter 4, or open the `ArchModel_IntroMat_01.max` file from the `Scenes` folder of the ArchModel project downloaded from the book's web page at `www.sybex.com/go/3dsmax2014essentials`. This file has the room with the lounge chair and couch set up. If you are using your own project file, it will look different because of the furniture you placed in the scene in Chapter 4. When you open this file, the couch is the only furniture visible; the other models have been hidden. Follow these steps:

> **1.** Open the Slate Material Editor (M). In the Material/Map Browser, open the Materials ➢ Standard rollout, and double-click Standard. This will add the Standard Material to the Active View area.

The black areas of the shader may throw you off at first, but keep in mind that a metallic surface is ideally black when it has nothing to reflect. Metals are best seen when they reflect the environment. The Metal shader requires a lot of reflection work to make the metal look just right.

2. Double-click the thumbnail with the sphere showing. This enlarges it and makes your material easier to view.

NAVIGATION IN ACTIVE VIEW

The Active View area uses the same navigation tools as the viewports. At the lower right of the Slate interface are the navigation tools. Keyboard short-cuts and the middle mouse button and wheel also work the same as in the viewports. The Navigator is another way to navigate in the Active View area. The Navigator panel changes the view of your material nodes; the colored box called the Proxy View area corresponds to the currently viewable area in the Active View area.

3. Double-click again on the node title bar; this adds the node parameters to the Parameter Editor.

4. In the Parameter Editor, at the top of the rollout, change the name to **Gray/Green Woven Fabric**.

5. In the Blinn Basic Parameters rollout, select the color swatch next to Diffuse. This brings up the Color Selector.

6. Set Red to 35, Green to 25, and Blue to 15. Click OK.
   In the material node, the sphere in the thumbnail will change color.

▶

It is always best to name your materials precisely. Calling the material Couch might be confusing if you want to use the same material on the curtains or a chair.

Applying the Material to the Couch

In the scene, select the couch. In Chapter 4, after the couch was merged into the room file, it was grouped. You can add materials to objects that are grouped; it can save time by applying the materials to all the pieces at the same time. We don't want to do that, so with the Couch selected, follow the steps below:

1. On the menu bar, choose Edit ➢ Group ➢ Ungroup. Hold Alt on the keyboard and click on the couch feet to deselect them.

2. In the Slate Material Editor toolbar, click the Assign Material To Selection icon (▨).

When you compare the material in the viewport to the material on the couch, you should not see a difference, as shown in Figure 10.4, but the best way to view the material is by rendering the viewport.

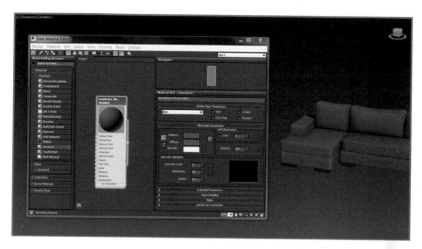

FIGURE 10.4   Material in the Material Editor and on the couch in the viewport

3. In the Perspective viewport, use the keyboard shortcut Z to fit the couch model into the viewport. In the main toolbar, click the Render Production button (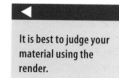), or press F9 for Render Last. The result is shown in Figure 10.5.

> ◀
>
> It is best to judge your material using the render.

FIGURE 10.5   The render of the couch with a Standard material applied

Adding a Bitmap

The couch material needs some refinement. It looks flat and too perfect, which in this instance isn't a good thing. A material with just color is not enough; what is needed is a map. Two map types are available, 2D and 3D:

▶ 2D maps are two-dimensional images that are mapped onto the surface of 3D objects; the simplest 2D maps are bitmaps (aka image files).

▶ 3D maps are patterns generated procedurally in three dimensions using the 3ds Max software.

Using a map to replace the diffuse color is a way to create a more realistic material because you are using actual images. Using maps in other material components can have various effects, such as making a material look bumpy and controlling its transparency.

1. In the Slate Material Editor, open the Blinn Basic Parameter rollout and click the small gray box next to the Diffuse color swatch, as shown in Figure 10.6.

    This is a shortcut to the Diffuse Color Map in the Maps rollout, which you can find if you look lower in the Parameter Editor.

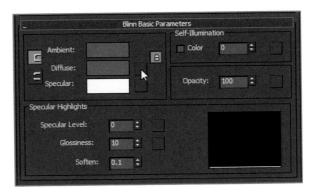

FIGURE 10.6 The shortcut button to add an image or bitmap to your material

2. This brings up a separate Material/Map Browser; in the Maps ➢ Standard rollout, choose Bitmap and click OK (Figure 10.7).

3. In the Select Bitmap Image File dialog box, navigate to the sceneassets\images folder in the ArchModel project, select the GrayGreenWovenFabric.tif image file, and click Open.

If you don't see this map, make sure the Files Of Type field is set to TIF Image File or All Formats.

▶

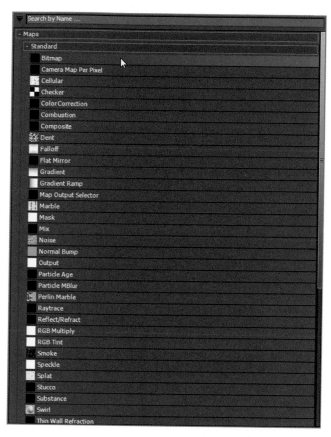

FIGURE 10.7 Choose Bitmap in the Material/Map Browser ➢ Maps ➢ Standard rollout to add an image to your material.

In the Active view area, an additional node has been added to the main material node. The green node is the Bitmap node, which holds the fabric image.

4. In the Slate Material Editor's toolbar, click the Show Shaded Material In Viewport icon ( ).

In the viewport, the couch shows the fabric image applied, as shown in Figure 10.8. This improves the color and adds some color variations.

The image is projected onto the surface of the couch model. How the image looks on the model depends on what are known as mapping coordinates. Right now the bitmap doesn't know how to lay on the surface, so it doesn't look right.

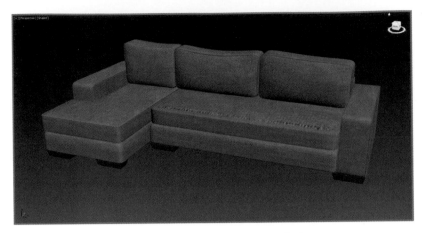

FIGURE 10.8   The couch with the fabric image applied

Introduction to Mapping Coordinates

An image map is two-dimensional; it has length and width but no depth. 3ds Max geometry, however, extends in all three axes. Mapping coordinates define how and where image maps are projected onto an object's surfaces and whether the maps are repeated across those surfaces.

Mapping coordinates can be applied to objects in several ways. When primitive objects are created and the Generate Mapping Coords option is checked at the bottom of the Parameters rollout, the appropriate mapping coordinates are created automatically. The next way is by applying a UVW Map modifier, which is commonly used to apply and control mapping coordinates. You select the type of mapping projection, regardless of the shape of the object, and then set the amount of tiling in the modifier's parameters. The mapping coordinates applied through the UVW Map modifier override any other mapping coordinates applied to an object, and the Tiling values set for the modifier are multiplied by the Tiling value set in the assigned material.

Using a UVW Mapping Modifier

You are going to use a modifier to replace those coordinates on the geometry. The UVW Mapping modifier allows you to change the bitmap by transforming the UVW Mapping modifier gizmo:

1. Select the main seat cushion on the couch, and enter Isolate Selection mode (💡); the icon is under the timeline at the bottom of the interface (or press Alt+Q).

2. In the Modify panel, select UVW Map from the Modifier List drop-down.

> You can also access Isolate Selection by right-clicking the selected object and choosing Isolate Selection from the quad menu ➤ Display.

In the modifier stack, you can see the UVW Map modifier stacked on top of the editable poly. You will also see a flat orange gizmo running through the seat cushion.

3. Go to the UVW Map modifier parameters, and in the Mapping section, select Box for the projection type.

4. In the Alignment section, click the Bitmap Fit button, as shown in Figure 10.9.

FIGURE 10.9
The Alignment section for the UVW Map modifier parameters

This will take you to the Select Image dialog box.

5. Navigate to the sceneassets\images folder in the ArchModel project and select the GrayGreenWovenFabric.tif file. Click Open.
   This will change the size of the UVW Mapping gizmo to the size and aspect of the image rather than the geometry.

The UVW Map modifier has also changed the image on the couch. The size is more consistent throughout the couch, but the size of the fabric texture is too big. Now let's adjust the UVW Map gizmo:

1. In the modifier stack, click the plus sign in the black box next to the UVW Map modifier and select Gizmo.

2. The box gizmo will turn yellow when in sub-object gizmo mode. You will now be able to transform the gizmo to the correct size.

3. Switch to the Scale tool (press **R**), and scale down the gizmo to 70 percent.

4. In the Modifier Stack, click the UVW Map modifier again to exit.
   Now that the couch fabric is where it should be, it is time to add the UVW Map modifier to the remaining pieces of the couch.

5. Exit Isolate Selection mode.

6. Select one of the back couch cushions, and in the Modifier List, choose UVW Map Modifier4.

7. In the Alignment section, click the Acquire button. Then click on the previous couch seat cushion. The Acquire UVW Mapping dialog will appear. Select Acquire Relative and click OK.

   Acquire takes the UVW information from the seat cushion and copies it onto the back cushion. This is a great time-saver.

8. Repeat the process on the remaining cushions.

The final results are shown in Figure 10.10.

FIGURE 10.10   The final results of the couch mapping

The couch is not finished just yet; look closely at the couch feet. If you compare the current scene couch to the image of the real couch, you'll see that the feet should be a dark wood, not just the default material on them now. Continue with your current file or open `ArchModel_IntroMat_02.max` file from the `Scenes` folder of the ArchModel project downloaded from the book's web page. Then follow these steps:

1. Open the Slate Material Editor if it isn't already open.

2. In the Material/Map Browser, choose Materials, and click and drag a Standard material into the Active View area.

3. Double-click the title bar of the material to add it to the Parameter Editor.

4. Change the name to **Dark Red Wood**.

5. Expand the Maps rollout and click the None button across from Diffuse Color.

   This brings up a separate Material/Map Browser.

6. Choose Bitmap, and in the Select Bitmap Image File dialog box, navigate to the sceneassets\images folder in the ArchModel project and select the DarkRedWood.jpg image file.

7. Apply the material by clicking and dragging from the node's output socket to the couch foot, as shown in Figure 10.11.

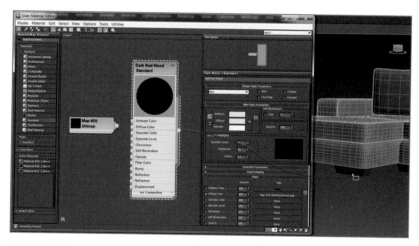

FIGURE 10.11 Apply the Dark Red Wood material by clicking and dragging from the node's output socket to the couch foot.

8. In the Material Editor, click the Show Shaded Material In Viewport icon.

   The material shows now, but the image has no detail. This is because it needs to have UVW Mapping applied.

9. Select the foot; then, in the Modify panel's Modifier List, add a UVW Map modifier to the couch foot.

10. Change the mapping type to Box, and select Bitmap Fit under Alignment.

11. Navigate to the DarkWood_Grain.jpg image file. The material now looks correct on the couch foot.

12. Apply the Dark Red Wood material to the remaining couch feet.

Applying a Bump Map

You are almost done with the couch. One important feature of the couch is the bumpiness on the surface of the fabric, as shown in Figure 10.12. This bumpiness changes all the specular and reflective properties on a surface.

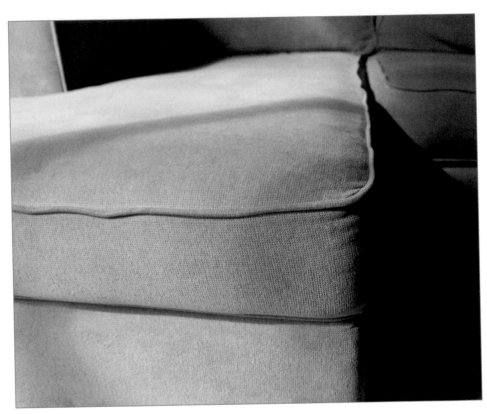

FIGURE 10.12   The couch fabric showing the subtle surface bumpiness

> Bump mapping is very common in computer graphics (CG). It adds a level of detail to an object fairly easily by creating bumps and grooves in the surface and giving the object a tactile element.

Bump mapping uses the intensity values (the brightness values) of an image or procedural map to simulate bumpiness on the surface of the model without changing the actual topology of the model itself. You can create some surface texture with a bump map; however, you will not be able to create extreme depth in the model. For that, you may want to model the surface depth manually or use displacement mapping instead. To add a bump map to the couch, follow these steps:

1. In the Slate Material Editor's Active View area, locate the Couch Fabric material. Double-click the title bar to load the material into the Parameter Editor.

2. In the Maps rollout, click the None button next to the bump map, and in the Material/Map Browser, choose Bitmap.

3. Navigate to the `sceneassets\images` folder in the ArchModel project, and select the `GrayGreenWovenFabric_bmp.tif` image file.

4. In the Maps rollout, increase Bump Amount from 30 (the default) to 60.

5. Render to see the results.

You should now see a texture on the couch that resembles the real bumpiness, as shown in Figure 10.13.

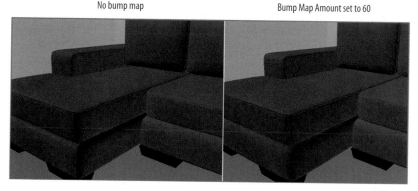

No bump map   Bump Map Amount set to 60

FIGURE 10.13 The couch fabric without the bump map (left); and with the bump map (right)

Applying the Material to the Lounge Chair

In this section, we will be adding materials to the lounge chair. Mapping the lounge chair is in some ways very much like mapping the couch. Continue with your current file or open the `ArchModel_IntroMat_03.max` file from the `Scenes` folder of the ArchModel project downloaded from the book's web page. Figure 10.14 shows the lounge chair that was modeled in Chapter 4.

The file has the lounge chair centered in the viewports, and the chair group is open so you can select the individual pieces. If you are continuing with your file, create the Cushion material using the techniques discussed in the previous section. Then follow these steps:

1. In the Slate Material Editor, add a Standard material to the Active View area.

2. Choose Bitmap from the Material/Map Browser and navigate to the `sceneassets\images` folder in the ArchModelproject.

If you double-click the input socket of the Diffuse Color map on the Standard Material node, the Material/Map Browser will open.

FIGURE 10.14 The lounge chair

3. Select the Leather.tif file, and rename the material **Leather**.

4. Select the lounge chair cushion, and apply the Leather material by clicking the Assign Material To Selection button in the toolbar.

5. On the Material Editor toolbar, click the Show Shaded Material In Viewport icon.

6. In the Specular Highlights group, change Specular Level to **20** and Glossiness to **10**. This will give the leather material a bit of gloss.

7. Repeat steps 1 through 6 but add the bitmap to the bump map channel.

8. When the Select Bitmap Image File dialog box opens, choose Leather_Bmp.tif.

9. In the Modify panel's Modifier List, add a UVW Map modifier.

10. Change the Mapping type to Box, and in Alignment, select Bitmap Fit. Navigate to the Leather.tif bitmap to change the size of the UVW Map gizmo.

    The size of the map is now the proper height-to-width ratio, but it is too large.

11. In the Modifier Stack, click the plus sign in the black box and select Gizmo.

12. Using the Scale tool, scale the gizmo until it looks correct, as shown in Figure 10.15.

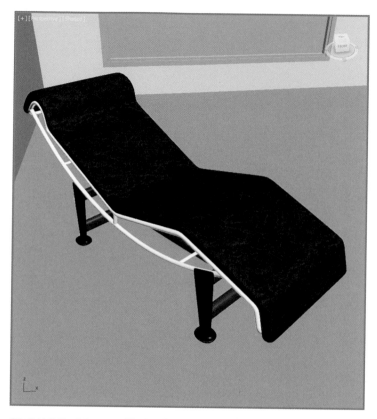

FIGURE 10.15   The Leather texture is applied to the chair cushion.

Applying a Reflection

Reflection occurs when light changes direction as a result of "bouncing off" a surface like a mirror. In the following steps, you will create reflections on the lounge chair frame; what you are going to create is a chrome material that has 100% reflections:

1. In the Material Editor, drag a Standard material from the Material/Map Browser to the Active View area.

2. Double-click the title bar of the material to add it to the Parameter Editor.

3. Rename the material **Chrome**, and change the diffuse color to black (R: 0, G: 0, B: 0).

4. In the Specular Highlights group, change Specular Level to **90** and Glossiness to **80**. This will give the chrome material a bit of gloss.

A reflection creates the illusion of chrome, glass, or metal by applying a map to the geometry so the image looks like a reflection on the surface. A Raytrace map provides reflections on a material. Raytrace reflects the actual surroundings in the scene.

5. In the Material/Map Browser rollout, go to the Maps rollout ➢ Standard, choose Raytrace from the list, and drag the Raytrace map to the Reflection input socket.

6. Apply the Chrome material to the lounge chair.
   You won't be able to see the mirror effect of the chrome in the viewport; you will have to render.

7. Click the Render Production button. The result of the render is shown in Figure 10.16.

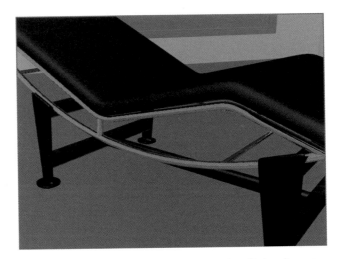

FIGURE 10.16   The Chrome material applied to the lounge chair frame

In the figure, the chrome doesn't look smooth. It has a noisy, broken-up look to it. You can correct this by controlling the anti-aliasing. Anti-aliasing smoothes the jagged edges that occur along the edges of diagonal and curved lines when a scene is rendered. SuperSampling performs an additional anti-aliasing pass on the material and can improve the image quality. The Standard material has a SuperSampling rollout to allow control of the anti-aliasing filters.

8. In the Chrome material, select the SuperSampling rollout. Uncheck Use Global Settings and check Enable Local Supersampler.

9. Choose Max 2.5 Star from the drop-down menu, and then render.
   You should see the difference in the reflections, as shown in Figure 10.17.

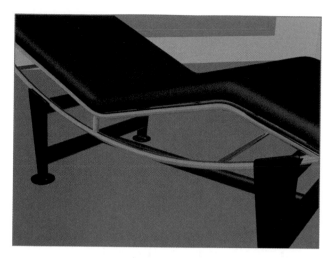

FIGURE 10.17 Final reflections on the chair frame

SuperSampling Filters

SuperSampling Filters is an anti-aliasing technique, the process of eliminating jagged and pixelated edges (aliasing). It is a method of smoothing images rendered in imagery. There are four SuperSampling filters:

Adaptive Halton   Samples along both the X- and Y-axes according to a random pattern.

Adaptive Uniform   Samples regularly, from a minimum quality of 4 samples to a maximum of 36.

Hammersley   Samples regularly along the X-axis, but along the Y-axis it spaces them according to a random pattern.

Max 2.5 Star   The sample at the center of the pixel is averaged with four samples surrounding it.

Creating a Material for the Lounge Chair Base

The last material is the material that is on the base of the chair. This should be a very simple material to create, a matte black material. Follow the steps learned throughout this chapter. Use a Standard material, and make the diffuse color black. Set Specular Level to **20** and Glossiness to **15**. Name the material **Base** and apply this material to all the objects from the base, as shown in Figure 10.18.

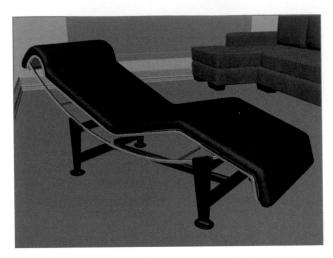

FIGURE 10.18   The final materials applied to the lounge chair

Mapping the Window and Doors

The window and doors are special 3D primitive objects. They are a collection of multiple objects attached together: a frame, mullions, and glass. You can edit those objects within the Architecture Engineering and Construction (AEC) object's parameters. You also have the ability to add materials to the individual pieces within the attached whole.

Creating a Multi/Sub-Object Material

The Multi/Sub-Object material (MSOM), which is in the Compound Materials category, lets you assign different materials at the sub-object level of your geometry. In the case of the AEC window, it is already divided into separate sub-object levels, so you just have to apply the material and identify the different parts. Continue with your current file or open the `ArchModel_furniture_04.max` file from the `Scenes` folder of the ArchModel project. Then follow these steps:

1. In the Slate Material Editor, drag a Multi/Sub-Object material from the Material/Map Browser into the Active View area.

2. Double-click the title bar to add the material to the Parameter Editor. Click the Set Number button and change Number Of Materials to 5, as shown in Figure 10.19. Change the name to **Window/Door**.

> Multi/Sub-Object is just a material that gathers other materials together.
>

> The number parameter allows you to control how many materials can be plugged into the Multi/Sub-Object material.

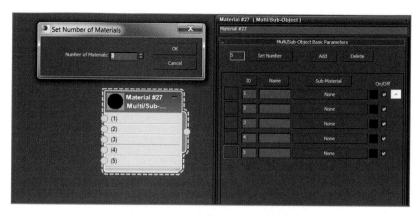

FIGURE 10.19   Multi/Sub-Object material and parameters

3. Drag a Standard material from the Material/Map Browser to the Active View area, and then from the output socket of the Standard material, drag it to the input socket of the MSOM, as shown in Figure 10.20.

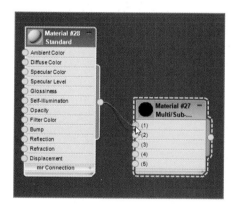

FIGURE 10.20   Adding a Standard material to the Multi/Sub-Object Material node

4. Double-click the new Standard material's title bar to add it to the Parameter Editor. Click the Diffuse color swatch to open the color selector; create a red color, and click OK.

5. Repeat the process until you have five Standard materials with five different diffuse colors plugged into the 1 through 5 input sockets of the MSOM.

The finished node is shown in Figure 10.21. The Standard Material node has been minimized for the figure.

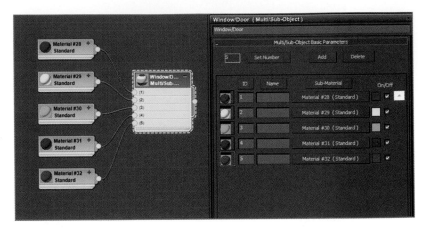

FIGURE 10.21 Finished MSOM with five Standard materials added

The numbers in the MSOM parameters are material IDs. Most objects do not have material IDs by default. They have to be created by converting the object to an editable polygon, selecting a group of polygons, and adding a material to that selected group. AEC objects like the window and doors already have them assigned; they just have to be identified.

6. Apply the MSOM to the window in the living room area, as shown in Figure 10.22. The colors show clearly which section of the window corresponds to which ID number.

   Now we will begin creating the glass material.

7. The colored materials that were just created are not needed. Select and delete them.

8. Starting with the glass, click the material bar for ID #3 in the MSOM parameters.

   This loads that material's parameters. Rename the material **Window Glass.**

9. In the Blinn Basic Parameters rollout, change Opacity to 0.

   If you render, you will see a black hole where the green used to be. That is because you are seeing the default color applied to the background in a render. That means the glass is see-through now.

10. In the Maps rollout, click the Reflection Map button.

FIGURE 10.22 The Multi/Sub-Object Material applied to the window object shows the different colors applied to the different parts of the window.

11. From the Material/Map Browser, choose Raytrace, and then change Reflection Amount to **10**.

   When the scene renders, the Reflection amount will appear to be very high; this is a bit of an illusion because of the black in the background. In Chapter 14, lighting will be covered, and this issue will be addressed more thoroughly; for now, you will just change the background color.

12. In the Rendering menu, choose Environment And Effects ➢ Environment And Exposure Settings, click the color swatch under Background, and change it to a light gray.

13. Render the Perspective viewport.

   Now the reflection looks more appropriate. Eventually, an image of an outdoor scene will be placed behind the glass. For now, let's continue with the MSOM for the window. Window frames and mullions come in many colors and textures, but for this example you are going to use a shiny white plastic.

14. Double-click the MSOM title bar to load the material into the Parameter Editor, and then select any of the material IDs (other than #3).

15. Rename the material **Shiny White Plastic**.

16. Change the Diffuse color to White, and then in the Maps rollout add a Raytrace node to the Reflection map and change the Amount to 10, as you did in step 11.

17. Drag from the output socket of the Shiny White Plastic material to the input of the Multi/Sub-Object material's IDs that were deleted, as shown in Figure 10.23.

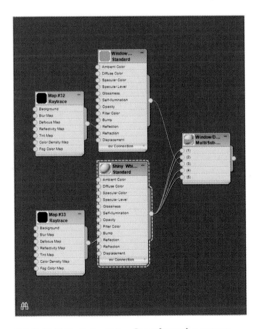

FIGURE 10.23 Drag from the output socket of the Shiny White Plastic material into the input socket of the remaining ID slots of the Multi/Sub-Object material.

This places a clone of the Shiny White Plastic material into the three remaining material slots and completes the window material, as shown in a render in Figure 10.24.

FIGURE 10.24 The completed window

The same technique used for the window can be used for the doors, but if you want the doors to be just a plain solid color or simple wood, apply a Standard material to the entire Door object. We used the White Shiny Plastic material for the door and baseboard molding. We'll return to this room in Chapter 14 when we look at lighting. Meanwhile, finish assigning materials to the rest of the scene.

THE ESSENTIALS AND BEYOND

Creating materials can give you a sense of accomplishment because it is essentially the last step in making the object look as you envisioned—aside from lighting and rendering.

Finding the right combination of maps, shader types, and material types can make a world of difference in the look of your scenes. In this chapter, you learned the basics of materials, you mapped part of the room and furniture you modeled in Chapter 3 and Chapter 4, and you readied it for its next step: lighting in Chapter 14.

ADDITIONAL EXERCISES

▶ Using the collection of images in the `sceneassets/images` folder of the ArchModel project, add materials to the floor and ceiling.

▶ Create an MSOM for the walls and use the colors you want. The actual colors can be seen in Figure 3.3 in Chapter 3. Now you will take an extra step with the walls. The Wall object has IDs like the Window object because it is an AEC object, but the IDs are not where you want them. You need to convert the object to an editable polygon.

CHAPTER 11

Textures and UV Workflow: The Soldier

Autodesk® 3ds Max® materials simulate the natural physics of how we see things by regulating how objects reflect and/or transmit light. You define a material by setting values for its parameters or by applying textures or maps. These parameters define the way an object will look when rendered. In this chapter and in Chapter 14, "Introduction to Lighting: Interior Lighting," you will discover that materials and lights work closely together.

In this chapter, you will apply material and maps to the soldier model from Chapters 7 through 9. You will first set up the model to accept textures properly through a process called *UV-unwrap*. This allows you to lay out the colors and patterns for the soldier's uniform and general look. This process essentially creates a flat map that can be used to paint the textures in a program such as Photoshop.

The textures (i.e., the maps) you'll use for the soldier have already been created in Photoshop. We will show you how to prepare the model for proper UVs and how to apply the maps you have already painted. We will not demonstrate the actual painting process in Photoshop because that discussion goes beyond the scope of this book.

This chapter includes the following topics:

▶ **UV unwrapping**

▶ **Seaming the rest of the body**

▶ **Applying the color map**

▶ **Applying the bump map**

▶ **Applying the specular map**

UV Unwrapping

Set your project to the Soldier project downloaded from the companion web page at www.sybex.com/go/3dsmax2014essentials. Open the scene file SoldierTexture_ v01.max from the scenes folder of the project, or use your own final model scene files from Chapter 9, "Character Poly Modeling: Part III." When you open the file, a Gamma & LUT Settings Mismatch dialog might appear. You want to adopt the file's gamma and LUT settings, which is the default option, so you only have to click OK. Keep in mind that any design changes you made to your own soldier model may cause discrepancies in the UV unwrapping and mapping steps in the following sections.

You will begin by creating seams to define the shapes of the arms so you'll know where to paint the sleeves of the uniform in an image editing program like Adobe Photoshop.

Begin defining UVs with the following steps:

1. Change the viewport rendering type to Shaded and Edged Faces (F4) in your viewports.

2. With your model selected, go to the Modify panel, and from the Modifier List, choose Unwrap UVW .

3. Expand the Unwrap UVW modifier in the modifier stack by clicking the plus sign in the black box next to the Unwrap UVW title. Enter Polygon mode.

4. At the bottom of the Configure rollout, uncheck Map Seams, as shown in Figure 11.1.

FIGURE 11.1
Uncheck Map Seams in the Configure rollout.

5. In the Peel rollout, click the Point-To-Point Seams button, as shown in Figure 11.2. This tool lets you reroute the seams to where you want them.

▶ In the SoldierTexture_ v01.max file, the image planes are hidden; if you want them back, right-click in the viewport and choose Unhide All from the context menu.

▶ Unchecking Map Seams turns off the green highlight on the edges; it is generated by default and is not useful in its current state.

FIGURE 11.2
Click the Point-To-Point
Seams button.

6. With Point-To-Point Seams enabled, click on the center of a pair of intersecting edges about where you want to define the left shoulder, as shown in Figure 11.3 (left image).

   A dashed-line "rubber band" appears next to your cursor, letting you know that the tool is waiting for the next point to be selected.

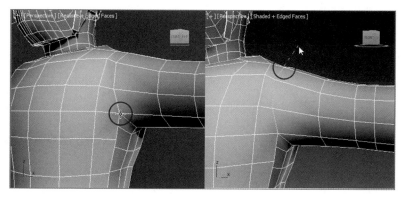

FIGURE 11.3   Pick this edge intersection to begin defining the seam (left). Choose the next point at the upper shoulder (right).

7. Select the next intersecting edges in the loop around the shoulder. This creates a blue highlight across the edges, as shown in Figure 11.3 (right image).

8. Continue around the shoulder until you have a complete loop, ending with the intersection you started with in step 6.

9. Select the bottommost edge intersection on the underarm and continue selecting edge intersections all the way to the middle point of the wrist, as shown in Figure 11.4.

   You will have to switch to Wireframe view (press F3) or See-Through mode (Alt+X) to pick the last point, as shown in Figure 11.5 (the figure shows the model in See-Through mode with wireframe showing for clarity), at the end of the forearm.

While Point-To-Point Seams is active, you can navigate using all the viewport navigation tools to look around the model. 3ds Max remembers the last intersection you clicked and draws an accurate seam at the next click.

Also, you can right-click and then start or continue the picks without overlapping them.

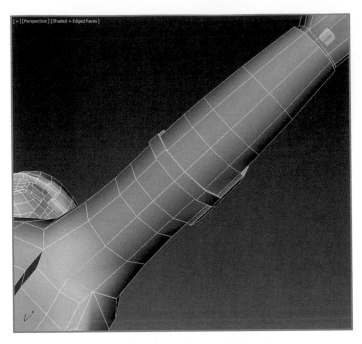

FIGURE 11.4   Select the intersections under the arm.

FIGURE 11.5   Switch to Wireframe view to pick the
last intersection for the forearm/wrist.

10. Right-click to deactivate the Point-To-Point Seams tool's rubber banding but still keep the button active; then continue cutting a new set of UVs for the right arm, just as you did for the left arm.

11. Right-click and box out areas under the arms on both sides, as shown in Figure 11.6.

In Figure 11.6, you can see the seams block out the area under the arm and continue down to the belt line and across the top of the belt line around the waist. If you pick a point by mistake, you can use the Undo Scene Operation button.

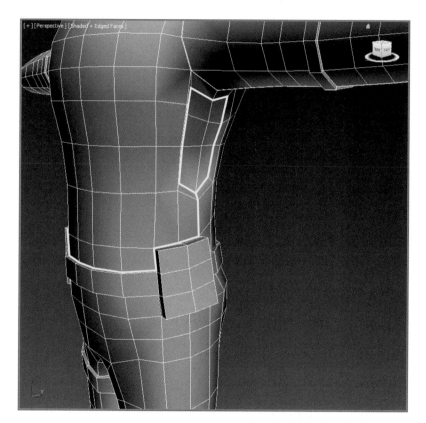

FIGURE 11.6   Add these seams to define the torso areas under the arm.

12. Using the Point-To-Point Seams tool, cut seams for the two gloves lengthwise down the middle from wrist to wrist. Begin at the wrist on the side of the thumb and work your way around to the opposite side of the wrist.

You can see this progression for the left-hand glove start in Figure 11.7. Figure 11.8 shows the seam working around the hand.

Remember, you may need to enter Wireframe view (press F3) to select the proper edge intersection points.

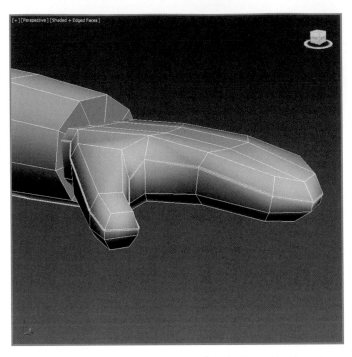

FIGURE 11.7   Cut a new seam along the glove, starting as shown.

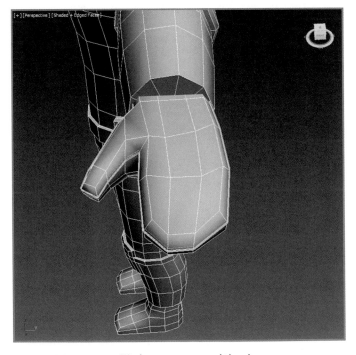

FIGURE 11.8   Work your way around the glove.

13. In the Edit UVs rollout, select the Open UV Editor button.

14. In the top right of the window, in the drop-down menu, choose CheckerPattern (Checker) from the list, even if it already appears in the menu,t as shown in Figure 11.9. This will apply a low-contrast checker map to the soldier, as shown in Figure 11.10.

15. Save your work now before continuing with the next section.

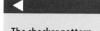

The checker pattern will disappear when the Edit UVWs dialog box is closed.

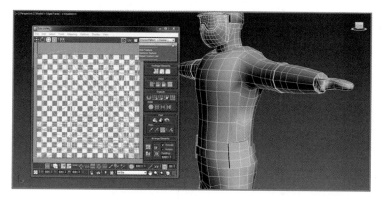

FIGURE 11.9 Choose CheckerPattern (Checker) from the drop-down list.

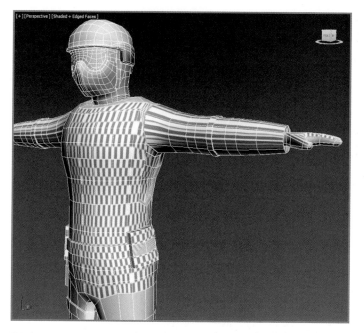

FIGURE 11.10 A low-contrast checker pattern is added to the soldier model.

Pelting the Arms UVs

This section contains a set of steps to unfold the UVs for the arms into usable patterns to paint the textures, starting with the left arm. You can pick up with the scene file SoldierTexture_v02.max from the scenes folder of the Soldier project on the book's companion web page to check your work so far or to skip to this point.

1. With Polygon mode selected in your Unwrap UVW modifier and Point-To-Point Seams toggled off, click on a polygon on the left forearm of your model, and then in the Peel rollout, click the Expand Polygon Selection To Seams icon (). This will select all the faces that were included when creating seams for the arm, as shown in Figure 11.11.

> Remember, the checker pattern applied to the soldier will show only if the Edit UVWs dialog box is open. The low-contrast checker will appear only when you select CheckerPattern (Checker) again, otherwise you will see the black and white checkers.

> In the SoldierTexture_v02.max file, the image planes are hidden; if you want them back, right-click in the viewport and choose Unhide All from the context menu.

The selected area is shaded in red.

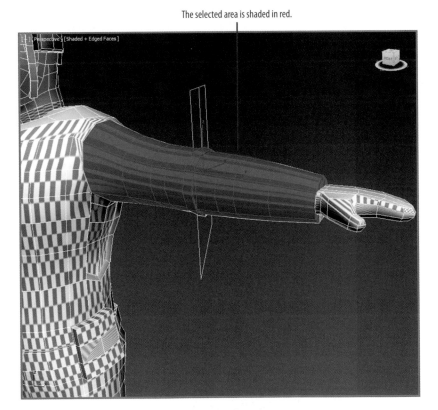

FIGURE 11.11   The arm's faces are selected.

You need to unfold the UVs to create the pattern to paint on in Photoshop (or another image editor).

2. To unfold the UVs into a usable pattern, click the Pelt Map icon ( ) in the Peel rollout. The Pelt Map dialog box opens.

3. In the Edit UVWs dialog box, click the View menu and toggle off Show Grid and Show Map to simplify the UV view, as shown in Figure 11.12. Before moving on, take a look at the checkerboard pattern on the arm of the soldier to recognize how it changes once you pelt.

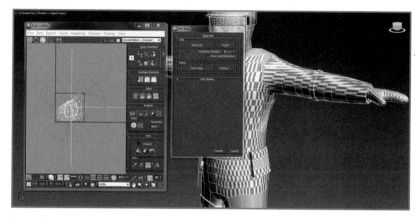

FIGURE 11.12 The Edit UVWs and Pelt Map dialog boxes showing the left arm UVs

4. To unfold the map, click the Start Pelt button in the Pelt Map dialog box. Doing so moves the UVs in the Edit UVWs dialog box in real time.

5. This procedure keeps unfolding the UVs until you stop it, so wait a couple of seconds for the UVs to stop moving and then click Stop Pelt.

You're almost done with the arm; however, if you check the checkerboard texture in your viewport, you can see that some of the checks are bigger than others. To fix this, complete the remaining steps.

6. Click the Settings box next to the Start Relax button in the Pelt Map dialog box. The Relax Tool dialog box opens. Change the drop-down option to Relax By Polygon Angles, as shown in Figure 11.13.

FIGURE 11.13 Set the drop-down menu to Relax By Polygon Angles.

7. Now, click the Start Relax button in the Relax Tool dialog box.

8. Wait until the UVs stop moving and then click Stop Relax; then click Apply.

9. Close the Relax Tool dialog box.

10. Check your texture in the viewport; it now shows the checkerboard the way you want it.

11. Click the Commit button at the bottom of the Pelt Map dialog box, or your changes won't take effect.

12. Close the Edit UVWs dialog box.

13. Repeat steps 1 through 12 for the right arm.
    You can see in Figure 11.14 that both arms are now laid out—pelted and relaxed.

14. Save your work now before continuing with the next section.

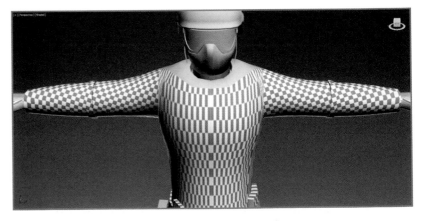

FIGURE 11.14 Both arms are pelted and relaxed.

Unwrapping and Using Pelt for the Head

By performing the steps in this section, you'll unfold the UVs for the head. You can pick up with the scene file SoldierTexture_v03.max from the scenes folder of the Soldier project downloaded from the book's web page to check your work so far or to skip to this point.

Since it is a bit hard to see where to seam, the file SoldierTexture_v03.max has the Edit UVWs dialog box closed.

The head poses a problem: Each part (helmet, goggles, and mask) is a separate object that was merged with the head in Chapter 9 and then attached into one editable polygon. That means when you look closely at the geometry, there is some object penetration, making it difficult to clearly see some of the areas you need to seam. You will use a sub-object visibility technique to control what you are viewing in the following steps:

1. Select the soldier, and in the Modify panel's modifier stack, expand Editable Poly and select Element.

   When you do this, you will get the warning shown in Figure 11.15.

Element mode allows you to select separate objects that are attached together into a single object.

FIGURE 11.15   Topology dependency warning

2. Click Yes.

3. Select the helmet, select the modeling ribbon ➤ Visibility, and click Hide Unselected.

   Doing so hides all unselected elements in the model, leaving the helmet as the only visible object.

TOPOLOGY DEPENDENCY WARNING

Every time you move between the Unwrap UVW modifier and the Editable Poly modifier, you will see this warning; if that gets annoying, check the Do Not Show This Message Again option. The warning tells you that any changes you make to that level of the model will ripple throughout the rest of the stack and may mess up other parts of your work. Since you are simply using Element mode to hide parts of the head of the model to make the seaming easier to see, you need not worry that anything will change.

4. Exit Element mode by selecting the Graphite Modeling Tools tab ➢ Polygon Modeling and clicking the Element mode button or by clicking Editable Poly in the modifier stack.

5. Now go back up to the Unwrap UVW modifier and click Polygon.

6. Select a polygon on the helmet and then move down to the Peel rollout and click the Point-To-Point Seams button.

7. Following the line in Figure 11.16, create a new seam on the helmet.
   Because you are in Polygon mode in Unwrap UVW, the helmet will be shaded in red to show you have selections. It can be difficult to see the seams you are trying to create. In the viewport, you can turn off Shade Selected Faces (F2).

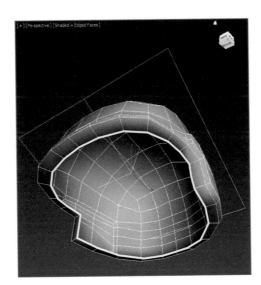

FIGURE 11.16 Create a new seam on the helmet.

8. When the seam has been created, click Editable Poly and select Element mode in the modifier stack. Select Yes in the warning that appears.

9. In the Visibility panel, click the Unhide All button, and then select the goggles, click the Visibility panel, and click the Hide Unselected button.

10. Repeat steps 4 through 7 on the goggles using Figure 11.17 as your guide for the seams.

11. Repeat the process individually for the mask, the head, and the helmet straps, using Hide Unselected to isolate each of the three elements as you work on them.

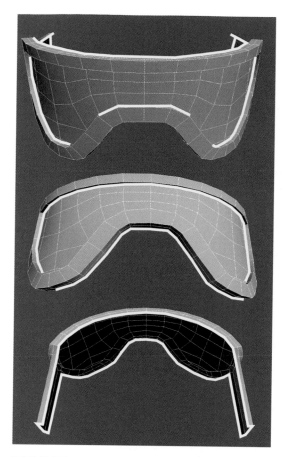

FIGURE 11.17 Guide for the seams on the goggles

12. Then follow the same process as before to create the seams shown in Figure 11.18 for the face mask, Figure 11.19 for the head, and Figure 11.20 for the helmet straps.

13. Open the Edit UVWs dialog box.

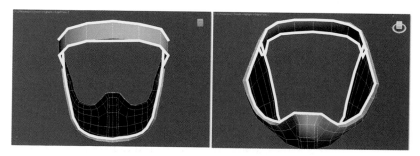

FIGURE 11.18 Seams for soldier face mask

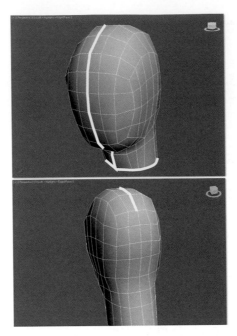

FIGURE 11.19   Seams for the soldier head

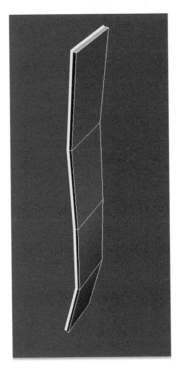

FIGURE 11.20   Seams for
the soldier helmet straps

Seaming the Rest of the Body

Use the Point-To-Point Seams tool to block out the rest of the model's parts and then use the Pelt Map dialog box as you did for the arms. Refer to Figure 11.21 and Figure 11.22 for the placement of seams on the model's body. Then save your work.

FIGURE 11.21 Follow these outlines to create the rest of the model's seams.

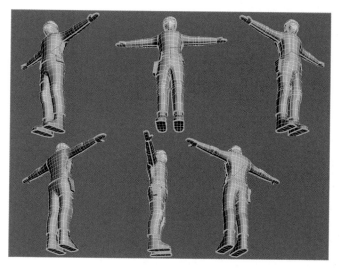

FIGURE 11.22 Follow these outlines taken from a different vantage point to create the rest of the model's seams.

Unfolding the Rest of the Body

You can pick up with the scene file `SoldierTexture_v04.max` from the `scenes` folder of the Soldier project downloaded from the book's web page to check your work so far or to skip to this point.

1. With the soldier selected, enter Polygon mode, and then click a single polygon on the helmet.

2. In the Peel rollout, click the Expand Polygon Selection To Seams icon ( ). Doing so selects all the polygons associated with the seams you created for the helmet.

3. Click the Pelt Map icon ( ) to open the Edit UVWs dialog box and the Pelt Map dialog box.

   a. First, click Start Pelt. You will see the UVs moving around.

   b. When they stop moving, click the Stop Pelt button.

4. Now, click the Settings button next to the Start Relax button.

5. Make sure the drop-down menu is set to Relax By Polygon Angles, click Apply, and then close the Relax Tool dialog box.

6. Click the Start Relax button again, and when the UVs stop moving, click Stop Relax.

   For the remaining objects, you don't have to go into the Relax Tool dialog box—just click Start Relax.

7. Click the Commit button.

   If the checker pattern is not showing, select CheckerPattern (Checker) from the Unwrap UVW modifier so the pattern shows. The checker pattern on the helmet should look organized and even.

8. Now that you are finished with the helmet, make your way down the body using Pelt and Relax to lay out the UVs on the remaining parts of the body, checking each one off as you go.

9. Save your work.

You can pick up with the scene file `SoldierTexture_v05.max` from the `scenes` folder of the Soldier project to check your work so far or to skip to this point.

As you can see in Figure 11.23, when the UVs are finished, the squares in the checker pattern on different parts of the soldier are different sizes. In the following steps, you will set them all to be the same, showing that the UVs are now uniform:

1. In the Modify panel, click the Polygon button if it isn't already selected.

2. Click away from the soldier model and drag a selection box around the whole model to select all the polygons, as shown in Figure 11.23.

3. In the Unwrap UVW modifier, go to the Edit UVs rollout and click the Open UV Editor button.

    What you will see is a mess; these are all the unwrapped UVs piled on top of each other.

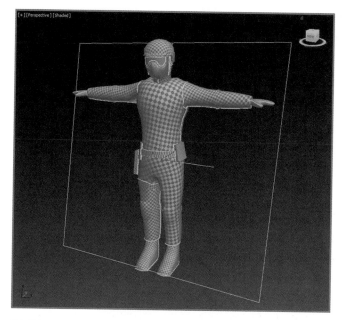

FIGURE 11.23 Soldier model with all the polygons selected

4. In the Edit UVWs menu, choose Tools ➢ Relax, and then click Start Relax.

5. Be patient and wait for the movement to slow down or stop before clicking Stop Relax, and then close the Relax Tool dialog box.

    This will relax all of your UVs together uniformly, ensuring that they all have the same UV real estate. This is important so that all the elements carry the same relative texture space, as shown in Figure 11.24.

6. Keep the Edit UVWs dialog box open, and deselect the UVs by clicking away from the model. Figure 11.25 shows what you should see now.

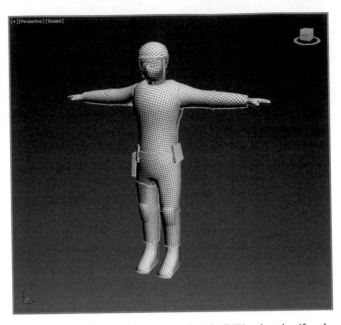

FIGURE 11.24 Soldier model with all UVs relaxed uniformly

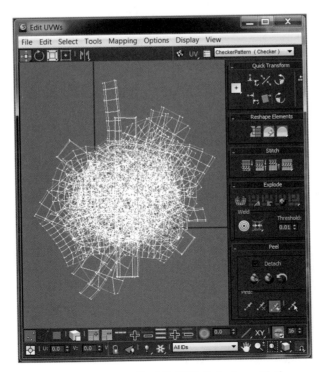

FIGURE 11.25 The Edit UVWs dialog box with the soldier UVs in a pile

Because you are still in Polygon mode in the Unwrap UVW modifier, if you click anywhere on the pile of UVs, you will select a face. What you want to do now is select an individual element's full set of UVs so that you can lay them out separately, giving them some space on the flat blank canvas that can be used later for painting the textures for those parts of the body. The easiest way is to follow these steps:

1. Click Select By Element UV Toggle, as shown in Figure 11.26.

FIGURE 11.26 Click Select By Element UV Toggle.

2. Select a polygon, and then go to the toolbar at the bottom of the Edit UVWs dialog box.

At this point, you can select all the UVs associated with an element (such as the vest only), as shown in Figure 11.27. This will help you know what parts you are moving around in the Edit UVWs dialog box. Also in the Edit UVWs dialog box, you can use all the navigation tools you use in the viewports to pan and zoom. In the following steps, you will start placing the UVs for each element within the thick blue-bordered box in the Edit UVWs dialog box to lay out the entire soldier's UVs for textures.

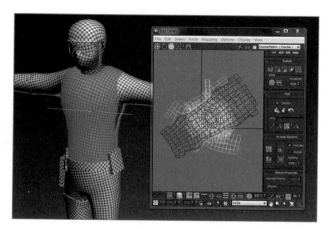

FIGURE 11.27 Select an element in the Edit UVWs dialog box and it will appear as selected on the model.

1. In the Edit UVWs dialog box, drag a selection box around all the UVs.

2. From the Arrange Elements rollout on the right side of the Edit UVWs dialog box, change the Padding Type-In field to 0.0 and then click the Pack Normalize button, as shown in Figure 11.28.

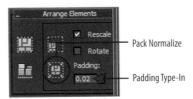

FIGURE 11.28
The Arrange Elements rollout

Now you should be able to see the blue-bordered box in the Edit UVWs dialog box with the UVs laid out, as shown in Figure 11.29. The UV layout can vary depending on many factors, as we said from the beginning.

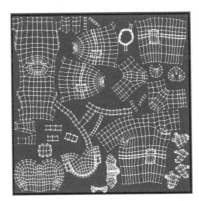

FIGURE 11.29   **UVs placed within the UV space**

The goal is to fit the UVs into this box without going outside of it and without overlapping any of the UVs. Anything outside this box ends up tiling (or having no texture at all), and any overlapping UVs share parts of the texture from another element. Either way, that's not good. Once you have the layout, you can select and move UVs around.

3. In the Edit UVWs dialog box, select Tools ➢ Render UVW Template to open the Render UVs dialog box, shown in Figure 11.30.

4. Click the Render UV Template button to create an image of your UVs, as shown in the Render Map dialog box. Remember, the layout of the UV rendered image can vary, as shown in Figure 11.31.

FIGURE 11.30
In the Render UVs dialog box,
leave the settings at their default.

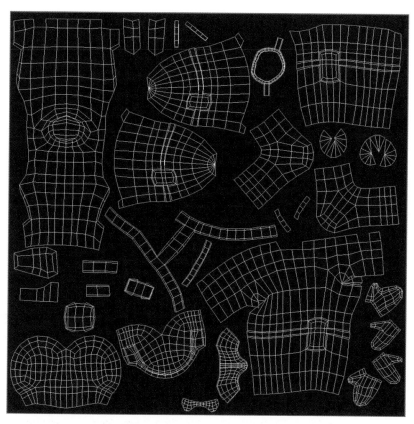

FIGURE 11.31 The layout of the UV rendered image can vary.

5. Save the UV layout image by clicking the Save Image icon in the Render Map dialog box, as shown in Figure 11.32. Save the UVs in the `sceneassets/images` folder.

FIGURE 11.32
Save the UV layout image.

Once the UVs are saved, you can close all the UV image boxes and the Edit UVWs dialog box. Now this image can be opened in your favorite image editor and you can use the pieces as guides to paint the soldier's textures.

With the UV layout image saved, you can go into Photoshop (or the image-editing software of your choice) and create a texture to place on your model. For example, we took the UV image into Photoshop, and with a combination of painting and cutting and pasting of photos, we created the final map for the soldier, as shown in Figure 11.33.

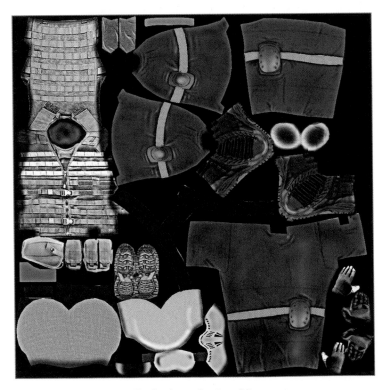

FIGURE 11.33   **The final map for the soldier**

The texture map, as you can see, places painted parts of the soldier's body according to the UV layout you just created. For example, you can clearly see the soldier's vest painted in the upper-left corner of the texture image file.

Applying the Color Map

Save your work before continuing with the next set of steps. You can pick up with the scene file SoldierTexture_v06.max from the scenes folder of the Soldier project to check your work so far or to skip to this point.

Now it is time to use the map you put so much effort into creating:

1. Open the Slate Material Editor (M).

2. In the Material/Map Browser, expand the Materials rollout, and on the Standard rollout, drag and drop a Standard material to the View 1 window.

3. Double-click on the Diffuse Color input socket of the material to open the Material/Map Browser.

4. In the Maps rollout, expand the Standard rollout and click Bitmap.

5. When the Select Bitmap Image File dialog box appears, navigate to the \sceneassets\images folder for the Soldier project and select the Soldier_Color.tif file.

6. Apply the material to the soldier and click Show Shaded Material In Viewport. Rename the material **Soldier**.

    The result is shown in Figure 11.34. Bam! Now wasn't all that hard UV work worth it? If the blue seams are showing, go back to the Modify panel and select Unwrap UVW. Go to the Configure rollout and uncheck Peel Seams.

The more you unwrap UVs for models, the easier it becomes to anticipate how to paint the textures.

FIGURE 11.34   The soldier with the material applied

Applying the Bump Map

Bump mapping makes an object appear to have a bumpy or irregular surface by simulating surface definition. When you render an object with a bump-mapped material, lighter (whiter) areas of the map appear to be raised on the object's surface, and darker (blacker) areas appear to be lower on the object's surface, as shown in Figure 11.35.

Normal mapping is a technique used for faking the lighting of bumps and dents. A normal map is usually used to fake high-resolution geometry detail while it's actually mapped onto a low-resolution mesh for efficiency. This vector is called a *normal* (or simply, a direction), and it describes a high-resolution surface's slope at that very point on the surface. The RGB channels of a normal map control the direction of each pixel's normal, enabling you to fake a high degree of surface resolution when applied to a low-polygon mesh. A normal map for the soldier is shown in Figure 11.36.

FIGURE 11.35 Bump map created in Photoshop by desaturating the original color map to create light and dark areas that conform to the original color texture

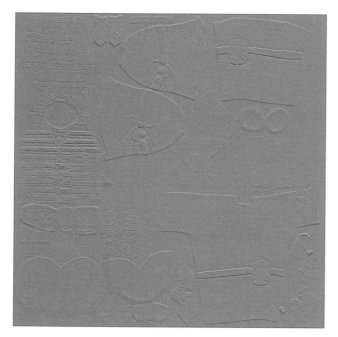

FIGURE 11.36 Normal map created in Photoshop and based on the original color map

You can use one or both of these mapping techniques to create additional surface detail. Bump maps are simpler to create because you can usually take the color map and just desaturate it to make a grayscale image file. We have both a normal map and a bump map for you to use. You will continue with the Soldier material you created in the previous exercise as you add these new maps in the following steps:

1. Double-click on the Bump input socket of the material to open the Material/Map Browser.

2. Under the Maps rollout, expand the Standard rollout and choose Normal Bump.

3. Double click on the title bar of the Normal Bump node to bring up the Parameters rollout shown in Figure 11.37, and then click the None button next to Normal. Doing so once again brings up the Material/Map Browser.

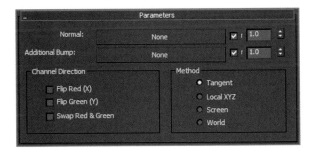

FIGURE 11.37 The Normal Bump node's Parameters rollout

4. Under the Maps rollout, expand the Standard rollout and choose Bitmap.

5. When the Select Bitmap Image File dialog box appears, navigate to the /sceneassets/images folder of the Soldier project and select the Soldier_Normal_V01.tif file.

6. Back in the Normal Bump parameters, click None next to Additional Bump to open the Material/Map Browser.

7. Under the Maps rollout, expand the Standard rollout and choose Bitmap.

8. When the Select Bitmap Image File dialog box appears, navigate to the /sceneassets/images folder of the Soldier project and select the Soldier_BS_V01.tif file.

9. Double-click on the material's title bar to show the main material parameters.

10. In the Maps rollout, set the Bump Amount to 100.

The normal map is applied and finished. See Figure 11.38 for images that compare the soldier rendered with and without the normal map. You may notice that the normal and bump maps have created a lot more detail in the soldier's body, particularly in his vest. You will notice the difference even better in your own renders.

FIGURE 11.38 The left image is a render of the soldier without the normal and bump maps. The right image is rendered with the normal and bump maps.

Applying the Specular Map

Highlights in objects are reflections of a light source. *Specular* maps are maps you use to define a surface's shininess and highlight color, without the complex calculations of reflections in the render. The higher a pixel's value (from black to white, or 0 to 1, respectively), the shinier the surface will appear at that location.

You will be adding a specular map to the soldier to further the amount of detail you can get from the render. You are going to reuse the image that you used for the bump map to give the soldier a bit of bling on his vest and buckles:

1. In the Slate Material Editor, drag from the output socket of the Additional Bump bitmap to the Specular Color input socket of the Soldier material already in your scene, as shown in Figure 11.39.

2. Use the Specular Level Amount spinner in the Maps rollout to increase or decrease the shininess as much as desired.

Placing the map into the Specular Color slot allows for iridescence and flexibility.

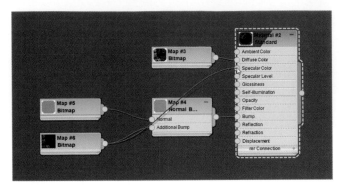

FIGURE 11.39 Dragging from the Additional Bump bitmap to the Specular Color slot

The final render of the soldier is shown in Figure 11.40. You can see the improvement to the look of the soldier's vest with the added specular color map.

FIGURE 11.40 Final render of the soldier

You will use the soldier for rigging and animation with Character Studio in Chapter 12, "Character Studio: Rigging."

THE ESSENTIALS AND BEYOND

In this chapter you set up the soldier's UV layout using UV unwrapping and the Pelt toolset. Then you assigned materials and maps created specifically for the soldier.

ADDITIONAL EXERCISE

▶ Create a new uniform color scheme for the soldier to make him/her more suitable for jungle camouflage and map it.

CHAPTER 12

Character Studio: Rigging

At one time or another, almost everyone in the 3D community wants to animate a character. This chapter examines the toolsets used in the process of setting up for character animation using Character Studio, a full-featured package that is incorporated into the Autodesk® 3ds Max® 2014 software and used mostly for animating bipedal characters, including humans, aliens, robots, and anything else that walks on two feet—though you can have characters with more than two feet in certain situations.

This chapter includes the following topics:

▶ **Character Studio workflow**

▶ **Associating a biped with the soldier model**

Character Studio Workflow

Character Studio is a system built into the 3ds Max program to help automate the creation and animation of a character, which may or may not be exactly a *biped* (two-footed creature). Character Studio consists of three basic components: the Biped system, the Skin modifiers, and the Crowd system. Biped and Skin are used to pose and animate a single character, and the Crowd system is used to assign similar movements and behaviors to multiple objects in your 3ds Max scene. This chapter covers the Biped and Skin features; the Crowd system is beyond the scope of this book.

The first step in the Character Studio workflow is to build or acquire a suitable character model. The second step is to *skin* (bind) the character model to the skeleton so the animation drives the model properly.

Models should typically be in the reference position known as the da Vinci pose, where the feet are shoulder width apart and the arms are extended to the sides with the palms down, as shown in Figure 12.1. This allows the animator to observe all of the model's features, unobstructed by the model itself, in at least two viewports.

FIGURE 12.1   A bipedal character in the reference position

In 3ds Max parlance, a *biped* is a predefined, initially humanoid structure. It is important to understand that you animate the biped that is associated with your model and not the model itself. Once the model is bound to the skeleton, the biped structure *drives* the model. You use the Skin modifier to create that relationship between the skeleton and the model.

General Workflow

The better the biped-to-model relationship, the easier the animation will be.

There are four different biped types you can choose from: Skeleton, Male, Female, and Classic, as shown in Figure 12.2. They all consist of legs, feet, toes, arms, hands, fingers, pelvis, spine, neck, and head. After your model is ready, you will create a biped and, using its parameters and the Scale transform, fit the biped closely to the model.

Once the biped is fit snugly to the model, you select all the components of the model, not the biped skeleton, and apply the Skin modifier in a process often referred to as *skinning*. It may take a while to properly test and refine the relationship between the model and the biped to get it to an acceptable level.

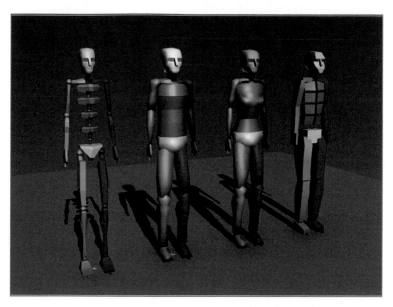

FIGURE 12.2 Skeleton, Male, Female, and Classic bipeds (from left to right)

BONES AND SKIN

The Bones system has capabilities similar to those found in Character Studio. Bones is a series of linked, hierarchical components that are used to control the displacement of a model, similar to the Biped method. The Bones system requires a more tedious setup process to create a skeleton than the Biped method and is not covered.

The final step is animating your character. You can accomplish this by adding to the biped any combination of default walk, run, and jump cycles included with Character Studio; applying any kind of freeform animation to the character; and finally, refining the animation keyframes in the Dope Sheet.

Don't expect the default walk, run, and jump cycles to create realistic motion, though. They are just starting points and must be tweaked to achieve acceptable movements.

The best way to start is to jump in and examine the tools available. In the next sections, you will work with a biped and adjust the parameters and components to modify it.

The Dope Sheet displays animation keys over time on a horizontal graph. It simplifies editing animation timing by displaying them in a spreadsheet format.

Associating a Biped with the Soldier Model

The purpose of a biped is to be the portal through which you add animation to your model rather than animating the model itself using direct vertex manipulation or deforming modifiers. Any motion assigned to a biped is passed through it to the nearest vertices of the associated model, essentially driving the surfaces of the model. For this reason, it is important that the biped fit as closely as possible to the model.

Creating and Modifying the Biped

In the following steps, you'll create and adjust a biped to fit to a character model. Set your project to the Soldier project available for download from this book's web page at www.sybex.com/go/3dsmax2014essentials. You can then open the CSSoldier01.max file from the Scenes folder of the Soldier project. It contains a completed soldier model in the reference position.

To start, follow these steps:

1. With the soldier model file open, select the Perspective viewport, and set the viewport rendering type to Shaded + Edged faces (F4).

2. Select the character, and use Alt+X to make the model see-through.

3. Right-click in a viewport and choose Freeze Selection. This will prevent you from inadvertently selecting the soldier instead of the biped.

> Opening or merging a scene whose gamma or LUT settings differ from the settings in the active file generates a dialog that gives you the choice of using the current settings or adopting those of the file you are loading; always choose Adopt.

VIEWING FROZEN OBJECTS

If your background color is similar to the default shade of gray used to depict frozen objects, the model may seem to disappear against the background. There are several solutions to this situation:

▶ You can go to Object Properties, turn off Show Frozen In Gray, turn on See-Through, and set all viewports to Realistic or Shaded mode.

▶ You can change the viewport background color in the Customize User Interface dialog box (Customize ➢ Customize User Interface ➢ Colors).

Follow these steps to create and adjust a biped:

1. From the command panel, select Create ➤ Systems ( ) ➤ Biped. When you click Biped, the parameters will appear below.

2. Go to Body Type, and from the drop-down menu choose Male.

3. In the Perspective viewport, click at the soldier's feet and drag to create the biped.

4. Create a biped with a height about the same as the soldier's. This will make most of the biped's parts similar in size to those of the soldier, as shown in Figure 12.3.

The first click sets the insertion point. Dragging defines the height of the biped system and defines all of the components. All of the biped's components are sized relative to the its Height parameter.

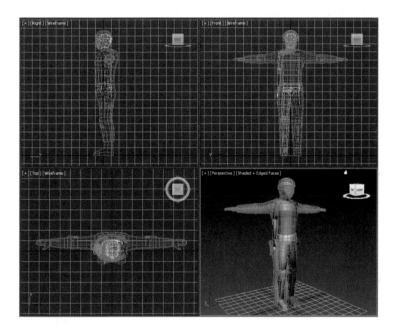

FIGURE 12.3 Create a biped about the same height as the soldier model.

5. With the biped still selected, in the Command panel, click the Motion tab ( ) and in the Biped rollout, enter Figure mode, as shown in Figure 12.4.

Changes to the biped's features or pose must be made in Figure mode to be retained by the system.

FIGURE 12.4
Enter Figure mode
in the Biped rollout.

6. Then in the Structure rollout, change the parameters to match Figure 12.5. The number of spine links should be set to 3. Change the number of toes to 1 and toe links to 1. Because the soldier is wearing boots, a single, wide toe will suffice. Change the number of fingers to 2 because with mittens you only need one finger and a thumb.

FIGURE 12.5
Change the biped from the Structure rollout.

7. Use the Body Vertical and Body Horizontal buttons in the Track Selection rollout and the Move Transform gizmo to position the biped's pelvis in the same location as the model's pelvis, as shown in Figure 12.6.

   With the pelvis located properly, scaling the legs or spine to match the model's proportions will be much easier.

8. Check to make sure the location is correct in all of the viewports. There are two important factors when creating a biped skeleton:

   ▶ The first is to place the joints accurately at the 3D mesh's joints.

   ▶ The other is to modify only one side of the model and then use mirroring to copy to the other side.

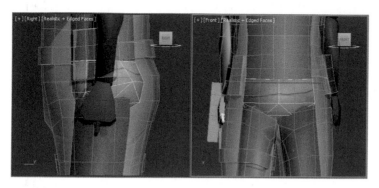

FIGURE 12.6   Match the positions of the biped pelvis and the model pelvis.

9. Select Scale in the main toolbar; make sure the coordinate system is set to Local. This will be set for the Scale tool only, as shown in Figure 12.7.

FIGURE 12.7
Set the coordinate
system to Local.

10. In the Front viewport, select the pelvis and scale its width so that the biped's legs fit inside the soldier's legs. Scale the pelvis in the Right viewport so that it roughly encompasses the soldier's lower region, as shown in Figure 12.8.

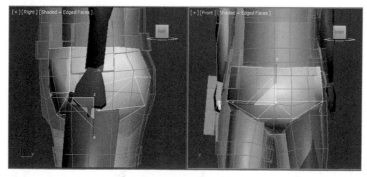

FIGURE 12.8   Scale the pelvis to fit.

11. Select the biped's left thigh, and then scale it along the X-axis until the knee aligns with the soldier's knee. Scale it on the Y- and Z-axes until it is similar in size to the soldier's thigh.

12. Select the biped's left calf. In the Right viewport, rotate the calf to match the model (move the calf if necessary) and then scale it on the X-axis until the biped's ankle matches the soldier's ankle. Scale the calf to match the proportions of the soldier's calf.

You may need to select the left foot and use the Move transform, in the Front viewport, to orient the calf to the model.

13. Continue working down the leg by scaling the biped's foot to match the soldier's. Be sure to check the orientation of the foot in the Top viewport.

14. Scale and move the biped's toe to match the model's boot. Be sure to scale the toe links on the Z-axis, as shown in Figure 12.9.

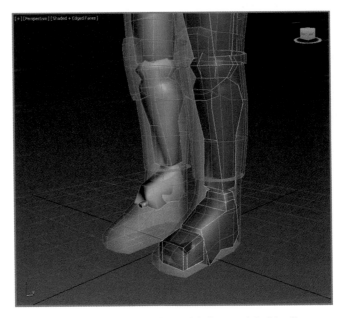

FIGURE 12.9   Match the model's boot and the biped's toe.

15. Double-click the left upper leg to select it and all of the objects below it in the hierarchy, from the thigh down to the toe.

16. In the Motion panel, open the Copy/Paste rollout.

17. Postures must be saved as collections prior to being pasted: Click the Create Collection button, as shown in Figure 12.10, and then rename the collection from the default Col01 to **Left Leg**.

FIGURE 12.10
Create the collection to paste
the left leg hierarchy.

18. Click the Copy Posture button just below the Posture button to copy
the selected posture to the Clipboard.

A preview of the copied posture will appear in the Copied Postures
area of the command panel, as shown in Figure 12.11.

FIGURE 12.11
Copy the posture. The
selected objects will
show in red in the preview.

19. Click the Paste Posture Opposite button ( ).

The size, scale, and orientation of the selected objects will be applied to the reciprocal objects on the opposite side of the biped.

Adjusting the Torso and Arms

Similar to the method used to adjust the legs, you will use the Scale and Rotate transforms to fit the biped to the model. The locations of the arms rely on the scale of the spine links. You can continue with your file from the previous exercise or open CSSoldier02.max from the Scenes folder of the Soldier project available on the book's web page. Just make sure your project is set to the Soldier project. Then follow these steps:

1. In your scene (or the one from the web page), select the biped and then access Figure mode if needed.

2. Ctrl+click to select each of the spine links in turn (Ctrl+click to add to the selection without losing the previous one) and then rotate and scale them to fit the soldier's torso.

Only the lowest spine link can be moved, and this will move all of the links above it as well. Each spine link should be scaled up slightly on the X- and Y-axes to move the biped's clavicles to match the models, as shown in Figure 12.12. (For this image only, the arms have been hidden so the placement of the clavicles can be seen clearly.)

3. Move, rotate, and scale the left clavicle as required, placing the biped's shoulder joint in the proper location.

4. Scale and rotate the left upper arm and left forearm using the same techniques you used to adjust the biped's legs to fit the arm with the model. Pay close attention to the placement of the elbow and wrist joint, as shown in Figure 12.13

5. Scale and rotate the left hand as required to fit the model.

> Once the fingers have been adjusted, you cannot go back and change the number of fingers or finger links. If you do, all modifications to the fingers will be lost.

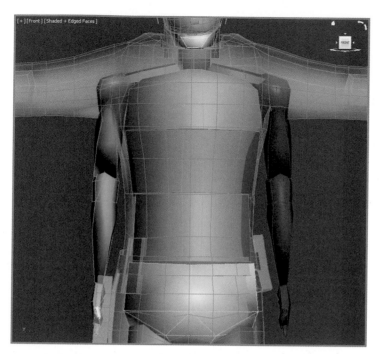

FIGURE 12.12 Scale the spine links up to place the clavicles in position.

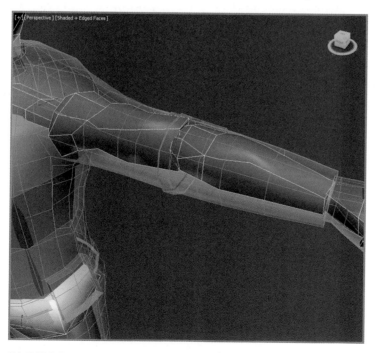

FIGURE 12.13 Arm positioned within the 3D mesh

6. The hands need only two fingers (the second finger is actually the thumb) and two links each. Adjust the biped's fingers to match the model's fingers, as shown in Figure 12.14.

   This can be one of the most tedious tasks in character animation, depending on the complexity and orientation of the model's fingers. Take your time and get it right. (Would you rather do it right or do it over?)

7. When you are done, copy the collection and then paste the posture to the right side of the biped and make any required changes.

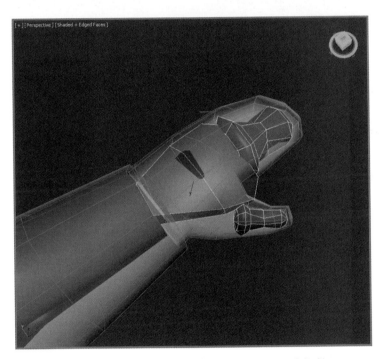

FIGURE 12.14   Match the biped's fingers to the model's fingers.

Adjusting the Neck and Head

The neck and head will seem easy to adjust when compared to the hands. You need to make sure the neck links fill the soldier's neck area, and scale the head to fit. Follow along here:

1. In the Structure rollout, increase the number of neck links to 2.

2. Move, scale, and rotate the neck links to match the proportions of the model's neck.

3. Move and scale the head to the approximate size of the soldier's head, as shown in Figure 12.15.

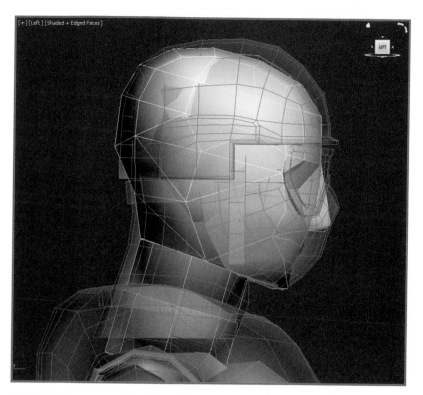

FIGURE 12.15   Matching the head

That's it. The biped has been created and adjusted to fit the 3D model, and half the battle is over. Next, you will tie the biped to the model and make adjustments to the skinning process. Now would be a good time to save your work and take a break.

Applying the Skin Modifier

The Skin modifier is the tool used to skin the 3D model to the biped so that all of the biped's animation is passed through to the model. It's important to remember that the modifier is applied to the model and not to the biped. Continue with the previous exercise's file or open CSSoldier03.max from the Scenes folder of the Soldier project on the book's web page to follow these steps:

1. Right-click in any viewport and select Unfreeze All from the quad menu to unfreeze the soldier model.

2. Then select the soldier and use Alt+X to exit See-Through mode and turn off Edged Faces (F4).

3. In the Modify panel, expand the Modifier List and select the Skin modifier.

4. In the Skin parameters, select the Add button next to bones. From the Select Bones dialog, select all the biped objects and click the Select button.

Testing the Model

The most time-consuming part of the process is complete. You have created a biped and adjusted all of its component parts to fit your model. The next step is to add animation that will allow you to test the skinning once it has been applied.

Before we get into fixing the skin, you need to add a little extra animation. Select the soldier model and right-click in the viewport to get the quad menu. Choose Hide Selection. Then follow these steps:

1. Select the model, right-click again, and from the quad menu, choose Hide Selected.

2. Move the timeline to frame 0. Turn on the Auto Key button (Auto) below the timeline.

3. Select the entire biped: The best way to do this is to select the Select By Name tool ( ) from the Main toolbar, and then from the Select From Scene dialog box, select all the Biped objects and click OK.

4. Go to the Motion panel ( ), and click the Figure Mode button ( ) to exit.

> You cannot animate a biped in Figure mode.

5. Select the Move tool and move the biped just a bit.
   The purpose of this is to create a keyframe of this original pose so that when you add animation, this pose won't be lost. The biped should still be in the same position as before—just give the Move tool a wiggle.

6. Select the right upper arm, Ctrl+click the left upper arm on the biped, and then set the coordinate system for the Move tool to Local, as shown earlier in Figure 12.7.

7. Move the timeline to frame 15, and rotate the arms –55 degrees on the Z-axis (the blue wire in the rotate gizmo).

8. Now select the right and left lower arms on the biped and rotate −55 degrees on the Z-axis.

9. Move the timeline to frame 30 and select the upper arms again, but this time rotate 45 degrees on the X-axis (green wire).

10. Now move to frame 50 and select the lower arms and upper arms. In the timeline, Shift+click the keyframe at frame 0, and then drag it to frame 50. This copies the keyframe at frame 0 to frame 50.

11. Add similar keyframes to repeat the same animation to fill 100 frames.

Using the same technique, add animation to the legs, chest, and head. The animation does not have to be elaborate. The purpose of the animation is to test the skinning when applied to the model. When you are finished, turn off the Auto Key button, unhide the soldier, and play the animation. Most likely you will see some problem with the skin—mostly around the feet, upper arms, and groin, as shown in Figure 12.16.

FIGURE 12.16   The problem areas with the skin

Tweaking the Skin Modifier

Each element in the biped has an area of influence, called an *envelope*. It determines which parts of the model it affects. The biped's left foot, for instance, should control the movement of only the model's left foot and the lower part of the ankle. In this case, the envelopes extend to affect some of the vertices on the opposite side. You can continue with your file from the previous exercise or open CSSoldier04.max from the Scenes folder of the Soldier project available on the book's web page. The animation in CSSoldier04.max might be a bit different than yours, but it will still work to check the Skin modifier. To fix the envelopes, follow this procedure:

1. Select the soldier model, and in the Skin parameters, click the Edit Envelopes button.

   You will see a color gradient around the pelvis. The gradient shows how heavily weighted the vertices on your mesh are to a given envelope, as shown in Figure 12.17. The biped bone is represented in the viewport as a straight line with vertices at either end. Envelopes are represented by two concentric capsule-shaped volumes; vertices within the inner volume are fully affected by that bone, and then the weighting falls off increasingly for vertices that lie outside the inner volume and inside the outer volume. The weight values appear as a colored gradient with red for the higher weights and blue for the lowest values, with orange, yellow, green in between.

2. Select the Bip001 R UpperArm object: You can select the object from the name list in the Skin parameters or just click on the representation of the bone on the model. Select the vertices at the end of the bone and move it toward the clavicle to make the envelope smaller, as shown in Figure 12.18.

   As the vertex moves, the gradient that represents the influence changes so the yellow-red color is moving up the arm. You want the influence to be on the upper arm only. Repeat this step on the other side of the bone, bringing it in toward the center of the bone.

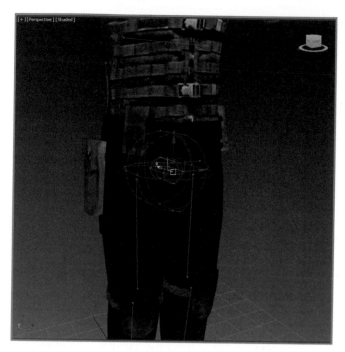

FIGURE 12.17 The soldier after the Edit Envelopes button is active

Move this point in this direction.
This will change the envelope's influence.

FIGURE 12.18 Select the bone vertex and move it to make the envelope smaller.

3. Select the points on the outer envelope and move them in on both sides of the bone, as shown in Figure 12.19. The final result is shown in Figure 12.20.

4. Move to frame 30 in the animation.

   In this frame you can really see the problem with the arm. Even though you edited the envelope for the upper arm, you can't see any improvement in the deformity. The previous exercise showed how to edit the envelope; now let's figure out where the trouble really lies with the upper arm. There is one bone that is affecting the upper arm: the Bip001 Spine2 bone.

5. Select the Bip001Spine2 bone: This bone's envelope is huge! It is influencing almost the whole upper body. Select a vertex on either end of the bone and move it in; immediately you will see the arms reacting.

6. Now scale down the size of the outer envelope so that the gradient has some yellow on the inside and blue between the capsules, as shown in Figure 12.21.

7. Now select and edit the remaining two spine bones.

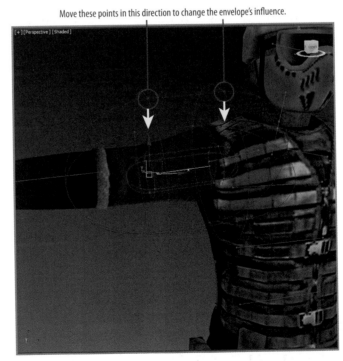

FIGURE 12.19 Make the outer envelope smaller by selecting and moving the points.

FIGURE 12.20   The edited envelope for the upper arm

FIGURE 12.21   The Bip001 Spine2 bone after the envelope
has been edited

The feet are the next area with problems, and a bit more of a challenge to fix.

8. Move to frame 88 in the animation. This frame shows that the part of the mesh on the inside of the feet is getting pulled.

9. Select the Bip001 R Foot bone, and move the time slider back to frame 0; it will be easier to edit the envelope when the foot isn't so distorted.

    Look closely at the bone. As shown in Figure 12.22, the bone is actually sideways.

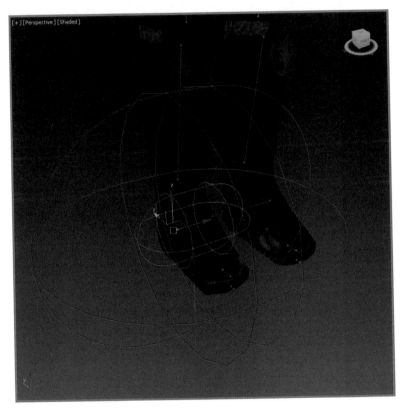

FIGURE 12.22   The envelope at the foot is set widthwise to the foot instead of lengthwise.

10. Move the points on the bone so they run from the toe to the heel, and then edit the envelopes so that the gradients are isolated on the foot, as shown in Figure 12.23.

FIGURE 12.23 The edited envelope for the right foot

11. Continue editing the bones and envelopes for the right side and middle of the model.

Once you are finished, the next step is to mirror the results to the left side of the body.

12. Select the BIP001 R Foot bone, and in the Mirror Parameters rollout of the Skin modifier, click the Mirror Mode button.

13. Then set Mirror Offset to –8.3, as shown in Figure 12.24. This moves the mirror plane along the X-axis

14. Then click the Paste Blue To Green Bones button axis. This pastes the envelope settings from blue bones to green. ().

15. In the Skin parameters, click the Edit Envelopes button to exit.

16. Play the animation again and pay attention to any areas where you see parts of the mesh pulling or distorting.

17. Go back to that area's envelope and edit until you are happy with the results.

FIGURE 12.24
In the Mirror Parameters
rollout, set Mirror Offset
to −8.3.

Weighting the Accessories

Now let's improve the skinning on the accessories, starting with the gun holster on the right side of the belt of the soldier, by adjusting the weight setting for the vertices. This technique is another way of editing the skinning on a character. You can choose to use the vertex weighting technique in conjunction with editing envelopes or use it exclusively. You can continue with your file from the previous exercise or open CSSoldier05.max from the Scenes folder of the Soldier project available on the book's web page. Follow these steps:

You select elements when you work with the accessories that are individual objects attached to an overall model.

1. Select Edit Elements, and in the Select section of Skin modifier's Parameters rollout, uncheck Envelopes and Cross Sections. Check Vertices and Select Element, as shown in Figure 12.25.

FIGURE 12.25
Uncheck the Envelopes and
Cross Sections boxes and
check the Vertices and
Select Element boxes.

2. Drag a selection box around the gun holster.

 The selected vertices appear as white hollow boxes, as shown in Figure 12.26. If other vertices are selected, then Alt+click or Alt+drag to deselect it.

FIGURE 12.26 The gun holster element is selected, showing the vertices for weighting.

3. In the Weight Properties section, click the Weight Table button; this will open the Skin Weight Table dialog box.

4. In the Skin Weight Table dialog box, in the Options menu, choose Show Affected Bones. At the bottom of the dialog box is a drop-down menu; choose Selected Vertices.

5. On the left of the Skin Weight Table dialog box under Vertex ID, drag from the top of the list down to the bottom to highlight all the vertices in the list. Then highlight at the top of the dialog box Bip001 Pelvis.

6. Click one of the numbers in the list below Bip001 Pelvis, type in 1, and then press Enter.

All the numbers in the list change to 1, while the numbers in the other lists change to 0, as shown in Figure 12.27. You just put all the weight of the gun holster on the pelvis and removed it from the thigh and spine.

7. Close the dialog box when you're finished.

FIGURE 12.27   Vertex weighting moved to the pelvis in the Skin Weight Table dialog box

Now if you play the animation, you will see that the gun holster looks stiff and doesn't move with the leg. Continue using the Skin Weight Table dialog box to edit the various soldier accessories, including the face mask, belt pouches, and anything that looks deformed and shouldn't.

Testing the Model

Continue with your file from the previous exercise or open CSSoldier06.max from the Scenes folder of the Soldier project available on the book's web page. This file has the completed rig with all the animation deleted. Follow these steps to test the model:

1. To delete any animation, select all the biped bones, drag a selection around the keyframes, and delete them in the timeline.

2. Select any element of the biped and click the Motion tab of the command panel.

3. Enter Footstep mode ( ).

   The rollouts change to display the tools for adding and controlling a biped's motion.

4. In the Footstep Creation rollout, make sure the walk gait is selected and then click the Create Multiple Footsteps button (![icon]) to open the Create Multiple Footsteps dialog box.

   In the dialog box that appears, you will assign Footstep properties for the number of steps you want, the width and length of each step, and which foot to step with first.

5. Set Number Of Footsteps to 8, leave the other parameters at their default values, and click OK.

6. Zoom out in the Perspective viewport to see the footsteps you just created. Look at the time slider, and note that the scene now ends at frame 123; that's 23 more frames than the 100 frames the scene had at the beginning of this chapter. The 3ds Max software recognized that it would take the biped 123 frames, or just over 4 seconds, to move through the eight steps that it was given.

7. Click the Play Animation button in the Playback Controls area. What happens? Nothing. The biped must be told explicitly to create animation keys for the steps that you have just added to the scene.

8. Drag the time slider back to frame 0.

9. In the Footstep Operations rollout in the command panel, click the Create Keys For Inactive Footsteps button (![icon]).

   The biped will drop its arms and prepare to walk through the footsteps that are now associated with it.

10. Click the Play Animation button again.

    This time the biped walks through the footsteps with its arms swinging and its hips swaying back and forth.

> You cannot be in both Footstep mode and Figure mode at the same time.

Controlling the View

Now the problem is that if you zoom in on the biped and play the animation, it walks off the screen so you cannot see the end of the walk cycle. What good is that? Motion cycles can be very linear and difficult to track, so Character Studio contains the In Place mode to follow a biped's animation. In the In Place mode, the biped will appear to stay in place while the scene moves around it in relation.

> The In Place mode cannot be used in a Camera viewport.

To set up In Place mode follow these steps:

1. Go to frame 0 and then zoom in on the biped in the Perspective viewport.

2. At the bottom of the Biped rollout, click the Modes And Display text with the plus sign to the left of it. This is a small rollout located inside of another rollout that expands to show additional display-related tools. It is hidden and difficult to find, as shown in Figure 12.28.

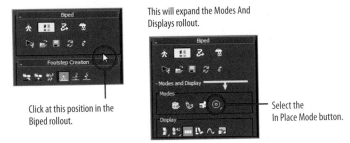

This will expand the Modes And Displays rollout.

Click at this position in the Biped rollout.

Select the In Place Mode button.

FIGURE 12.28   In the Biped rollout, click at the bottom to reveal the Modes And Display rollout.

3. In the Modes And Display rollout, click the In Place Mode button (⊙), as shown in Figure 12.28.

4. Click the Play Animation button again.
   This time the biped will appear to be walking in place while the footsteps move underneath it.

5. Stop the animation playback when you're ready.

IN PLACE MODE

Using the In Place mode helps you work out the way a character moves without having to navigate throughout 3D space with your viewport, so you won't need to hunt down your biped. The In Place mode is great for tweaking your animation cycle because the viewport moves with the character in 3D space and you can concentrate on how its body is moving.

6. Exit Footstep mode, and then select the entire biped by double-clicking Bip001. If it is too difficult to do, use the Select By Name menu (H).

7. Right-click in any viewport and choose Hide Selection from the quad menu to hide the biped and obtain an unobstructed view of the model.

8. Click the Play Animation button.

Your soldier will walk through the scene. It should be similar to the rendered soldier shown in Figure 12.29.

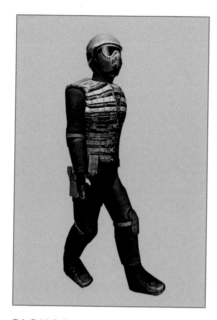

FIGURE 12.29 The rendered soldier during a walk cycle

Skinning a character is a detail-oriented task, and it requires lots of experimentation and trial and error—and patience. Character Studio is a complete character-animation package, and we've barely scratched the surface here. There are tools for saving biped configurations and sequences of animation. You can mix animation sequences from different files to create an entirely new motion. When the model does not skin as well as you need, you can use envelopes to refine the skinning process further, define vertices to be excluded from a specific Biped object's influence, or include bulge conditions to define the model's behavior depending on the angle between subsequent biped elements. The list goes on.

It's important to realize that animation requires nuance, and the best animation with the simplest rig and setup will beat a mediocre animation created with a more wonderful, complicated, and ingenious setup.

The Character Studio tutorials and help system that ship with the 3ds Max program are very thorough, and you should find the information there to expand your skills once you have a solid footing with the basics.

THE ESSENTIALS AND BEYOND

This chapter introduced you to the basics of Character Studio and biped setup for the soldier character. You used Skin to apply the biped setup to the geometry of the soldier and adjusted the envelopes for the best animation results.

ADDITIONAL EXERCISES

▶ Try adjusting the proportions of the soldier model to create a new character design and adjust the biped accordingly.

▶ Try adding a tail to the biped for an interesting creature.

CHAPTER 13

Character Studio: Animation

Character animation is a broad and complex field; in fact, the character animation computer generated specialty is one of the toughest specialties to master. To use one word, good character animation comes down to *nuance*. When you animate a character, you have to have a keen eye for detail and an understanding of how proportions move on a person's body. Setting up a computer-generated character to walk *exactly* like a human being is amazingly complicated.

Character systems such as Character Studio make it a breeze to outfit characters with biped setups and have them moving in a walk cycle very quickly.

This chapter introduces you to the basics of using Character Studio and bones for animation. Further investigation into these tools is a must if you want your animation to be full of life and character.

This chapter includes the following topic:

▶ **Animating the soldier**

Animating the Soldier

Bipeds can be animated in several ways, including footstep-driven animation and freeform animation. With *footstep-driven animation,* you add visible Footstep objects to your scene and direct the biped to step onto those footsteps at particular points in time. Footsteps can be added individually or as a set of walk, run, or jump steps; they can be moved or rotated to achieve the desired result and direction. When you use footstep-driven animation, the legs and feet of the biped are not the only things animated; the hips, arms, tails, and all other components are animated as well. However, this approach is rarely the complete solution to your animation needs.

Freeform animation is when you animate the components of the biped manually, as you would animate any other object, such as a bouncing ball.

Animation keys that are added to the selected Biped objects appear in the track bar, just like other objects, where they can be moved, modified, or deleted to adjust the animation.

Adding a Run-and-Jump Sequence

At the end of the previous chapter, you finished rigging the soldier model and added footsteps to check the model. New footsteps can be appended to any existing footsteps. In the next exercise, you will add footsteps to the existing animation cycle.

Continue with the previous soldier model or open the CSSoldierComplete00 .max file in the Scenes folder of the Soldier project on the book's web page at www.sybex.com/go/3dsmax2014essentials. This file has most of the biped bones hidden. The objects that are visible in the file are the soldier model; Bip001, which is the diamond shape that sits at the pelvis area of the soldier character and acts as the center for your biped rig, and the footsteps which hold the animation that was added in the previous chapter. Follow these steps:

> ▶
>
> If you have trouble, you can either press the H key or click the Select By Name icon (🖻) found on the main toolbar, which opens the Select From Scene dialog box.

1. Select the Bip001 object in the Select From Scene dialog box, and click OK.

2. Then on the Motion panel, choose Footstep mode (👣)

3. Click the Run icon (🏃) in the Footstep Creation rollout.
   This will apply a run gait to any footsteps you add to your current footsteps using the Create Multiple Footsteps dialog box.

4. Click the Create Multiple Footsteps icon (👣) to open the Create Multiple Footsteps dialog box.

5. Change the number of footsteps to 10 and click OK.

6. In the Footstep Operations rollout, click the Create Keys For Inactive Footsteps icon (🎬) to associate the new footsteps with the biped.

7. Click the Play Animation button. In this file the In Place Mode icon (◉) is active. The biped will appear to stay in place while the scene moves around it. The biped walks through the first 8 steps and then runs through the next 10.
   As you can see, the run sequence meets the definition of a run, but it is far from realistic. In the next exercise, you'll learn how to add to

or modify a biped's motion with freeform animation to make a better cycle. For now, click the Stop Animation button to turn off the animation.

8. Click the Jump button in the Footstep Creation rollout, and then click the Create Multiple Footsteps button.

9. In the Create Multiple Footsteps dialog box, set the number of footsteps to 4 and click OK.

10. Click the Create Keys For Inactive Footsteps icon to associate the new jump footsteps with the biped.

11. Click the Play Animation button.

The biped will walk, run, and then end the sequence with two jumps, as shown in Figure 13.1.

Because a jump is defined as a sequence with either two feet or zero feet on the ground at a time, four jump steps will equal two actual jumps.

The Actual Stride Height parameter in the Create Multiple Footsteps dialog box determines the height difference from one footstep to the next. This is how to make the biped climb stairs.

[+][Perspective][Shaded]

FIGURE 13.1 Soldier model with the Jump sequence added

Adding Freeform Animation

When you set your keys initially, you will need to edit them to suit good timing and form. When one part of the body is in one movement, another part of the body is in an accompanying or supportive or even opposite form of movement. When you are walking and your right leg swings forward in a step, your right arm swings back and your left arm swings out to compensate.

You can easily add or modify the biped's existing animation keys with freeform animation using the Auto Key button and the Dope Sheet. The following exercises contain examples of freeform animation.

Moving the Head

The following steps will guide you through the process of creating head movement for your biped. Continue with the previous soldier model or open the CSSoldierComplete01.max file in the Scenes folder of the Soldier project on the book's web page at www.sybex.com/go/3dsmax2014essentials. Because you will be working with the biped a lot in this exercise, the biped components have been unhidden and the soldier model has been hidden. If you are using your own file you need to do the same:

1. Select the Bip001 object, and if necessary, exit the Footstep mode by clicking the Footstep Mode icon.

2. Drag the time slider to frame 50, approximately the point when the biped lifts its left foot off footstep number 2.

3. Select the biped's head and note the animation keys that appear in the track bar, as shown in Figure 13.2.

4. In the track bar, select the two keys on either side of the current frame. You can do that using either of the following methods:

   ▶ Drag a selection box around both keys directly on the track bar.

   ▶ Select one key, and then holding the Ctrl key, select the other key.

5. Once the two keys are selected, right-click either key and then delete them as shown in Figure 13.3.

6. Click the Auto Key button or press the N key to turn it on. This will allow you to begin creating the animation.

Footsteps are numbered, starting with the number 0 and initially alternating from the left to the right side. They are also color-coded, with blue footsteps on the left and green footsteps on the right.

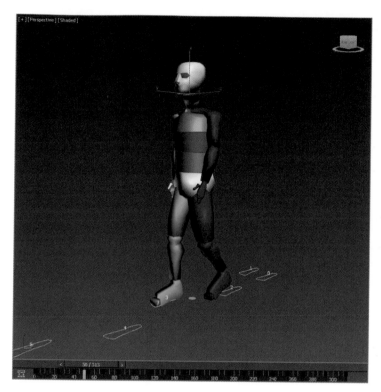

FIGURE 13.2 Selecting the head of the biped reveals all of that object's animation keys in the track bar.

FIGURE 13.3 Delete the keys on either side of frame 50.

7. Click the Rotate button and rotate the head, as shown in Figure 13.4, to the left and up, as if the character sees somebody in a second floor window offscreen.

FIGURE 13.4 Rotate the head to the left and up.

A new key will be created at frame 50, recording the time and value of the head's rotation.

8. Scrub through the time slider by moving it back and forth, watching the head rotate from a neutral position to the orientation that you created and then rotate back to the neutral position.

9. Select all the keys between frame 50 and frame 100 (but not keys at frames 50 and 100), and delete them. Doing so will make room for the new key that you are about to create.

10. Select the key at frame 50, hold down the Shift key, and drag a copy of the key to frame 90, as shown in Figure 13.5. Use the readout at the bottom of the window to drag the key with precision. Copying the key will cause your biped to hold that neck pose for 40 frames, or about 1⅓ seconds.

FIGURE 13.5
Drag to copy the key.

11. Scrub the time slider to review the animation.

12. Select the biped's left upper arm.

> If animation keys are too close together, the animation could appear jerky.

13. In the track bar, select and delete all keys between frames 50 and 100. If you scrub the time slider or play the animation, the biped will hold its arm unnaturally stiff for 60 frames because you deleted the animation keys between two points where it holds its hand forward. That's okay; you're just making room for some new keys.

The animation keys for the arms define their swing motion.

14. Move the time slider to frame 60. This is the location for the first new animation key.

Moving the Arms

Now it's time to animate the arms, which are essential components in any walk cycle. To do so, follow these steps:

1. Rotate the upper arm upward, so that it points to the location at which the head is looking.

2. Continue adjusting the biped's left arm, hand, and finger until they appear to be pointing at something, as shown in Figure 13.6.

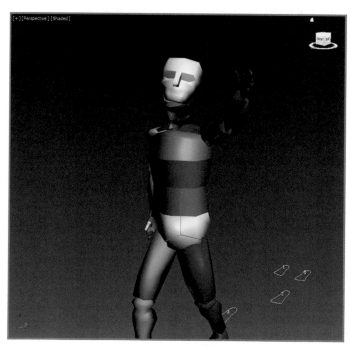

FIGURE 13.6 Rotate the biped's arm, hand, and finger to assume a pointing posture.

3. Double-click the left upper arm to select it and all of the components below it in the hierarchy.

4. In the track bar, select the key at frame 60, hold down the Shift key, and drag it to frame 85 to create a copy.

5. Drag the time slider and watch the Perspective viewport.
    The biped will walk for a bit, notice something offscreen, point at it, and drop its arm while looking forward again before breaking into a run and then a jump.

6. Click the Auto Key button to turn it off.

Completing the Motion Sequence

> Remember to make sure the Auto Key button is turned on to record all the changes that you make as you animate your character.

Continue with the previous soldier model or open the CSSoldierComplete02 .max file in the Scenes folder of the Soldier project on the book's web page at www.sybex.com/go/3dsmax2014essentials.

For additional practice, add keys to the animation of the biped's arms when it jogs through the run cycle. For example, when the left foot is fully extended and the heel plants on the ground, the right arm should be bent at the elbow and swung forward and slightly in front of the biped's body. As the right foot swings forward during the next step, the right arm should swing backward and assume a nearly straight posture. Bend each of the spine links and swing both arms backward to prepare the biped for each of the jumps. Use the Body Vertical button in the Track Selection rollout to lower the pelvis into a prelaunch position, as shown in Figure 13.7, before the biped launches into its upward motion.

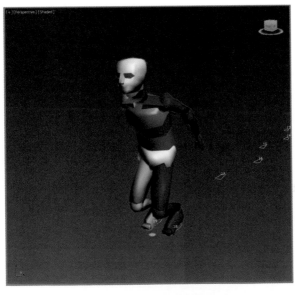

F I G U R E 1 3 . 7   Use the Body Vertical button to position the biped for a jump.

Modifying Animation in the Dope Sheet

To change the animation that is generated with Character Studio, you will edit the keyframes of the biped once you are happy with the base animation cycle. For this, you need to use the Track View–Dope Sheet. The Track View–Curve Editor, as you have already seen in Chapter 5, "Introduction to Animation," is used to edit the function curves between animation keys; however, the Track View–Dope Sheet interface is cleaner and is used to edit the specific value and position of the keys. It is not a different set of keyframes or animation; it's just a different way of editing them.

Access to editing the footstep keys is available only in the Dope Sheet.

In the next exercise, you will add individual footsteps and modify the footstep timing in the Dope Sheet to make the biped dance and jump.

Adding Footsteps Manually

In the following steps, you will manually add footsteps to your biped character. Open the CSSoldierComplete03.max file in the Scenes folder of the Soldier project on the book's web page at www.sybex.com/go/3dsmax2014essentials. This is the rigged and skinned soldier biped with no footsteps applied. Then follow these steps:

1. Select a biped component and enter the Footstep mode.

2. In the Footstep Creation rollout, click the Walk button and then the Create Footsteps (At Current Frame) icon ( ).

3. In the Top viewport, click in several locations around the biped to place alternating left and right footsteps to your liking.

4. Change the gait to Jump, and then click the Create Footsteps (Append) icon ( ) to create additional footsteps. Create about 12 footsteps in all.

5. When you are done, use the Move and Rotate transforms to adjust the footstep locations and orientations as desired. Your Top viewport should look similar to Figure 13.8.

6. In the Footstep Operations rollout, click the Create Keys For Inactive Footsteps icon and then play the animation.

Character Studio doesn't have a collision-detection feature, so it is very possible that limbs will pass through one another, which would be quite uncomfortable in real life. If this happens, the footsteps must be modified to eliminate these conditions. If necessary, move any footsteps that cause collisions or other unwanted conditions during the playback.

FIGURE 13.8   Manually place the footsteps in the
Top viewport.

Using the Dope Sheet

In Chapter 5, you experimented with the Track View–Curve Editor and learned
how to adjust the values of animation keyframes. When the Track View is in
Dope Sheet mode, frames are displayed as individual blocks of time that may or
may not contain keys. Although you cannot see the flow from key to key that
the Curve Editor displays with its curves, the Dope Sheet mode has its advan-
tages. For one, the Dope Sheet has the ability to add Visibility tracks to control the display of an object, as well as Note tracks for adding text information
regarding the keys as reminders.

Using the Track View–Dope Sheet, you can adjust the point in time when a foot
plants on or lifts off the ground, how long the foot is on the ground, and how long
the foot is airborne. Rather than appearing as single-frame blocks in the Dope
Sheet as other keys do, footstep keys appear as multiframe rectangles that identify
each foot's impact time with the footstep. Let's try the Dope Sheet on for size here:

1. Make sure you are in Footstep mode. This will select the biped's footsteps.

2. In the main toolbar, choose Animation ➢ Motion Editors ➢ Track
   View–Dope Sheet. The Dope Sheet will open.

3. In the Navigation pane on the left, scroll down until you find the
   Bip001 Footsteps entry, and expand it.

The footstep keys appear as rectangles in the Key pane. As expected, the left keys are colored blue and the right keys are colored green.

4. If necessary, click the Zoom Region icon ( ) in the lower-right corner of the Dope Sheet window and drag a zoom window around the footstep keys, as shown in Figure 13.9. The region will expand to fit the Key pane.

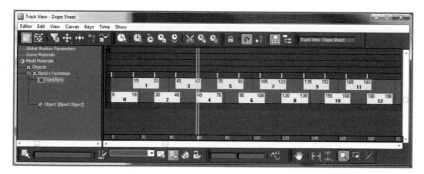

FIGURE 13.9   Zoom to the Footstep keys.

5. Select a few footsteps in the viewport or select the green- and blue-colored rectangles (holding Ctrl to select multiple footsteps).

The white dot on the left side of a selected key identifies the frame when the heel of the biped's foot first impacts the footstep. The white dot on the right side of a selected key identifies when the biped's foot lifts off a footstep, as shown in Figure 13.10. A blue key (rectangle) overlapping a green key (rectangle) indicates that both feet are on the ground. A vertical gray area with no footstep indicates that the biped is airborne and neither foot is on the ground.

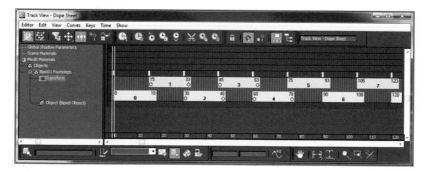

FIGURE 13.10   The dots indicate when contact begins and ends. You can drag a dot to change the duration of contact.

You can't move the end of one footstep key beyond the beginning of another one, and you must maintain a one-frame gap between same-side footsteps.

It is possible to move a footstep beyond the limits of the active time segment in the Dope Sheet. Use the Alt+R key combination to extend the active time segment to include all existing keys.

6. Select the first key (numbered 0), place the cursor over the right edge of the key, and then drag the dot to the right to extend the length of time the biped's foot is on the ground.

    The double vertical line in the Dope Sheet's Key pane is another time slider that allows you to scrub through the animation.

7. Drag the Dope Sheet's time slider to a point in time when the biped is airborne.

    Increasing the airborne time by increasing the gap between footsteps will also boost the height to which the biped rises, acting against the gravitational force pushing it downward.

8. Select the last four jump keys and drag them to the right to create a gap approximately 30 frames wide, as shown in Figure 13.11. Doing so will cause the biped to be airborne for about one second.

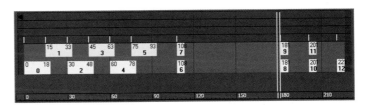

F I G U R E   1 3 . 1 1   Create a key gap to get your biped airborne.

9. Move the time slider to the frame when both feet are planted before the jump starts, and turn on the Auto Key button.

10. Deselect any keys by clicking a blank area in the Key pane.

11. Prepare the biped to leap as follows:

    a. Be sure to choose Local as the reference coordinate system for the Rotate transform.

    b. Select the Bip001 object and move it downward, causing the biped to bend its knees more.

    c. Rotate the spine links, neck, and head to bend the torso forward and tuck the chin.

    d. Rotate both arms backward into a pre-jump posture, as shown in Figure 13.12.

12. Move the time slider forward until the biped is at the apex of the jump.

13. Rotate the biped's components into positions you like, such as the split shown in Figure 13.13.

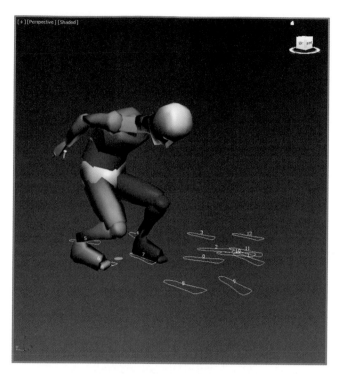

FIGURE 13.12   Prepare your biped to jump.

FIGURE 13.13   Position your biped in mid-jump.

14. Delete any animation keys that may interfere with your desired motion, and turn off Auto Key.

The `CSSoldierComplete04.max` file in the `Scenes` folder of the Soldier project contains the completed exercise so you can check your work. This file has the soldier model unhidden and the biped hidden.

15. Play the animation and see how it looks; modify where needed.

As you saw, there are several ways to animate a biped, including the footstep-driven method, the freeform method, and a combination of techniques. You can also modify the animation in the track bar, with the Auto Key button, and with Track View–Dope Sheet.

THE ESSENTIALS AND BEYOND

This chapter introduced you to animating characters with Character Studio. Character Studio has tools for animating 3D characters and is an environment in which you can quickly and easily build skeletons (also known as character rigs) and then animate them, thus creating motion sequences.

ADDITIONAL EXERCISES

▶ Add different head or arm movements to the current animation on your soldier.

▶ Animate the soldier character running and dodging enemy fire.

CHAPTER 14

Introduction to Lighting: Interior Lighting

Light reveals the world around us and defines shape, color, and texture. Lighting is the most important aspect of Computer Graphics (CG), and it simply cannot be mastered at a snap of the fingers. The trick to correctly lighting a CG scene is to understand how light works and to see the visual nuances it has to offer.

In this chapter, you will study the various tools used to light in the Autodesk® 3ds Max® software. This chapter will serve as a primer on this important aspect of CG. It will start you on the path by showing you the tools available and giving you opportunities to begin using them.

This chapter includes the following topics:

▶ **Three-point lighting**

▶ **3ds Max lights**

▶ **Lighting a still life in the interior space**

▶ **Selecting a shadow type**

▶ **Atmospheres and effects**

▶ **Light Lister**

Three-Point Lighting

Three-point lighting is a traditional approach to lighting a television shot. After all these years, the concepts still carry over to CG lighting. In this setup, three distinct roles are used to light the subject of a shot. The scene should, in effect, seem to have the following elements:

▶ Only one primary or *key* light to define lighting direction and create primary shadows

▶ A softer light to fill the scene and soften the shadows a bit

▶ A back light to make the subject pop out from the background

This does not mean there are only three lights in the scene. Three-point lighting suggests that there are three primary angles of light for your shot, dependent on where the camera is located.

Three-point lighting ensures that your scene's main subject for a particular shot is well lit and has highlights and a sense of lighting direction using shadow and tone. Figure 14.1 shows a plan view of the three-point lighting layout. The subject is in the middle of the image.

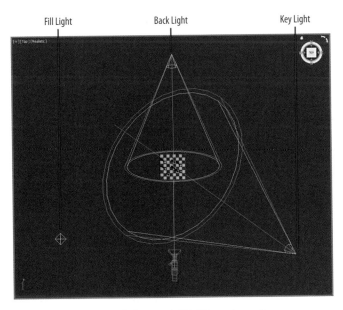

FIGURE 14.1   A three-point lighting schematic

3ds Max Lights

The 3ds Max program has two types of light objects: photometric and standard. *Photometric lights* are lights that possess specific features to enable a more accurate definition of lighting, as you would see in the real world. Photometric lights have physically based intensity values that closely mimic

In the absence of lights, a scene is automatically lit by *default lighting* so you can easily view an object in Shaded or Realistic mode and test-render without creating a light first. Default lighting is replaced by any lights you add.

the behavior of real light. *Standard lights* are extremely powerful and capable of realism, but they are more straightforward to use than photometric lights and less taxing on the system at render time. In this book, we will discuss only standard lights.

Standard Lights

The 3ds Max lights attempt to mimic the way real lights work. For example, a light bulb that emits light all around itself would be an *omni* light in 3ds Max terminology. A desk lamp that shines light in a specific direction in a cone shape would be a spotlight. Each of the different standard lights casts light differently. We will look at the most commonly used lights.

The 3ds Max program has a total of eight light types in its Standard Light collection:

Target spotlight	Omni light
Target direct light	Skylight
Free spotlight	mr area omni light
Free direct light	mr area spotlight

The last two on this list begin with *mr* to signify that they are mental ray–specific lights (see Chapter 16, "mental ray," for more about mental ray). An advanced renderer, mental ray is commonly used in production today. It offers many sophisticated and frequently complex methods of lighting that enhance the realism of a rendered scene. In this chapter, we will cover only the first five standard lights.

Target Spotlight

A *target spotlight*, as shown in Figure 14.2, is one of the most commonly used lights because it is extremely versatile. A spotlight casts light in a focused beam, similar to a flashlight. This type of lighting allows you to light specific areas of a scene without casting any unwanted light on areas that may not need that light. You can control the size of the *hotspot*, which is the size of the beam before it starts losing intensity.

The light is created with two nodes, the light itself (*light source*) and the target node, at which the light points at all times. This way, you easily are able to animate the light following the subject of the scene, as a spotlight would follow a singer on stage. Select the target and move it as you would any other object. The target spot rotates to follow the target.

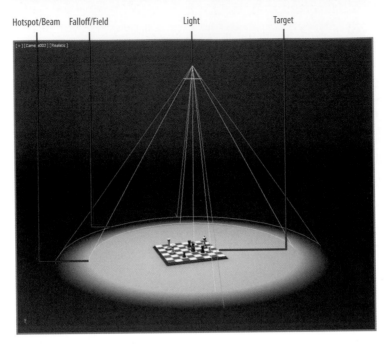

FIGURE 14.2 A target spotlight

Similarly, you can animate the light source, and it will orient itself accordingly to aim at the stationary target. Select the box at the end (the target) to point the light. To move (and animate) the entire light, do the following:

1. Select the line that connects the light source and the target.

2. Select the top of the light (tip of the cone) to access the parameters of the light.

3. Create a target spot by going to the Create panel and clicking the Lights icon (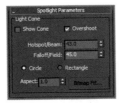). In the drop-down menu, choose Standard.

4. Click the Target Spot button, and in the Front viewport, click and drag to create a target spotlight.

5. Go to the Modify panel and open the Spotlight Parameters rollout, shown in Figure 14.3.

FIGURE 14.3
The Spotlight Parameters rollout

The falloff, which pertains to standard lights in 3ds Max software, is represented in the viewport by the area between the inner, lighter yellow cone and the outer, darker yellow cone. The light diminishes to 0 by the outer region, creating a soft area around the hotspot circle (where the light is the brightest), as shown in Figure 14.4.

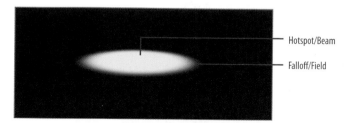

Hotspot/Beam

Falloff/Field

FIGURE 14.4   The falloff of a spotlight

Target Direct Light

A *target direct light* has target and light nodes to help you control the direction and animation of the light. It also has a hotspot and beam, as well as a falloff, much like the target spot. However, whereas the target spot emits light rays from a single point (the light source) outward in a cone shape, the target direct light casts parallel rays of light within its beam area. This helps simulate the lighting effect of the sun because its light rays (for all practical purposes on Earth) are parallel. Figure 14.5 shows a target direct light in a viewport.

Because the directional rays are parallel, the target direct lights have a beam in a straight cylindrical or rectangular box shape instead of a cone.

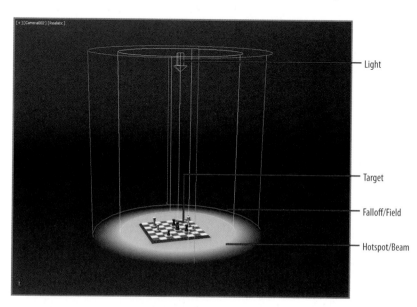

Light

Target

Falloff/Field

Hotspot/Beam

FIGURE 14.5   A target direct light

You can create and select/move parts of a target direct light in much the same way as a target spot. In the Directional Parameters rollout, you'll find the similar parameters for the target direct light. Although the spotlight and the directional light don't seem to be very different, the way they light is strikingly different, as you can see in Figure 14.6. The spotlight rays cast an entirely different hotspot and shadow than the directional light, despite having the same values for those parameters.

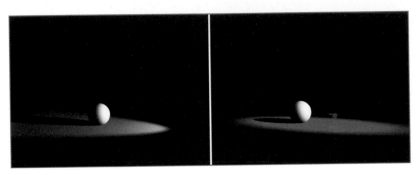

FIGURE 14.6   A target spot (left) and a target direct spot (right)

Free Spot or Free Direct Light

Free spotlights and *free direct lights* are virtually identical to target spots and target direct lights, respectively, except that the free spot and direct lights have no Target object. You can move and rotate the free spot however you want, relying on rotation instead of a target to aim it in any direction, as shown in Figure 14.7.

FIGURE 14.7   Free spot (left) and free direct (right) lights

To create a free spot or direct light, follow these steps:

1. Go to the Create panel ➢ Lights, and from the drop-down menu, choose Free Spot or Free.

2. Click in a viewport; this will create the light oriented in that viewport.

3. Now use the Move and Rotate tools to position the free spot or direct light however you want.

Another difference between a free spot or direct light and a target spot or direct light is that whereas the length of the target spotlight is controlled by its target, a free spot or direct light instead has, in the General Parameters rollout, a parameter called Targ. Dist. The default is 240 units.

Free Spot and Free Direct (including target spot and target direct) are great for key lighting because they are very easy to control and give a fantastic sense of direction. In the General Parameters rollout, there is a drop-down menu allowing you to change your chosen light type to another type. You can also change a free light to a target light by checking the Targeted box.

Adjusting the length of a free spot or free direct light will not matter when the light is rendered; however, seeing a longer light in the viewports can help you line up the light with objects in the scene.

Omni Light

The 3ds Max *omni light* is a point light that emanates light from a single point in all directions around it. Figure 14.8 shows an omni light. Unlike the spot and directional lights, the omni light does not have a special rollout, and its General Parameters rollout is much simpler.

FIGURE 14.8 An omni light is a single-point-source light.

Omni lights are not as good for simulating sunlight as directional lights are. In Figure 14.9, the omni light in the image on the left creates different shadow and lighting directions for all the objects in the scene, and the directional light in the image on the right creates a uniform direction for the light and shadow, as would the sun here on Earth.

FIGURE 14.9　Omni light (left) and directional light (right)

Omni lights are good for fill lights as well as for simulating certain practical light sources.

▶

Try to avoid casting shadows with omni lights, because they will use a lot more memory than spot-lights when casting shadows.

1. In the Create Panel ➤ Lights, choose Standard from the drop-down menu and then choose Omni.

2. In any viewport, click to create the omni.

3. The omni can be moved and positioned quickly and easily using the Select And Move tool.

Lighting a Still Life in the Interior Space

▶

The ArchModel file is a version of the room built in earlier chapters. Models and more materials have been added to beef up the file.

Now that you have an overview of how lights work in a 3ds Max scene, let's put them to good use and light the room from Chapter 10, "Introduction to Materials: Interiors and Furniture," and create a basic light setup for the scene. Set your current project to the ArchModel project you copied to your hard drive from this book's web page, www.sybex.com/go/3dsmax2014essentials. Open ArchModel_Light_Start.max from the Scenes folder of the ArchModel project.

We will start with a still-life scene set up in the dining room:

1. Go to the Create panel and select the Lights to bring up the selection of lights you can create.

2. Click the drop-down menu and choose Standard, as shown in Figure 14.10.

FIGURE 14.10
Choose Standard from
the Lights drop-
down menu.

3. Select Target Spot and go to the Front viewport.

4. Click and drag from the ceiling above the dining room table to the floor below the table. In the command panel, rename the light **Key Light**.

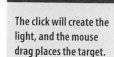

The click will create the light, and the mouse drag places the target.

5. In the Top viewport, use the Select And Move tool to select the light and the target by dragging a selection box around both.

6. Move them so they are over the dining room table in the Top viewport, as shown in Figure 14.11.

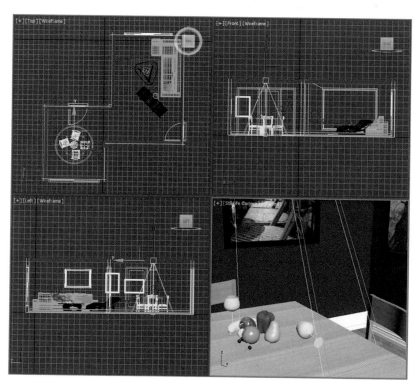

FIGURE 14.11   The spotlight's position in the room

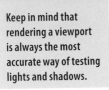

7. Go to the Modify panel. In the Intensity/Color/Attenuation rollout, set the Multiplier to **1.2**.

   The Multiplier acts as a dimmer switch for the key light. This light will have shadows and give the scene its main source of light and direction.

8. In the Still Life Camera viewport, click the Shading Viewport Label menu to expand it. Choose Realistic from the list.

9. Click the Shading Viewport Label menu again, go down to Lighting And Shadows, and choose Illuminate With Scene Lights, as shown in Figure 14.12.

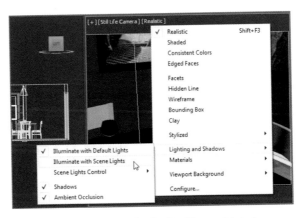

FIGURE 14.12   The Shading Viewport Label menu

Now the Still Life camera can be used to judge the lights and shadows for this scene.

10. Go to the Modify panel and expand the Spotlight Parameters rollout.

11. Set Hotspot/Beam to **40** and Falloff/Field to **100**.

    As you can see in the Still Life Camera viewport, the light spread out farther toward the walls.

12. Now render by clicking on the Render Production button (⬛), which is on the main toolbar.

The image on the left in Figure 14.13 shows that the Realistic viewport setting is fairly accurate. The reflections and transparencies that are seen in the rendered image on the right are not shown in the Realistic viewport shading.

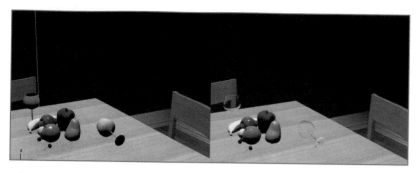

FIGURE 14.13 The Still Life Camera viewport set to Realistic, showing new Hotspot/Beam and Falloff/Field settings (left); the rendered scene (right)

A few things need to be added to the rendered scene to make it look more realistic. First, the scene needs shadows. Second, the area outside of the light is too dark; it looks too moody and mysterious. You need to add a fill light and back light to complete the lighting in the following steps:

1. Select the key light, if it isn't already selected.

2. In the Modify panel, go to the General Parameters rollout ➢ Shadows area and check the On box.

3. In the Still Life Camera viewport, a low-resolution version of the shadows appears, but a render of the scene will show it more accurately.

4. Render the scene. The result is shown in Figure 14.14.

FIGURE 14.14 It looks good, but the scene shadows are too soft.

5. Go to the Shadow Map Params rollout and change Size to 2048.
   This parameter adds more pixels to the shadow, which makes it more defined and less diffused.

6. Change Sample Range to 2.0; this parameter adds softness to the edge of the shadow. The default is 4.0, so lowering the number makes the edge sharper.
   Render the Still Life Camera viewport and compare the render with the Still Life Camera viewport. In the viewport, the shadow already looks better, but in the render, because the glasses are transparent, the shadow looks a bit weird—too dark and solid for a shadow for a transparent glass. To fix this issue, the shadow's density needs to be lowered. Adding a light to fill in the very dark shadows will correct this issue.

7. In the Create panel, select Lights➤ Omni, and in the Top viewport, click to create the omni light in the lower-right corner of the dining room.

8. In the Front viewport, move the omni light up so it is just below the ceiling of the dining room, and change the name to **Fill Light**.

9. In the Intensity/Color/Attenuation rollout, change the Multiplier to **0.2**.
   The omni is just a fill light in this scene that is used to simulate the indirect light you see in the real world. You don't want any shadows or specular highlights from this light; without them you can make sure the render looks as if there is only one light in the room. By default, shadows are always off, but you must turn off specular highlights manually.

10. With the omni light selected, go to the Modify panel and, under the Advanced Effects rollout, uncheck Specular.

11. Render again (press F9), and you'll see that the render looks better, but the still life's shadows are still dark, as shown in Figure 14.15.

FIGURE 14.15   Interior room with key light and fill light

To fix the darkness of the shadow, you will adjust the density of the shadow.

12. Select the key light, go to the Modify panel, and in the Shadow Parameters rollout, change the Object Shadows Dens parameter to 0.8.

13. Render the Camera viewport again (press F9) or select the Render Production icon ( ) in the main toolbar. The shadow looks much better, as shown in Figure 14.16.

FIGURE 14.16   Shadows with Density set to 0.8

This looks good, but the light is too even overall. The omni light needs to have what is called *decay* or attenuation applied. This means light over distance loses its intensity or energy. Standard lights don't do this by default; it has to be simulated within the parameters. For the room scene, you will be using attenuation.

14. Select the omni light. In the Intensity/Color/Attenuation rollout, click the Use and Show check boxes under Far Attenuation, as shown in Figure 14.17.

FIGURE 14.17 Check the Use and Show boxes for Far Attenuation.

When Use is checked, the circles appear when the light is selected, and Show makes them appear whether it is selected or not. This is best seen in the Top viewport, as shown in Figure 14.18. The Start value defines the start of the decay of the light. The End value defines when the light drops off to zero.

15. Set the Start value to **145.0** and the End value to **190.0** This gives some variation to the fill light, as shown in Figure 14.19.

Using shadows intelligently is important in lighting your scenes. Without the shadows in the scene, the still life would float and have no contact with its environment.

You can create the following types of shadows using the 3ds Max program:

▶ Advanced ray traced

▶ mental ray shadow map

▶ Area shadows

▶ Shadow map

▶ Raytraced shadows

Each type of shadow has its benefits and its drawbacks. The two most frequently used types are shadow map (which you've already seen) and ray traced shadows.

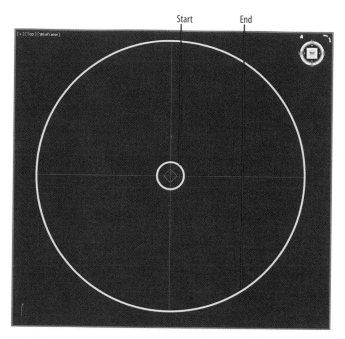

Start   End

FIGURE 14.18 Far Attenuation set on the fill light as viewed from the Top viewport with all the scene objects hidden

FIGURE 14.19 A still life rendered with Far Attenuation

Selecting a Shadow Type

To get shadows to respond to transparencies, you will need to use ray traced shadows instead of shadow maps.

Shadow Maps

Using a shadow map is often the fastest way to cast a shadow. However, shadow map shadows do not show the color cast through transparent or translucent objects.

When you are close to a shadow, to avoid jagged edges around it, use the Size parameter to make the resolution higher. The following parameters are useful for creating shadow maps:

Bias The shadow is moved, according to the value set, closer to or farther away from the object casting the shadow.

Size Detailed shadows will need detailed shadow maps. Increase the Size value, which in turn increases the detail of the shadow cast. Figure 14.20 compares using a low Shadow Map Size setting to using one four times larger. Notice how the shadows on the left (Size = 1024) are somewhat mushy and less noticeable, and the shadows on the right (Size = 4096) are crisp and clean. A size around 2048 is good for most cases. Scenes like this chessboard that have a large scale to them will require higher Size values, such as the 4096 that was used.

> Setting Shadow Map Size too high will increase the render time for little to no effect. The rule of thumb is to use the lowest size value that will get you the best result for your scene.

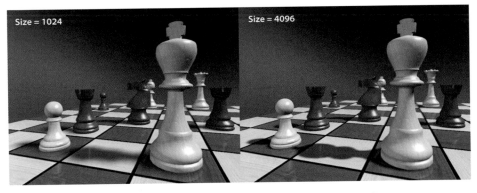

FIGURE 14.20 The Shadow Map Size setting affects the shadow detail.

Sample Range This option creates and controls the softness of the edge of shadow map shadows. The higher the value is, the softer the edges of the shadow will be.

raytraced Shadows

raytracing involves tracing a ray of light from every light source in all directions and tracing the reflection back to the camera lens. You can create more accurate shadows with raytracing than with other methods, at the cost of longer render times. Ray traced shadows are realistic for transparent and translucent objects. Figure 14.21 shows the still life rendered with a plane object casting a shadow over it. The plane has a logo mapped to its Opacity map channel, so it has alternating transparent and opaque areas defining the solid and transparent parts of the logo. On the left side of the image in Figure 14.21, the light is casting shadow map shadows; and on the right, the light is casting ray traced shadows.

FIGURE 14.21 Ray traced shadows react to transparencies, and shadow map shadows do not.

Use ray traced shadows when you need highly accurate shadows or when shadow map resolutions are just not high enough to get you the crisp edges you need. You can also use ray traced shadows to cast shadows from wireframe rendered objects.

The Ray Traced Shadow Params rollout controls the shadow. The Ray Bias parameter is the same as the Shadow Map Bias parameter in that it controls how far the shadow is from the casting.

Atmospheres and Effects

Atmospheric effects with lights, such as fog or volume lights, are created using the Atmospheres & Effects rollout in the Modify panel for the selected light.

Using this rollout, you can assign and manage atmospheric effects and other rendering effects that are associated with lights.

Creating a Volumetric Light

Let's create a fog light now:

1. Open the ArchModel_LightEnviro_Start.max scene file in the ArchModel project/scenes folder that you downloaded from the book's web page.

2. Go to the Create panel, select Lights, and in the drop-down list, select Standard, and then select the Target Direct light.

3. Go to the Left viewport and, clicking from the left outside of the room, position the light at a high angle from the window. Drag toward the living room window and set the light on the floor inside the room.

4. Select the Select And Move tool, and then in the Top viewport, click on the line that connects the light and its target, which will select both easily.

5. Select the light only, and then move the light so it is aligned with the living room window, as shown in Figure 14.22, and name the light **Sunlight**.

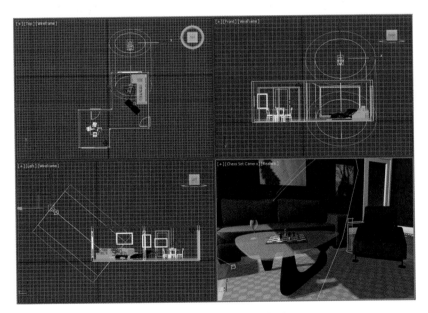

FIGURE 14.22   The light's position shown in all the viewports

6. Select the main Light object and go to the Modify panel.

7. In the Intensity/Color/Attenuation rollout, change the Multiplier to 1.2.

8. In the Directional Parameters rollout, change Hotspot/Beam to **60.0** and Falloff/Field to **63.0**.

   Looking at the Chess Set Camera viewport, you will see the light coming in through the window, but it is very dark everywhere else, as shown in Figure 14.23. More lights need to be added.

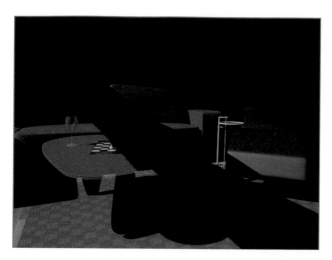

FIGURE 14.23 Interior room with the direct light in place as the sun.

9. In the Create panel, select Lights ➤ Omni, and place the light in a position near the Sunlight's position. Name the light **Fill Light_1**.

10. With the Omni light selected, go to the Modify panel, and in the Intensity/Color/Attenuation rollout, change the Multiplier to **0.5**.

11. In the Advanced Effects rollout, uncheck the Specular check box. This keeps the light on but does not show any specular highlights from this light.

Adding Shadows

Now you need some shadows in the scene:

1. Select the Sunlight light, and from the Modify panel, open the General Parameters rollout.

2. In the Shadows section, check the On box to enable shadows, and select Shadow Map from the drop-down list. Doing so turns on shadow map shadows for this light.

3. Go to the Shadow Map Params rollout and set the size to **2048** and change Sample Range to **2.0**; this will add some sharpness to the shadow's edge and make it more like a daylight shadow.

   If you perform a render, you won't see any shadows. This is because the window is blocking the light. The Window Glass object has a material that has its Opacity value turned down to 0. However, shadow map shadows don't recognize transparency in materials.

To solve this problem, you need to exclude the Window Glass object from the light. When the window was created, the glass was attached to the overall window object. It will take a few extra steps to access the glass and make it a separate object.

4. Select the FixedWindow001 object, and in the Graphite Modeling Tools tab ➤ Polygon Modeling, select Convert to Poly.

5. Enter the Element mode and click on the glass; it should become shaded in red.

6. In the Geometry (All) tab, select Detach, and in the type-in next to Detach As, change the name from Object001 to **Window Glass**.

Excluding an Object from a Light

The Exclude/Include dialog determines which objects are not illuminated by the selected light. Light exclusion is not found in nature, but this feature is useful when you need control over the lighting in your scene. Follow these steps:

1. Select the Sunlight light, and go to the Modify panel.
   In the General Parameters rollout, just below the Shadow type list, is the Exclude button.

2. Click the Exclude button to open the Exclude/Include window shown in Figure 14.24.

3. Click the Window Glass object and click the right arrow button in the middle of the window, as shown in Figure 14.24, to add the Window Glass object to the other side, excluding the object from receiving light and casting shadows. Click OK.

4. Render your scene to take a look.
   Now you can see shadows. You didn't exclude the whole window— just the glass. The window frame is still there and will cast nice detail.

5. Select the fill light. You need to set Attenuation on the light to vary the fill light and make it look more realistic.

6. In the Intensity/Color/Attenuation rollout, in the Far Attenuation section, check Use and set Start to **150.0** and End to **400.0**.
   The final results are still not there. The shaded areas facing the camera are still too dark, as shown in Figure 14.25. On a bright sunny day, the light coming through that big window would bounce light all over the room. Another fill light should do the trick.

Select the object in this box.   Click the right arrow button.   Add the object to this side.

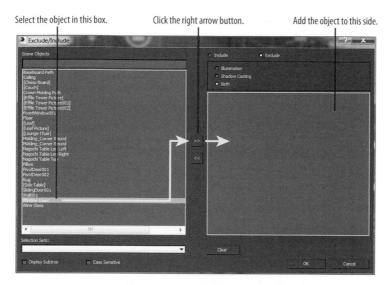

FIGURE 14.24 The Exclude/Include window allows you to exclude certain objects from being lit by the light in the scene.

FIGURE 14.25 Room with fill light set with attenuation

7. In the Create panel, select Lights ➢ Omni, and place the light behind the Chess Set Camera camera.

8. Move the light so it is just below the ceiling, as shown in Figure 14.26. Name the light **Fill Light_2**.

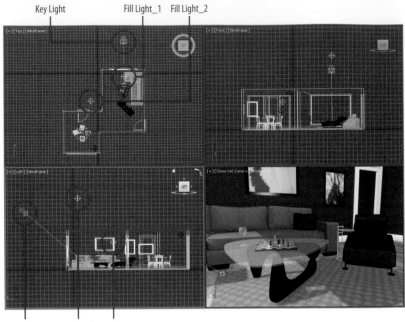

FIGURE 14.26   The position of Fill Light_2 shown in all four viewports

9. With the omni light selected, go to the Modify panel, and in the Intensity/Color/Attenuation rollout, change the Multiplier to 0.3.

10. In the Advanced Effects rollout, uncheck the Specular check box.

11. In the Intensity/Color/Attenuation rollout, in the Far Attenuation section, check Use and set Start to 48.0 and End to 180.0. The final results are shown in Figure 14.27.

FIGURE 14.27   The final results of the newly added fill light

Adding a Volumetric Effect

The whole point of this exercise is to add volume to the light. Volume light creates light effects based on the interaction of lights with atmosphere, like dust or smoke. This will give the scene some much-needed atmosphere:

1. Select the Sunlight light. In the Sunlight's parameters, go to the Atmospheres & Effects rollout.

2. Select Add from the rollout to open the Add Atmosphere Or Effect dialog box, select Volume Light, and click OK to add the effect to the light. Volume Light will be added to the rollout.

3. Render the scene. You should see a render similar to Figure 14.28.

FIGURE 14.28   Ooh! Volume light!

4. To adjust the volume light, go back to the Atmospheres & Effects rollout, select the Volume Light entry, and click the Setup button. This will bring up the Environment And Effects dialog box.

5. Scroll down to the Volume Light Parameters section to access the settings for the volume light, shown in Figure 14.29.

6. In the Volume section, change Density to .25. This lessens the intensity of the volume and makes it more realistic.

7. Change Max Light % to 10.0.

8. Render the camera; the results are shown in 14.30.

FIGURE 14.29 The Environment And Effects dialog box displays the Volume Light parameters.

FIGURE 14.30 The final results of the volume light in the interior room

You can use `ArchModel_LightEnviro_End.max` in the `Scenes` folder of the ArchModel project from the book's web page to see the results of this work and to adjust as you wish.

Volume Light Parameters

The default parameters for a volume light will give you some nice volume in the light for most scenes, right off the bat. If you want to adjust the volume settings, you can edit the following parameters:

Exponential   The density of the volume light will increase exponentially with distance. By default (Exponential is off), density will increase linearly with distance. You will want to enable Exponential only when you need to render transparent objects in volume fog.

Density   This value sets the fog's density. The denser the fog is, the more light will reflect off the fog inside the volume. The most realistic fog can be rendered with about 2 to 6 percent density value, depending on the scene.

Most of the parameters are for troubleshooting volume problems in your scene if it is not rendering very well. Sometimes you just don't know what that problem is and you have to experiment with switches and buttons.

The Noise settings are another cool feature to add some randomness to your volume:

Noise On   This toggles the noise on and off. Render times will increase slightly with noise enabled for the volume.

Amount   This is the amount of noise that is applied to the fog. A value of 0 creates no noise. If the amount is set to 1, the fog renders with pure noise.

Size, Uniformity, and Phase   These settings determine the look of the noise and let you set a noise type (Regular, Fractal, or Turbulence).

Adding atmosphere to a scene can heighten the sense of realism and mood. Creating a little bit of a volume for some lights can go a long way to improve the look of your renders. However, adding volume to lights can also slow your renders, so use it with care.

Light Lister

If several lights are in your scene and you need to adjust all of them, selecting each light and making one adjustment at a time can become tedious. This is where 3ds Max Light Lister comes in handy. Accessed through the menu bar by choosing

Lighting/Cameras ➢ Tools (Lights/Cameras Set) ➢ Light Lister, this floating palette gives you control over all of your scene lights, as shown in Figure 14.31.

FIGURE 14.31   The Light Lister dialog box

You can choose to view or edit all the lights in your scene or just the ones that are selected. When you adjust the values for any parameter in the Light Lister dialog box, the changes are reflected in the appropriate place in the Modify panel for that changed light.

THE ESSENTIALS AND BEYOND

This chapter reviewed key concepts in CG lighting, including three-point lighting. You learned about the various types of lights that the 3ds Max program has to offer, from default lights to target lights, and how to use them. You explored the common light parameters to gauge how best to control the lights in your scene before moving on to creating shadows. You ran through a set of short exercises in which you created a volume light for a fog effect, and you finished with a brief tour of the Light Lister dialog box.

Additional Exercises

▶ Try lighting the interior scene to evoke different moods: somber, jubilant, scary, and so forth.

▶ Add a new camera to the scene and light the scene again to see the various problems that arise.

▶ Change the lighting for a night scene.

CHAPTER 15

3ds Max Rendering

Rendering is the last step in creating your CG work, *but it is the first step to consider when you start to build a scene.* During rendering, the computer calculates the scene's surface properties, lighting, shadows, and object movement and then saves a sequence of images. To get to the point where the computer takes over, you'll need to set up your camera and render settings so that you'll get exactly what you need from your scene.

This chapter will show you how to render your scene using the Scanline Renderer in the Autodesk® 3ds Max® software and how to create reflections and refractions using raytracing.

This chapter includes the following topics:

▶ **Rendering setup**

▶ **Cameras**

▶ **Safe Frames**

▶ **Raytraced reflections and refractions**

▶ **Rendering the interior and furniture**

Rendering Setup

Your render settings and the final decisions you make about your 3ds Max scene ultimately determine how your work will look. If you create models and textures with the final image in mind and gear the lighting toward elegantly showing off the scene, the final touches will be relatively easy to set up.

The Render Setup dialog box is where you define your 3ds Max render output. You can open this dialog box by taking one of the following actions:

▶ Click the Render Setup icon (▧) in the main toolbar.

▶ Select Rendering ➢ Render Setup.

▶ Press F10.

You've already seen how to render (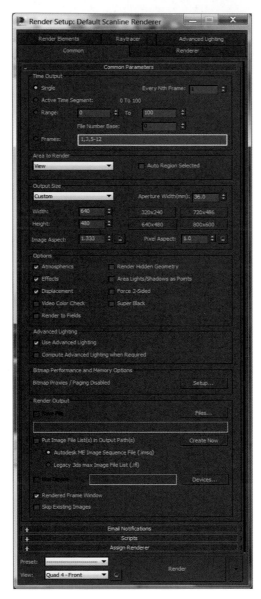) a frame in your scene to check your work. The settings in the Render Setup dialog box are used even when the Render Production button is invoked, so it's important to understand how this dialog box works. Figure 15.1 shows the Common tab in the Render Setup dialog box.

FIGURE 15.1 The Common tab in the Render Setup dialog box

Common Tab

The Render Setup dialog box is divided into five tabs; each tab has settings grouped by function. The Common tab stores the settings for the overall needs of the render—for example, image size, frame range to render, and type of renderer to use. Some of the most necessary render settings are described here:

Time Output   In this section, you can set the frame range of your render output by selecting one of the following options:

>   **Single**   Renders the current frame only
>
>   **Active Time Segment**   Renders the current range of frames
>
>   **Range**   Renders the frames specified

Output Size   The image size of your render, which is set in the Output Size section, will depend on your output format—that is, how you want to show your render.

>   **Resolution**   By default, the dialog box is set to render images at a resolution of 640×480 pixels, defined by the Width and Height parameters, respectively.
>
>   **Image Aspect**   Changing the Image Aspect value will adjust the size of your image along the Height parameter to correspond with the existing Width parameter. For example, regular television is 1.33:1 (simply called 1.33) and a high-definition (HD) television is a wide screen with a ratio of 1.78:1 (simply called 1.78). The resolution of your output will define the screen ratio.

In the Output Size section of the Render Setup dialog box, there is a drop-down menu for choosing presets from different film and video resolutions. The image quality and resolution of a render affect how long a render will take.

Options   The Options section lets you access several global toggles. You can toggle the rendering of specific elements in your scene. For example, if you are using atmospherics (volume light) or effects (lens flare) and don't want them to render, you can clear the appropriate boxes.

Render Output   Use the Render Output section to indicate that the file should be saved. The image format can be selected to be a single image file or a sequence of image files (such as Targa or TIFF files) that form a sequence, or it can be a movie file such as a QuickTime.

In addition to turning down the resolution for a test render, you can use a lower-quality render or turn off certain effects, such as atmospherics.

Choosing a Filename

Name your rendered images according to the scene's filename. This way, you can always know from which scene file a rendered image was produced.

To specify a location and file type for the render, click the Files button in the Render Output section. This will open the Render Output File dialog box shown in Figure 15.2. Select the folder to which you want to render, and set the filename. You can set the file type using the Save As Type drop-down menu.

FIGURE 15.2   The Render Output File dialog box defines how the render saves to disk.

Rendered Frame Window

When you click the Render button at the bottom of the Render Setup dialog box, the Rendered Frame window opens (Figure 15.3).

The Rendered Frame window shows you how the frames look as the renderer processes through the sequence of frames. A collection of quick-access buttons on the frame is also available in the Render Frame window.

Render Processing

When you click the Render button in the Render Setup dialog box, the Rendering dialog box shown in Figure 15.4 appears. This dialog box shows the parameters being used, and it displays a progress bar indicating the render's progress. You can pause or cancel the render by clicking the appropriate button.

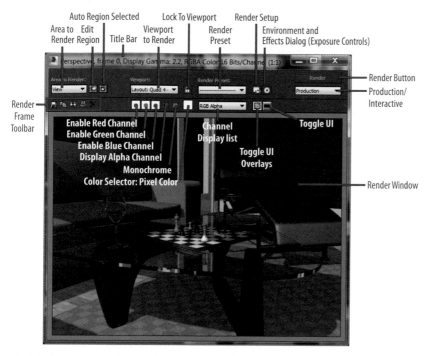

Area to
Render Region — Edit Region
Auto Region Selected
Title Bar
Viewport to Render
Lock To Viewport
Render Preset
Render Setup
Environment and
Effects Dialog (Exposure Controls)

Render Frame Toolbar

Render Button

Production/
Interactive

Enable Red Channel
Enable Green Channel
Enable Blue Channel
Display Alpha Channel
Monochrome
Color Selector: Pixel Color

Channel
Display list

Toggle UI

Toggle UI
Overlays

Render Window

FIGURE 15.3 The Rendered Frame window

FIGURE 15.4 The Rendering dialog box shows you everything you want to know about your current render.

Assign Renderer

Five types of renderers are available by default (without any additional plug-ins installed). The Default Scanline Renderer is the default renderer and is already assigned and appears in the Assign Renderer rollout. To access the Choose Renderer dialog box, shown in Figure 15.5, click the ellipsis button (![...]) to the right of Production. Only four renderers appear because the Default Scanline Renderer is already assigned. Mental ray rendering is covered in Chapter 16, "mental ray."

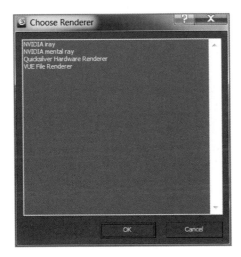

FIGURE 15.5 The Choose Renderer
dialog box

Rendering the Bouncing Ball

Seeing is believing, but doing is understanding. In this exercise, you will render the Bouncing Ball animation from Chapter 5, "Introduction to Animation," to get a feel for rendering an animation using the 3ds Max program. Just follow these steps:

1. Set your Project folder to the BouncingBall project that you down-loaded to your hard drive from the companion web page at `www.sybex.com/go/3dsmax2014essentials`.

2. Open the `Animation_Ball_02.max` file in the `Scenes` folder. Let's render a movie to see the animation.

3. Open the Render Setup dialog box, and in the Time Output section, select Active Time Segment: 0 To 100.

4. In the Output Size section, select the 320×240 preset button and leave Image Aspect and Pixel Aspect as is.

5. Leave the Options group at the defaults, and skip down to the Render Output section.

6. Click the Files button to open a Render Output File dialog box, and navigate to where you want to save the output file, preferably into the `renderoutput` folder in your BouncingBall project.

7. Name the file **Bouncy Ball**, and click the drop-down menu next to Save As Type to choose MOV QuickTime File (*.mov) for your render file type.

   Apple's QuickTime movie file format gives you a multitude of options for compression and quality. The quality settings for the QuickTime file are not the same as the render quality settings.

   After you select MOV QuickTime File and click the Save button, the Compression Settings dialog box, shown in Figure 15.6, opens.

By default, the 3ds Max program renders your files to the `renderoutput` folder in the current project directory.

Normally, you would render to a sequence of images rather than a movie file; however, for short renders and to check animation, a QuickTime file works out fine.

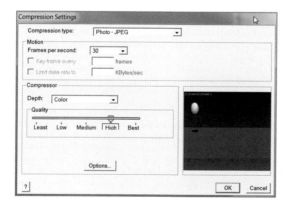

FIGURE 15.6 QuickTime compression settings affect the quality of the rendered QuickTime video file.

8. Set the parameters for the QuickTime file as indicated:

   Compression Type: Photo–JPEG

   Frames Per Second: 30

   Compressor Depth: Color

   Quality: High

9. Click OK to close the Compression Settings dialog box.

10. Skip down to the bottom of the Render Setup dialog box, and verify that the drop-down menu is set to Production.

11. Select the viewport you want to render in the View drop-down menu. You need to render Camera01.

12. Click Render.

13. After the render is complete, navigate to your render location (by default, it is set to the renderoutput folder for the BouncingBall project).

14. Double-click the QuickTime file to see your movie.

Cameras

The 3ds Max cameras, as shown in the Perspective viewport in Figure 15.7, capture and output all the fun in your scene. In theory, 3ds Max cameras work as much like real cameras as possible.

The *camera* creates a perspective through which you can see and render your scene. You can have as many cameras in the scene as you want. You can use the Perspective viewport to move around your scene as you work, leaving the render camera alone.

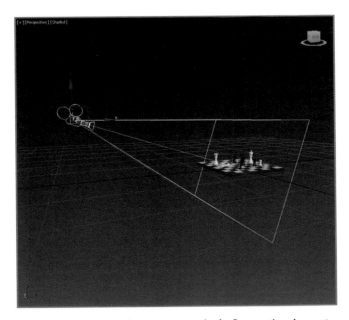

FIGURE 15.7   A camera as seen in the Perspective viewport

Creating a Camera

There are two types of 3ds Max cameras:

Target Camera   A *target camera*, much like a target spotlight, has a Target node that allows it to look at a spot defined by where the target is placed (or animated). A target camera is easier to aim than a free camera because once you position the Target object at the center of interest, the camera will always aim there.

Free Camera   On the other hand, *free cameras* have only one node, so they must be rotated to aim at the subject, much like a free spotlight. If your scene requires the camera to follow an action, you will be better off with a target camera.

You can create a camera by clicking the Cameras icon (🎥) in the Create panel and selecting either of the two camera types:

▶ To create a free camera, click in a viewport to place it.

▶ To create a target camera, click in a viewport to lay down the Camera node, and then drag to pull out and place the Target node.

Using Cameras

A camera's main feature is the *lens,* which sets the *focal length* in millimeters and also sets the *field of view (FOV)*, which determines how wide an area the camera sees, in degrees. By default, a 3ds Max camera lens is 43.456mm long with an FOV of 45 degrees. To change a lens, you can change the Lens or FOV parameters, or you can pick from the stock lenses available for a camera in its Modify panel parameters, as shown in Figure 15.8.

FIGURE 15.8 Stock lenses make it easy to pick the right lens for a scene.

The most interactive way to adjust a camera is to use the viewport navigation tools. The Camera viewport must be selected for the viewport camera tools to be available to you in the lower-right corner of the user interface (UI). You can move the camera or change the lens or FOV.

Talk Is Cheap!

The best way to explain how to use a camera is to create one, as in the following steps:

1. Set your project to the ArchModel project you have downloaded to your hard drive from this book's web page.

2. Open the ArchModel_Render_Start.max scene file in the Scenes folder.
   This scene is without a camera. Creating a camera is the same as creating a light. It's easier to create a camera in the Top viewport so you can easily orient it in reference to your scene objects.

3. In the Create panel, click the Cameras icon, select the target camera, and go to the Top viewport. Click from the window inside the room and drag toward the gap between the coffee table and the couch.
   The camera was created along the ground plane. You need to move the entire camera up.

4. In the Top viewport, select both the camera and target to move them as a unit by clicking the line that connects the camera and target in the viewport, and then in the Front viewport use the Move tool to relocate the camera higher in the scene.

5. To see the Camera viewport, select a viewport and press the C key.
   This changes the viewport to whatever camera is currently selected. The position of the camera and the way it looks in the Camera001 viewport is shown in Figure 15.9.

6. Now render the scene—press F9 or click the teapot icon (🫖) in the main toolbar—through the camera you just created and positioned.

Now that the camera is set up, take some time to move it around and see the changes in the viewport. To move the camera, select the Camera object. Use the Select And Move tool. Moving a camera from side to side is known as a *truck*. Moving a camera in and out is called a *dolly*. Rotating a camera is called a *roll*. Also change the Lens and FOV settings to see the results.

You can also change a camera by selecting the camera object and moving and rotating it just as you would any other object.

The first click creates the camera object. The mouse drag and release sets the location of the target, just like creating a target light.

If there are multiple cameras in your scene and none are selected, when you press C, you will get a dialog box that gives a list of the cameras from which you can choose.

Zooming a lens (changing the Lens parameter) is not the same as a dolly in or dolly out. The field of view changes when you zoom, and it stays constant when you dolly. They will yield different framing, or they will focus on the subject.

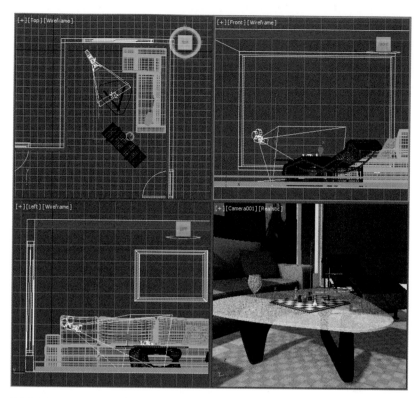

FIGURE 15.9 The position of the camera in the Top, Front, Left and Camera001 viewports.

Animating a Camera

Camera animation is done in the same way as animating any object. You can animate the camera or the target or both. You can also animate camera parameters such as Lens or FOV. Follow these steps to animate a camera:

1. In the scene you just worked in, select the camera.

2. Move the time slider to frame 30.

3. Press the N key to activate Auto Key, or click its button.

4. In the Top viewport, use the Move tool to move the camera farther away from the chess set; watch the Camera001 viewport to be sure you don't go outside the room. The direction or distance doesn't really matter just as long as it is different than the previous camera position.

5. Look in the Camera001 viewport, and then move the time slider through the animation. Press the N key again to turn off Auto Key.

The camera should just move away from the chess set toward the window, as shown in Figure 15.10. Don't worry if your camera position isn't the same as in the figure.

Move the camera from position 1 to position 2.

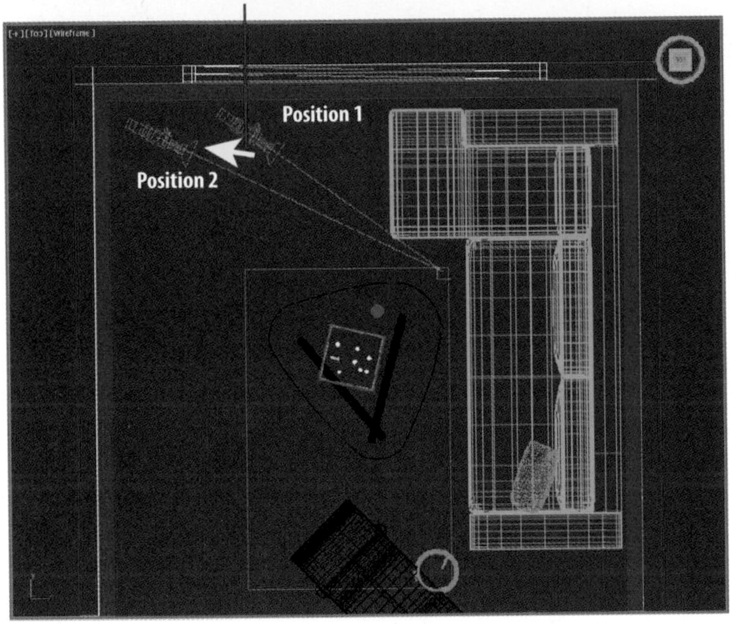

FIGURE 15.10   Move the camera in the Top viewport.

Clipping Planes

In a huge scene, you can exclude, or *clip*, the geometry that is beyond a certain distance from the camera by using *clipping planes*. This helps minimize the amount of geometry that needs to be calculated. Each camera has a clipping plane for distance (Far Clip), as shown in the left image in Figure 15.11, and for the foreground (Near Clip), as shown in the right image. The near clipping plane clips geometry within the distance designated from the camera lens.

▶

If you find that a model or scene you have imported looks odd or is cut off, check to make sure your clipping planes are adjusted to fit the extent of the scene.

To enable clipping planes, click the Clip Manually check box and set the distances needed. Once you turn on manual clipping planes, the camera displays the near and far extents in the viewports with red plane markers.

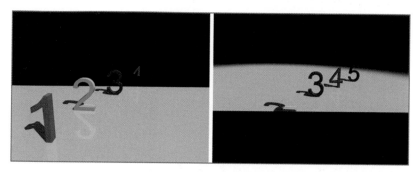

FIGURE 15.11 A far clipping plane cuts off the distant extents of a scene (left). A near clipping plane cuts off the extents directly in front of a camera (right).

Safe Frames

Safe Frames allow you to see the proportions of your rendered output within a viewport. Safe Frames display a series of rectangular frames in the viewport. This is particularly useful when you are rendering to output that doesn't match the viewport's aspect ratio. Follow these steps to enable Safe Frames view:

1. In the Camera viewport, click the General Viewport Label menu (**[+]**) and choose Configure Viewports near the bottom of the menu.

2. In the dialog box, choose the Safe Frames tab.
   This tab contains settings for frame types, as shown in Figure 15.12.

3. The default is to show only the Live Area Safe Frame. To have the other Safe Frames show, you check the boxes in the Safe Frames tab.

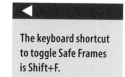

The keyboard shortcut to toggle Safe Frames is Shift+F.

The Live Area Safe Frame is the extent of what will be rendered. The Action Safe area is the boundary where you should be assured that the action in the scene will display on most if not all TV screens. The Title Safe area is where you can feel comfortable rendering text in your frame. Finally, the User Safe setting is for setting custom frames, as shown in Figure 15.13.

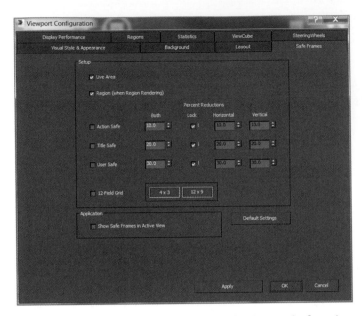

FIGURE 15.12 The Safe Frames tab in the Viewport Configuration dialog box

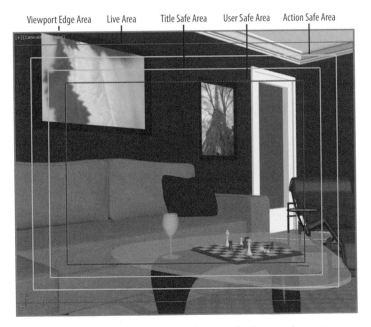

FIGURE 15.13 Safe Frames shown in the Camera viewport

Raytraced Reflections and Refractions

As you saw in Chapter 10, "Introduction to Materials: Interiors and Furniture," you can apply a raytrace map to a material's Reflection parameter to add a reflection to the object. To get a true reflection of the other objects in the scene, you will need to use the raytracing methodology. There are essentially two ways to create raytraced reflections in a scene:

▶ By using a raytrace map

▶ By using a Raytrace material

In many cases, the raytrace map looks great and saves tons of rendering time as opposed to using the Raytrace material.

Raytrace Material

In the following steps, you will learn how to use the Raytrace material to create reflection in a scene using the room built in Chapter 3 and Chapter 4.

1. Open the Material Editor; in the Material/Map Browser, select Materials ➤ Standard and drag Raytrace into the active view.

2. Double-click on the node title area to load the parameters into the Parameter Editor, and change the material name to **New Dark Wood**.

3. The parameters to create reflections are available through the Raytrace Basic Parameters rollout. Leave most of these parameters at their default values, but change the Reflect color swatch from black to white.

   This sets the reflection of the material all the way to the maximum reflectivity.

4. In the Material/Map Browser, choose Maps ➤ Standard and drag Bitmap to the Diffuse input socket of the Raytrace material.

   This will bring up the Select Bitmap Image File dialog box; you should see the images folder of the ArchModel project folder.

5. Choose DarkWood_Grain.jpg and then click Open.

6. Apply the Dark Wood raytrace material to the coffee table legs in the scene. Render the Camera viewport.

   The coffee table leg is very reflective; it looks like a mirror, as shown in Figure 15.14.

7. Go back to the Raytrace Basic Parameters rollout, select the color swatch next to Reflect, and change the Reflect color (RGB sliders

> Keep in mind that the amount of control you will have with a raytrace map is significantly less than with the Raytrace material.

only) so that R = 20, G = 20, and B = 20, which is a darker gray and will lessen the reflections.

FIGURE 15.14 The Raytrace material with reflections set to the maximum

8. In the Specular Highlight area, change Specular Level to 30 and Glossiness to 30. This will change how clear the reflection appears.

9. Go to the Raytracer Controls rollout, and in the Falloff End Distance area, check the box next to Reflect and change the value to 50.

   This parameter will fade the reflection over distance, which is more accurate, as shown in Figure 15.15.

FIGURE 15.15 More accurate reflections are added to the coffee table legs.

Raytrace Mapping

You can apply raytracing only to a specific map; you can't apply it to the entire material. In this case, you will assign a raytrace map to the Reflection map channel of a material to get truer reflections in the scene and at a faster render time than when using the material as you just did. Follow these steps:

1. In the Material Editor and in the Material/Map Browser, select Materials ➢ Standard and drag a Standard material to the View Area. Load the parameter into the Parameter Editor and change the name to **Hardwood Floors**.

2. In the Material/Map Browser, choose Maps ➢ Standard and drag a raytrace map into the Reflection input socket.

3. In the Material/Map Browser, choose Maps and drag a Bitmap map into the Diffuse Color input socket.

4. From the Select Bitmap Image File dialog box, choose Hardwood_honey.tif from the images folder.

5. In the Maps rollout, change Reflection Amount to **50**.

6. Apply the Hardwood Floors material to the Floor object in the scene by dragging from the output socket to the Floor object in the Camera001 viewport.

7. In the Material Editor toolbar, select the Show Shaded Material In Viewport button (▦).

8. So you can get the full force of the Hardwood Floors material, hide the rug: Select the Rug object in the scene, right-click over it, and from the quad menu, choose Hide Selection.

9. Render the Camera001 viewport; the floors look good but too reflective, and a falloff needs to be added.

10. Double-click on the Raytrace Map node to load the parameters into the editor.

11. In the Attenuation rollout, change Falloff Type to **Linear**, and then change Ranges: End to **50**. The results are shown in Figure 15.16.

12. Unhide the rug.

FIGURE 15.16   The reflection map with falloff

Take a look at the images created with reflections using the Raytrace material and those created using the Standard material with the raytrace map applied to reflection. They look almost the same. However, there is slightly better detail in the reflections created with the Raytrace material, but with longer render times.

Refractions Using the Raytrace Material

Creating raytraced refractions in glass can be accomplished using the same two workflows as for the raytraced reflections from the previous section. The Raytrace material renders better, but it takes longer than using a raytrace map for the refraction map in a material.

Now you will create refractions using the Raytrace material:

> Keep in mind that render times are much slower with refractions—so don't freak out.

1. In the same scene, change the Camera001 viewport to a Perspective viewport by following these steps:

   a. Select the Camera001 viewport and press P on the keyboard.

   b. Select the wineglass in the scene and then press Z on your keyboard.
   This will frame the wineglass in the Perspective viewport.

   c. Use Ctrl+C, which is a shortcut, to create a camera from a Perspective viewport.

   d. Name the camera **WineGlass Camera**.

2. In the Material Editor, drag a Raytrace material from the Material/Map Browser into the area. Name it **Wine Glass**, and apply the material to the wineglass.

3. Go to the Raytrace Basic Parameters rollout, and change the color swatch for Transparency from black to white.

4. Uncheck the box next to Reflect and change that spinner to 10. This sets a slight reflection for the material.

Black is opaque and white is fully transparent.

5. Take a look at the Index Of Refr parameter. This value sets the index of refraction (IOR) value that determines how much the material should refract. The value is already set to 1.55. Leave it at that value.

6. Go to the Extended Parameters rollout, shown in Figure 15.17. The Reflections section is at the bottom.

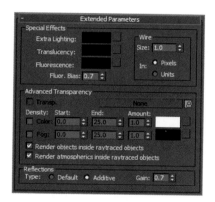

FIGURE 15.17 The Extended Parameters rollout for the Raytrace material

7. Select Additive and change Gain to 0.7. This gives a bit of reflective brightness for the clear wineglass.

8. Render the Camera viewport.

The render shows the Raytrace material on the wineglass refracting and reflecting, but you may notice the jagged edges or artifacts around the reflected objects. What you're seeing is aliasing in the reflections. Clone this rendered image by pressing the Clone Rendered Frame Window icon ( ), which is found in the Rendered Frame Window toolbar. This allows you to compare the before and after shots of the rendering. SuperSampling is an extra pass of anti-aliasing.

By default, the 3ds Max program applies a single SuperSample pass over all the materials in the scene. Follow these steps:

1. Go to the SuperSampling rollout and uncheck Use Global Settings.

2. Check Enable Local SuperSampler and keep it set to Max 2.5 Star. Leave the parameters at their defaults, as shown in Figure 15.18. Render the camera.

FIGURE 15.18
The SuperSampling rollout

Figure 15.19 it shows renderings before and after the SuperSampling was modified.

FIGURE 15.19   The wineglass with default SuperSampling (left); the SuperSampling modified (right)

3. In the Specular Highlight group, change Specular Level to 98 and Glossiness to 90.

4. Render the camera.

You will notice a very nice wineglass render. Change the Index Of Refr parameter on the material to 8.0 and you will see a much greater refraction, as shown in Figure 15.20. That may work better for a nice heavy bottle, but it is too much for the glass. An Index Of Refr parameter between 1.5 and 2.5 works pretty well for the wineglass.

FIGURE 15.20 A much more pronounced refraction is rendered with an IOR of 8.0.

Refractions Using Raytrace Mapping

Just as you did with the reflections, you will now use a raytrace map on the Refraction parameter for the Wine Glass material. In the following steps, you will create a new refractive material for the wineglass:

1. In the Material Editor, drag a Standard material from the Material/ Map Browser into the View Area. Name it **Wine Glass**.

2. Drag the raytrace map from the Material/Map Browser into the Refraction input slot.

3. Drag the raytrace map from the Material/Map Browser into the Reflection input slot.

4. Go to the Maps rollout and change Reflection Amount to **6**. This will reduce the amount of reflection.

5. Go to the SuperSampling rollout and uncheck Use Global Settings, check Enable Local SuperSampler, and keep it as Max 2.5 Star.

If the Reflection Map setting is enabled, it will take a long time to render the image. If you have a slower computer or perhaps are in a rush, uncheck the Reflection Map box in the Maps rollout of the reflection.

6. In the Specular Highlight group, change Specular Level to 98 and Glossiness to 90.

7. Apply the material to the Wine Glass object in the scene and render as shown in Figure 15.21.

FIGURE 15.21   Use the raytrace map on the Refraction parameter to create refraction in the wineglass.

In the raytrace map, you can control the IOR through the material parameters in the Extended Parameters rollout, in the Advanced Transparency section, shown in Figure 15.22.

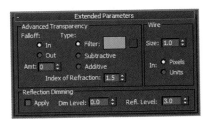

FIGURE 15.22   The Advanced Transparency section in the Extended Parameters rollout

The raytracing reflections and refractions slow down the render quite a bit. You can leave out the reflections if you'd like, but that will reduce the realistic look of the wineglass.

Rendering the Interior and Furniture

Let's take a quick look at rendering the short 30-frame sequence of the scene you did earlier in the chapter. You'll need to tweak a few of the scene settings, such as setting the furniture and the interior materials to have raytraced reflections for maximum impact. Let's go!

Adding Raytraced Reflections

The reflect/refract map was added to the reflections of some of the furniture. It is a way to add reflections, but is not as accurate as the raytrace map. The raytrace map calculates reflections as they work in the real world, reflecting the object's environment. Of course, in order for raytraced reflections to work, there has to be something around the object to reflect. The materials created for this scene have some reflect/refract maps that were added for these exercises; they are in the Material Editor. You need to go into any of those materials and switch out the reflect/refract maps with raytrace maps. For this section, you need to see a close-up of the chess set. Change the Wine Glass Camera to a Perspective viewport. Select one of the chess pieces and use the Zoom Extents shortcut (Z) to focus in on the chess piece. Follow these steps:

1. In the Slate Material Editor, at the bottom left of the View Area is an icon of a pair of binoculars. This is a search feature. Click it, and a type-in area appears.

2. Go to the Zoom To Results tool, and then type **Light Wood for Chess** in the type-in area and press Enter. The material will be zoomed in on the active view, as shown in Figure 15.23.

3. Select and delete the reflect/refract map that is plugged into the Reflection input node.

4. In the Material/Map Browser, select Maps ➢ Standard, drag a raytrace map into the area, and then drag from the output socket of the raytrace map into the input socket of the reflection map, as shown in Figure 15.24.

5. Double-click the title of the Light Wood for Chess material to load the parameters into the editor, and in the Maps rollout, change the Amount value for Reflection to **20**.

The Zoom To Results feature will frame the material in the active view area.

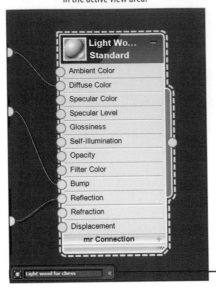

Type the material name in the Zoom To Results tool.

FIGURE 15.23   Frame the material using the Zoom To Results feature in the Material Editor.

FIGURE 15.24   Plug the raytrace map into the Reflection input socket of the Light Wood for Chess material.

If you want the reflective objects in the scene to have a higher amount of reflection, go back to the Maps rollout and make the Amount value for Reflection higher than 20.

▶

6. Render a frame, and you should see some reflections of the room.

7. Go through the materials in the Material Editor to add a raytrace map to the material's Reflection channels. If there is a reflect/refract map, delete it and follow the previous steps to replace it with a raytrace map.

Outputting the Render

You need to render out the entire 30 frames of the camera move. As you saw with the Bouncing Ball render earlier in the chapter, rendering out a sequence of images is done through the Common tab of the Render Setup dialog box:

1. In the Time Output section, click to select Range and change it to read 0 to 30, as shown in Figure 15.25.

FIGURE 15.25 The Time Output section setup for a range from 0 to 30

The resolution of the render is set in Output Size. The default resolution is 640×480.

2. Go to the Render Output section of the Render Setup dialog box and click Files to open the Render Output File dialog box.

   Typically, animations are rendered out as a sequence of images, but for simplicity's sake, you will render it out to an AVI.

3. In the Render Output File dialog box, choose where you want to store the rendered file and pick a name for the movie (Room_Raytrace.avi, for example).

4. Then, in the Save As Type drop-down menu, choose AVI File (.avi) and click Save. The AVI File Compression Setup dialog box will appear.

5. In the AVI File Compression Setup dialog box, select MJPEG Compressor for the compressor type, and set the Quality slider to 100.

   This Quality setting applies only to the compression of the AVI file and not to the render itself.

6. Click OK to return to the Render Output File dialog box, and click Save to return to the Render Setup dialog box.

7. Save your scene file, and you are ready to render! Just click Render in the Render Setup dialog box.

And go outside to play catch with your kids or hassle your spouse or sibling into a needless argument for a little while. Then run back inside and play the

If your computer isn't a powerful one, drop the size to 320×240, half the default size; and it will cost you one-fourth of the higher resolution's time to render.

Again, it is generally preferable to render to a sequence of images rather than a movie file; however, in this case, an AVI movie file will be best.

AVI file saved in the location you chose earlier. Then take a huge magnet and stick your monitor to your fridge door. Voilà! You are now ready to enter the world of rendering.

THE ESSENTIALS AND BEYOND

Rendering is the way you get to show your finished scene to the world, or whoever will stop and look. Nothing is more fulfilling than seeing your creation come to life, and that's what rendering is all about. One of the things you learned in this chapter was how to set up and render your scenes out to files. In addition, you took a tour of raytracing and cameras.

Rendering may be the last step of the process, but you should travel the entire journey with rendering in mind, from design and modeling to animation and lighting.

ADDITIONAL EXERCISES

▶ Try rendering different resolutions and qualities for your scene, and make note of the time each frame took so you can better evaluate which settings work best versus time involved in processing the render.

▶ Create multiple cameras of different areas of your scene. Play around with lenses and FOV. Animate the cameras and then render.

mental ray

This chapter will show you how to create materials and render your scene using mental ray.

This chapter includes the following topics:

▶ **mental ray renderer**

▶ **Final Gather with mental ray**

▶ **mental ray materials**

mental ray Renderer

mental ray is a popular general-purpose renderer that has fantastic capabilities. One of mental ray's strengths is its ability to generate physically accurate lighting simulations based on *indirect lighting* principles. *Indirect lighting* is when light bounces from one object in a scene onto another object. In addition, incandescence or self-illumination from one object can light other objects in the scene. *Direct light*, such as from an omni light, is not necessarily required. Another thing to consider is that mental ray's reflections and refractions take on very real qualities when set up and lighted well.

Enabling the mental ray Renderer

To enable mental ray, follow these steps:

1. Choose Rendering ➤ Render ➤ Render Setup (or use the shortcut, F10) to open the Render Setup dialog box.

2. On the Common tab, scroll down to the Assign Renderer rollout, and then click the ellipsis button for the Production entry shown in Figure 16.1.

FIGURE 16.1 The Assign Renderer rollout

This opens the Choose Renderer dialog box, shown in Figure 16.2.

FIGURE 16.2 Select NVIDIA mental ray
in the Choose Renderer dialog box.

3. In the Choose Renderer dialog box, highlight NVIDIA mental ray, and then click OK.

mental ray Sampling Quality

Once the mental ray renderer is enabled, click the Renderer tab in the Render Setup dialog box. The following is a brief explanation of the render settings most useful for you in your work.

Under the Sampling Quality rollout, shown in Figure 16.3, are the settings that let you control the overall image quality of your renders.

In the Sampling Mode drop-down list, there are three options to choose from. Unified/Raytraced (Recommended) is the default. This mode raytraces the scene using the same sampling method for both anti-aliasing and calculating motion blur. This results in far quicker rendering than the Classic/Raytraced method.

Once the NVIDIA mental ray renderer is assigned, you can make it the default renderer by clicking the Save As Defaults button on the Assign Renderer rollout. If mental ray is set as the default, the Render Setup dialog box opens with the mental ray controls in tabs. You will not need to do this for the exercises in this chapter.

Quality essentially sets the "noise level" at which the renderer stops sampling. Higher quality implies less noise. The Quality parameter sets the quality of rendering. The lower the values, the faster the render, but the render is much grainier, as shown in Figure 16.4. The higher the value, the smoother the images, as shown in Figure 16.5, but they take longer to render.

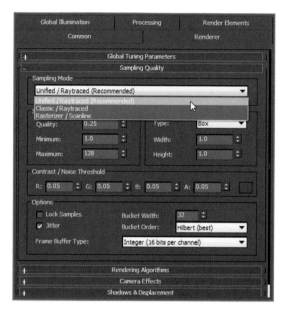

FIGURE 16.3 The Renderer tab shows mental ray's common settings.

FIGURE 16.4 A Quality setting of 0.01 renders a noisy image.

FIGURE 16.5   A Quality setting of 20.0 renders a smooth image.

Final Gather with mental ray

A popular feature in mental ray is *indirect illumination*—the simulation of bounced light (explained in the next section). Click the Global Illumination tab at the top of the Render Setup dialog box. There are four rollouts, the second of which we will explore further:

▶ Skylights & Environment Lighting (IBL)

▶ Final Gathering (FG)

▶ Caustics & Photon Mapping (GI)

▶ Reuse (FG And GI Disk Caching)

This type of rendering can introduce artifacts or noise in the render. Finding the right settings to balance a clean render and acceptable render times is an art form all its own and is rather difficult to master.

Final Gather is a method of mental ray rendering for estimating global illumination (GI). In short, *global illumination* is a way of calculating indirect lighting. This way, objects do not need to be in the direct path of a light (such as a spotlight) to be lit in the scene. mental ray accomplishes this by casting points throughout a scene. These light points are allowed to bounce from object to object, contributing light as they go, effectively simulating how real light photons work in the physical world.

Figure 16.6 shows the Final Gathering (FG) rollout. Some of the Final Gather options, including how to deal with quality and noise, are explained next.

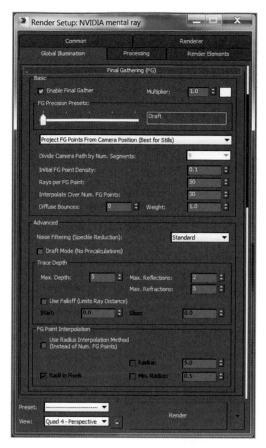

FIGURE 16.6 The Final Gathering (FG) rollout in the Global Illumination tab of the Render Setup dialog box

Basic Group

These are the most important parameters in the Basic group of the Final Gathering (FG) rollout; they set the accuracy and precision of the light bounces, thereby controlling noise.

FG Precision Presets Slider   Sets the accuracy level of the Final Gather simulation by adjusting settings for the renderer such as Initial FG Point Density, Rays Per FG Point, and Interpolate Over Num. FG Points. Use this slider first in setting how good your render's lighting looks. In the left image in Figure 16.7, three spheres are rendered with the Draft setting for Final Gather, while the right image is set to High. Notice that the right image is a cleaner render, and it also shows more of the background and the spheres than does the Draft quality in the left image. This slider will adjust the settings for several of the values covered in the following list.

FIGURE 16.7   The Draft setting produces a test render of the spheres (left). The High setting produces a better-quality render of the spheres (right).

Initial FG Point Density   This multiplier controls the density for the Final Gather points. This is one of the settings adjusted by the FG Precision Presets slider, but it can also be set manually. This value sets the quantity and density of FG *points* that are cast into the scene. The higher the density of these points, the more accurate the bounced light appears, at a cost of render time.

Rays Per FG Point   This value is controlled by the FG Precision Presets slider but can also be manually set. The higher the number of rays used to compute the indirect illumination in a scene, the less noise and the more accuracy you gain, but at the cost of longer render times.

Interpolate Over Num. FG Points   Interpolation is controlled by the FG Precision Presets slider as well as manual input. This value is useful for getting rid of noise in your renders for smoother results. Increasing the interpolation will increase render times, but not as much as increasing the Initial FG Point Density or Rays Per FG Point values.

Diffuse Bounces   The number of bounces governs how many times a ray of light can bounce and affect objects in a scene before stopping calculation. If you set the bounces higher, the light simulation will be more accurate, but the render times will be costly. A Diffuse Bounces setting of 1 or 5 is adequate for many applications. Figure 16.8 shows the same render of the spheres as Figure 16.7, but with a Diffuse Bounces value of 5. This render is brighter and also shows color bleed from the purple spheres onto the gray floor.

FIGURE 16.8   More diffuse bounces mean more bounced light.

Advanced Group

The Advanced group of settings gives you access to additional ways of controlling the quality of your Final Gather renders. Some are described next in brief. You should experiment with different settings as you gain more experience with Final Gather to see what settings work best for your scenes.

Noise Filtering (Speckle Reduction)   This value essentially averages the brightness of the light rays in the scene to give you smoother Final Gather results. The higher the filtering, the darker your Final Gather simulation, and the longer your render times will be. However, the noise in your lighting will diminish.

Draft Mode (No Precalculations)   This setting allows you to turn off a good number of calculations that mental ray completes prior to rendering the scene. Enabling this setting results in a faster render for preview and draft purposes.

Max. Reflections   This value controls how many times a light ray can be reflected in the scene. A value of 0 turns off reflections entirely. The higher this value, the more times you can see a reflection. For example, a value of 2 allows you to see a reflection of a reflection.

Max. Refractions   Similar to Max. Reflections, this value sets the number of times a light ray can be refracted through a surface. A value of 0 turns off all refraction.

The mental ray Rendered Frame Window

When you render a frame using the 3ds Max® program, the Rendered Frame window opens, displaying the image you just rendered. When you render with mental ray, an additional control panel is displayed under the Rendered Frame window, as shown in Figure 16.9.

FIGURE 16.9   The Rendered Frame window now shows several mental ray controls.

This control panel gives you access to many of the most useful settings in the Render Settings dialog box so you can adjust render settings easily and quickly.

mental ray Materials

For the most part, mental ray treats regular 3ds Max maps and materials the same way the Default Scanline renderer does. However, a set of mental ray–specific materials exists to take further advantage of mental ray's power.

The mental ray Arch & Design material works great for most hard surfaces, such as metal, wood, glass, and ceramic. It is especially useful for surfaces that are glossy and reflective, such as metal and ceramic.

To showcase these materials, let's retexture a few of the features from the room from Chapter 10, "Introduction to Materials: Interiors and Furniture." Follow these steps:

1. Set your project to the ArchModel project that you downloaded from the web page at www.sybex.com/go/3dsmax2014essentials. Open the ArchModel_mentalray_Start.max file from the Scenes folder.

    This file has NVIDIA mental ray already assigned as the renderer. The scene includes the room and the textured furniture. There are no lights in the scene, but because NVIDIA mental ray is the assigned renderer, it utilizes the default lights to generate a lighted scene, as shown rendered in Figure 16.10. mental ray renders the materials from the previous chapter. Some look the same, but others don't look so good—the coffee table in particular. Start with it.

FIGURE 16.10   The file rendered with mental ray

2. Open the Slate Material Editor at the top of the active view.
    You will see a tab called View 1; it holds all the materials you built in the previous chapters for the room.

3. To keep the materials separate and organized, create another tab for the mental ray materials. To create a new tab, right-click in the blank area next to the tab, as shown in Figure 16.11, and create a new view . Name it **mental ray.**

FIGURE 16.11 Create a new view.

Using Arch & Design Material Templates

In the Material/Map Browser, you will see an additional rollout, mental ray. This gives a whole new set of materials, including the Arch & Design material. Arch & Design materials have a special feature: templates. *Templates* provide access to already created materials and parameters for different types of materials, such as wood, glass, and metal. These templates can also be used as a starting point for material creation. We will use one to create the material for the tabletop and wineglass in the following steps:

1. Drag an Arch & Design material to the new active view from the mental ray material section of the Material/Map Browser.

2. Double-click on the title of the node; this will display the Arch & Design material in the Parameter Editor.

3. Name the material **Thick Glass.**

4. From the Parameter Editor, in the Select A Template drop-down menu, choose Glass (Solid Geometry), as shown in Figure 16.12.

5. Drag a wire from the Glass material's output socket to the tabletop and the wineglass in the viewport.

6. Render the Chess Set Camera viewport to see the new material on the coffee table.

   There is some blue in the glass; this is from the Refraction color.

7. Select the color swatch and change the color to achieve a colored tint to the glass. Change the color to white to get a clear glass, shown in Figure 16.13.

   Another Arch & Design material template is the Chrome template. We will use it to replace the chrome that already exists on the side table and lounge chair frames.

8. Press the C key on the keyboard.

   This will bring up the Select Camera dialog box, which includes a list of cameras in the scene.

FIGURE 16.12 The Thick Glass material applied to the tabletop and wineglass

FIGURE 16.13 Refraction color changed to white to achieve clear glass

9. Select the Lounge Chair/Table Camera. Click OK to close the dialog box.

10. In the Material Editor, create a new Arch & Design material and choose Chrome from the template list. Name it **Chrome**.

11. Apply it to the frame of the side table and the frame of the lounge chair.

12. The side table and lounge chair are grouped: Open the group to select the pieces that need to be chrome.

    When you apply the material, you will get an error window, shown in Figure 16.14, telling you that there is a material with the same name already applied. This material was a Standard material that was previously applied.

13. Select Replace It? from the dialog.

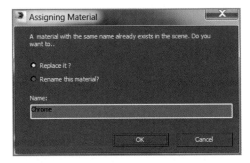

FIGURE 16.14   The message that warns you about assigning a duplicate material to an object

14. Render to see the new Chrome material applied to the frames, as shown in Figure 16.15.

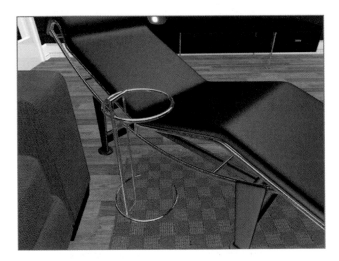

FIGURE 16.15   The new Chrome material applied to the chair frame and side table

Creating Arch & Design Materials

Using the Arch & Design material, we will create a new material for the floor. There is a template called Glossy Varnished Wood, but we are going to create the floor material from scratch. Press C on the keyboard and select the Floor Camera. Then follow these steps:

1. Switch from the Lounge Chair/Table Camera to the Floor Camera using C to bring up the Select Camera dialog.

2. Then in the Material Editor, drag an Arch & Design material to the new active area from the mental ray Materials rollout of the Material/Map Browser.

3. Double-click the title of the node to display the Arch & Design material parameters in the l Parameter Editor. Name the material **Hardwood Floors**.

4. Drag a bitmap from the Maps rollout into the input socket of the Arch & Design material. This will bring up an Explore window.

5. Choose the `Hardwood_honey.tif` file. Leave all the other parameters at the default.

6. Apply the material to the floor. Render the Floor Camera viewport. The results are shown in Figure 16.16.

FIGURE 16.16   Floor with the Arch & Design material applied

By default, Arch & Design materials have reflection enabled. The area below the Diffuse group in the Parameter Editor of the Slate Material Editor is the Reflection group of parameters. Reflections for this material are calculated using the Reflectivity and Glossiness values. The higher the Reflectivity value is, the clearer the reflections are. The Glossiness value controls the blurriness of the reflections from sharp (a value of 1) to completely blurred (a value of 0). When you blur your reflections, the blurrier they are, and the noisier they will be in the render. You can use the Glossy Samples value to increase the quality of the blurred reflections once you set Glossiness to anything less than 1. The floors should not be so reflective.

7. In the Reflection group, leave Reflectivity at **0.6** and change Glossiness to **0.6**.

8. Render the camera to see the results, as shown in Figure 16.17.

You can use the same techniques for creating Arch & Design materials for the other objects in the scene, like the base of the coffee table and the couch.

FIGURE 16.17 The Hardwood Floors material using the Arch & Design material

Multi/Sub-Object Material and Arch & Design

You can use the same technique for the window that you used in Chapter 10, but the difference now is that you will use the Arch & Design material instead of the Multi/Sub-Object material. The window is divided into two materials: shiny white for the frame and a shiny transparent material for the glass. Another way to apply a Multi/Sub-Object material is to apply the material to the selected sub-objects. First, select the window and then select the Graphite Modeling Tools tab ➢ Polygon Modeling ➢ Convert To Poly. Then select the polygons you want the material to be applied to and apply it to those selected polygons. For this exercise we will use this technique on the window:

1. Switch from the Floor Camera to the Window Camera by pressing C to bring up the Select Camera dialog box.

2. Select the Window and go to the Graphite Modeling Tools tab ➢ Polygon Modeling ➢ Convert to Poly.

3. Enter Element mode (🔲), and select all the polygons for the window frame. The simplest way to do this is to select the Window object, and then hold down Alt and click just the window glass; this will deselect the glass.

4. In the Slate Material Editor, you'll create a shiny white material: Drag an Arch & Design material to the mental ray active area, and change the Diffuse color to R = 1.0, G = 1.0, B = 1.0 and rename it **White Window Frame.**

    Based on what you know about reflections from the previous steps, the default reflections are too high, especially for the frame on the window.

5. In the Reflection group, change Reflectivity to 0.4 and Glossiness to 0.4.

6. Apply the material to the selected sub-objects using the Assign Material To Selection button (🔳).

    Now go to the main toolbar ➢ Edit menu and choose Select ➢ Select Invert; this will deselect the window frame and select the window glass.

7. Back in the Material Editor, drag an Arch & Design material to the mental ray active area.

8. Double-click the title bar of the new Arch & Design material to load it into the Parameter Editor.

9. In the Template drop-down menu, choose Glass (Thin Geometry), and select the Show Background In Preview icon (🔳). Rename the material **Window Glass.**

    This will place a checker pattern behind the sample sphere to make the transparency easier to edit.

10. Save the file now.

You can see that the window and frame look very similar to the Standard materials, but the coffee table and floor look significantly better than with their previous Standard material. When you're using mental ray, Arch & Design materials are superior. Sometimes the look of a particular object can change depending on the camera angle and lighting. Keep an eye on the window to see if the look maintains the realism you are after.

The Arch & Design material type is an elaborate construct of mental ray shaders, and with proper lighting it can make any render look special. If you open the ArchModel_mentalray_End.max file, you will see several examples of materials beyond what you created in the previous exercise, as shown in Figure 16.18. A few things have been added for some bling—some pictures, a vase, and a floor lamp. All these items can be found in the Chapter 04 Extra Furniture folder in the Scenes folder.

FIGURE 16.18   The final render of the mental ray materials

3ds Max Photometric Lights in mental ray Renderings

Many of the parameters for photometric lights are the same as or very similar to the standard lights you looked at in Chapter 14, "Introduction to Lighting: Interior Lighting." Here, you see the parameters that are specific to photometric lights. Photometric lights simulate real lighting by using physically based energy values and color temperatures. To learn about photometric lights, follow these steps:

1. Either continue with the file you are working with or open the ArchModel_mentalray_Light.max file from the Scenes folder of the ArchModel project from the book's web page.

2. Choose Objects ➤ Lights ➤ Target Light (Photometric) to create a photometric target light.

   When you click on the photometric target light, you will get a pop-up recommending that you use the mr (mental ray) Photographic Exposure Control, as shown in Figure 16.19.

3. Click Yes.

4. In the Left viewport, click to create the light, and then drag from the ceiling down to the floor. Make sure the light stays within the room.

5. Select the light. The easiest way to make sure you select both the light and the target is to select the blue string that runs between the two and then just use the Move tool.

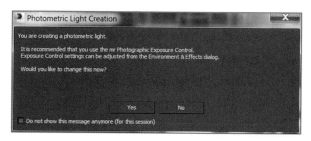

FIGURE 16.19   Select Yes in the Photometric Light Creation dialog box.

6. Switch to the Top viewport and move the light and its target so they are above the coffee table.

7. Once the light is in the room, change the viewport rendering type to Realistic in the Chess Set Camera viewport.

8. Go to the Modify panel. The first rollout under the modifier stack is Templates.

   This rollout gives you access to several light type presets to save you time in creating a light. Feel free to play around with the different presets and render the room frame a few times to see the differences before continuing with the exercise and the next step.

9. In the Select A Template drop-down menu, select Recessed 75W Wallwash (Web).

   A photometric light with a "web" distribution essentially defines the light's behavior and the light it casts. Lighting manufacturers provide web files that model the kinds of lights they make, so using these distribution patterns as templates will give you a lot of options in simulating real-world lights, such as this 75-watt recessed lamp. Figure 16.20 shows the distribution pattern for this light as shown in the Modify panel.

FIGURE 16.20 The Distribution (Photometric Web) rollout

10. You need to take care of some basic stuff now, so with the light still selected, open the General Parameters rollout and check the Targeted box.

    You originally created a targeted light, but when you used the template, it took away the target. Having a target on a light makes it easier to edit the light's position. Checking this box turns the target back on for the light.

11. Click the Shadows On box to turn it on. From the drop-down menu, choose Ray Traced Shadows.

12. Make the Window Camera viewport active, and on the menu bar, choose Rendering ➢ Environment And Effects ➢ Environment And Exposure Settings and click the Render Preview button in the Exposure Control rollout, shown in Figure 16.21.

    The preview may show as either very bright or very dark at first. If so, the preview function will work perfectly once you render a frame for the first time.

13. Under the mr Photographic Exposure Control rollout, select Exposure Value (EV) if it isn't already selected.

14. Set some different values for the EV and see what happens in the Render Preview dialog box. The higher the EV number, the darker the scene will be. Set the EV to 3 and render. When you change the exposure value, the Render Preview window updates. Render the Window Camera viewport, as shown in Figure 16.22.

15. You can continue to work with the EV to experiment with the luminance level. When you're finished experimenting, be sure to set the EV to 5 and close the Environment And Effects dialog box.

Exposure controls adjust output levels and the range of colors of a rendering. These controls are similar to real-world film exposure settings on a physical camera.

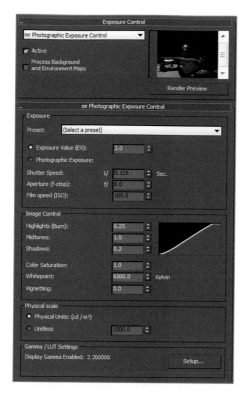

FIGURE 16.21 Exposure Control and mr Photographic Exposure Control rollouts in the Environment And Effects dialog box

FIGURE 16.22 The room so far

Photometric Light Parameters

Now let's look in the command panel at the photometric light's Intensity/Color/Attenuation rollout for the 75W light, as shown in Figure 16.23.

FIGURE 16.23
Photometric light's
Intensity/Color/Attenuation
rollout in the command panel

The Color group of parameters controls the color temperature of the light, which you can set either with a color value or in Kelvin units, just as with real-world photographic lights. In the drop-down menu, there are different color/temp settings. The default is D65 Illuminant (Reference White).

The Intensity group of parameters controls the strength or brightness of the lights measured in lm, cd, or lx at:

lm (lumen)   This value is the overall output power of the light. A 100-watt general purpose lightbulb measures about 1750 lm.

cd (candela)   This value shows the maximum luminous intensity of the light. A 100-watt general-purpose lightbulb measures about 139 cd.

lx at (lux)   This value shows the amount of luminance created by the light shining on a surface at a certain distance.

The parameters in the Dimming section are also used to control the intensity of the light. When the Resulting Intensity box is checked, the value specifies a multiplier that dims the existing intensity of the light and takes over control of the intensity. Picking up from the last step in the previous exercise, let's start to experiment with these values in the following steps:

1. With the 75W light still selected, go to the Modify panel, and in the Color group in the Intensity/Color/Attenuation rollout, click the radio button next to Kelvin and change the value to 4500.

   This will give the light a bit more warmth by adding more yellow/red.

2. In the Dimming group, uncheck the box next to the 100% spinner under Resulting Intensity to enable the Intensity parameter.

3. In the Intensity group, select cd and set the cd amount to 1000. This will brighten things up a bit.

4. Render the scene. The result is shown in Figure 16.24.

FIGURE 16.24 The room render with color and intensity changes

The scene still looks a bit dark and the shadows are very dark; they look like black holes. You will use Final Gather to brighten up the overall render. So far, you have used Final Gather's default settings. The one thing you need is for the rays that are generated by the light to bounce. The more bounces the light makes, the more luminance there is in the room—but more bounces slow down the render. For the best and most efficient results, try to balance the bounces with exposure control and the intensity of the light.

When you are rendering with mental ray, the mini Final Gather panel in the Rendered Frame window is available for quick changes.

Most of the controls in the Final Gather panel also have a home in the Render Setup dialog box, and changing the value in one area updates the corresponding value in the other area.

5. In the mini panel below the Rendered Frame window, shown in Figure 16.25, change FG Bounces to **7**.

6. Render and compare the resulting render shown in Figure 16.24 to Figure 16.26. Figure 16.26 shows the final render.

7. Save this file.

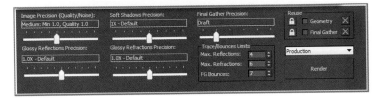

FIGURE 16.25 This mini panel gives you access to Final Gather controls to adjust your render easily.

FIGURE 16.26 The final mental ray render of the room's interior lighting

3ds Max Daylight System in mental ray Renderings

The Sunlight and Daylight System simulate sunlight by following the geographically correct angle and movement of the sun over the earth. You can choose location, date, time, and compass orientation to set the orientation of the sun and its lighting conditions. You can also animate the date and time to achieve very cool time-lapse looks and shadow studies. In essence, this type of light works really well with mental ray and Final Gather. In this exercise, you will use it in the most basic way, using all of its defaults:

1. Open the ArchModel_mentalray_Day_Start.max file from the Scenes folder of the ArchModel project on the book's web page.

   This is the file you ended with after applying the Arch & Design textures earlier in the chapter.

2. Choose Lighting/Cameras ➢ Create Lights ➢ Daylight System, as shown in Figure 16.27.

FIGURE 16.27
The Daylight System icon

3. A Daylight System Creation warning will appear, as shown in Figure 16.28, asking if you want to change the exposure controls to suit the Daylight System. Click Yes.

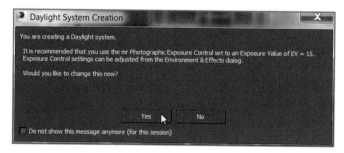

FIGURE 16.28 The Daylight System Creation warning

4. In a Top viewport, click and drag at the center of the scene.

   This will create a compass that is attached to the Daylight System. Make it the size of the room.

5. When you release the mouse button, move the mouse so the light is placed outside the walls of the room.

The Daylight System is supposed to simulate the sun and sky, so it needs to be outside the room.

6. With the light still selected, open the Modify panel, and in the Daylight Parameters rollout, change the drop-down menus under both Sunlight and Skylight to mr Sun and mr Sky, respectively.

7. When you change the Skylight parameter, a mental ray Sky warning will appear, asking if you want to place an mr Physical Sky environment map in your scene. Click Yes, as shown in Figure 16.29.

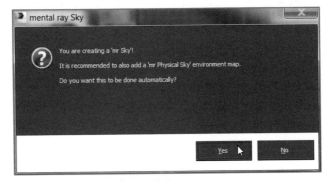

FIGURE 16.29   Add the mr Physical Sky environment map into the scene.

8. Also in the Daylight Parameters rollout, under Position, select Manual.

This will allow you to use the Move tool to move the light to where you want it. The default position represents noon. The lower the light is to the horizon in your scene, the more it will simulate darker skies at sunset.

9. Move the light so it is going through the window, as shown in Figure 16.30.

10. Select the Window Camera viewport and render.

As you can see, it is too dark. You are trying to simulate a sunny day, and beyond the direct light coming through the window, it's pretty dark, as shown in Figure 16.31.

A good tool to use in this situation is mr Sky Portal. It gives you an efficient way of using a scene's existing sky lighting within interior scenes that do not require costly Final Gather or GI, resulting in very long render times.

▶

A portal acts just like a mental ray area light. This light gets its brightness and color from the environment already in your scene.

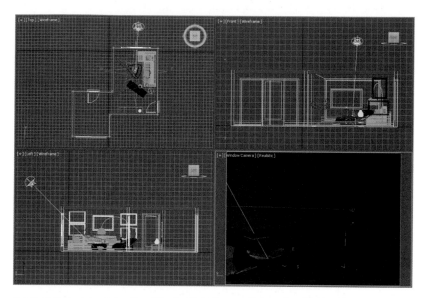

FIGURE 16.30 Move the Daylight System light so it will shine through the window.

FIGURE 16.31 Rendering with the Daylight System is too dark.

11. Choose Lighting/Cameras ➢ Create Lights ➢ mr Sky Portal (Figure 16.32).

FIGURE 16.32
Add the mr Sky Portal from
the Lighting/Cameras menu.

12. In the Front viewport, drag an mr Sky Portal so it fits the window size in the wall.

13. Then in the Top viewport, move the mr Sky Portal back so it is aligned with the opening of the window outside the room.

Make sure the arrow is pointing into the room, as shown in Figure 16.33. Figure 16.33 is shown with just the walls, window, Daylight System, and mr Sky Portal.

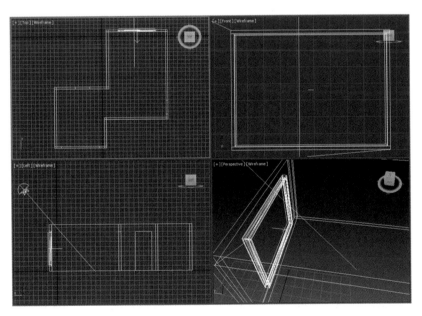

FIGURE 16.33   Move the mr Sky Portal to the window in the wall in the Top viewport.

14. Render the Window Camera viewport again.

That helps, but it is not enough; it is still too dark, so it's time to play with exposure controls.

15. Choose Rendering ➢ Environment and Effects ➢ Environment And Exposure Settings. Click Render Preview.

16. In the mr Photographic Exposure Control rollout, change Exposure Value (EV) from 15 (the default) to 10, as shown in Figure 16.34. You should see the render preview change to show the update.

17. Render the Window Camera viewport again to see the difference.
    It looks good but is still a bit dark, so it's time to add Final Gather bounces.

FIGURE 16.34   The mr Photographic Exposure Control rollout

18. In the Rendered Frame window, change FG Bounces to 5. Render the viewport again.

That's it! If you want to play around some more, try moving the light for a more dramatic shadow on the floor. Moving the light can have a dramatic effect on the luminance levels also, so be prepared to edit FG Bounces and Exposure Controls. The last render is shown in Figure 16.35. Don't be surprised if it takes a while to render.

Open the ArchModel_mentalray_Day_End.max file to compare it to your file.

FIGURE 16.35   The final render

THE ESSENTIALS AND BEYOND

In this chapter, you learned rendering techniques used with mental ray in 3ds Max 2014. You saw the quality settings and how they could help you with better renders. Finding the right balance of settings for a clean render is an art in itself. You also started lighting with Final Gather.

Additional Exercises

▶ Create new objects for the scene to which chrome and glass materials can be applied, and then play with rendering the scene to make these objects look photo-realistic.

▶ Experiment with different Final Gather settings to get the best look for the least render time in the chess set example.

▶ Try creating an outdoor scene and use the Daylight System to light.

Autodesk® 3ds Max® Certification

Autodesk certifications are industry-recognized credentials that can help you succeed in your design career—providing benefits to both you and your employer. Getting certified is a reliable validation of skills and knowledge, and it can lead to accelerated professional development, improved productivity, and enhanced credibility.

Certification Objective

This Autodesk Official Press can be an effective component of your exam preparation for the Autodesk® 3ds Max® 2014 certification exam. Autodesk highly recommends (and we agree!) that you schedule regular time to prepare, review the most current exam preparation road map available at www .autodesk.com/certification, use Autodesk Official Press books, take a class at an Authorized Training Center (find ATCs near you at www.autodesk .com/atc), take an assessment test, and use a variety of resources to prepare for your certification—including plenty of actual hands-on experience.

Table A.1 is for the Autodesk 3ds Max 2014 Certified Professional exam and lists the topics, exam objectives, and the chapter where the information for each objective is found—and in the chapters, you'll find certification icons like the one in the margin here to indicate where objectives are covered. This book will give you a foundation for the basic objectives covered on the exam, but you will need further study and hands-on practice to complete and pass the Professional exam.

Please refer to www.autodesk.com/certification for the most current exam road map and objectives.

Good luck preparing for your certification!

TABLE A.1   3ds Max 2014 exam objectives

Topic	Exam Objective	Chapter
Animation	Analyze the animation of an object using the Curve Editor	Chapter 5
	Change interpolation methods	Chapter 5
	Create a path animation and evaluate an object along the path	Not Covered
	Differentiate Dope Sheet from the Curve Editor	Chapters 5, 12
	Explain how to edit tangents with the Curve Editor	Chapter 5
	Identify Controller types	Chapter 5
	Identify playback settings	Chapter 5
	Identify the constraint used for an animation	Chapter 13
	Locate the value of keys in the Time Slider	Chapter 5
	Use animation passes and animation editors	Not Covered
Cameras	Differentiate camera types	Chapter 15
	Edit FOV (Field of View)	Not Covered
	Explain Near and Far Clip Plane for your camera	Chapter 15
Compositing	Demonstrate how to composite multiple layers together	Not Covered
	Demonstrate how to remap the color output for an image	Not Covered
Data Management / Interoperability	Differentiate common file types and usages	Not Covered
	Use the import feature to import model data	Chapter 3
Dynamics / Simulation	Use modifiers for soft body simulation	Not Covered

TABLE A.1   *(Continued)*

Topic	Exam Objective	Chapter
Lighting	Compare Attenuation and Decay	Chapter 14
	Differentiate light functions in a scene	Chapter 14
	Identify parameters for modifying shadows	Chapter 14
	Use the Daylight System	Chapter 16
	Use the Light Lister	Chapter 14
Materials / Shading	Identify Shader parameters	Chapter 10
	Identify standard materials	Chapter 10
	Use Blending Modes	Not Covered
	Use the Material Editor	Chapters 10, 11
Modeling	Differentiate reference coordinate systems	Chapters 1, 5
	Differentiate workflow	Chapters 2–4, 7–10
	Identify Clone types	Chapters 2–4, 7, 8
	Identify Vertex types	Chapters 2–4, 7, 8
	Use object creation and modification workflows	Chapters 2, 4, 7–9
	Use polygon modeling tools	Chapters 2–4, 7–10
	Use ProBoolean	Not Covered
Rendering	Differentiate Renderers	Chapter 16
	Identify pass types	Not Covered
	Identify rendering parameters	Chapter 16
	Use Render to render an effect pass	Not Covered

(Continues)

TABLE A.1 *(Continued)*

Topic	Exam Objective	Chapter
Rigging / Setup	Describe common Biped features	Chapter 12
	Identify Bones	Not Covered
	Identify Controller usage	Chapter 5
	Identify IK Solvers	Chapter 13
	Use Weight Table	Chapter 12
Scripting	Apply (run) Scripts	Not Covered
	Describe common use of scripts	Not Covered
UI/Object Management	Describe and use object transformations	Chapters 1, 2, 5
	Identify Selection Regions	Not Covered
	Describe View configuration and ViewCube navigation	Chapters 1, 2

INDEX

Note to the reader: Throughout this index boldfaced page numbers indicate primary discussions of a topic. *Italicized* page numbers indicate illustrations.

NUMERALS

2D maps, 216
2D Snaps Toggle button (S), 62, 65, 70
3D Cartesian coordinates, 43
3D maps, 216
90-degree angles, constraining line to, 39

A

accessories, weighting, 284–286, *285*
Acquire UVW Mapping dialog box, 220
Action Safe area, 343
Action View area
    in Material Editor, 210, *210*
    navigation in, 214
Adaptive Halton SuperSampling filter, 227
Adaptive Uniform SuperSampling
        filter, 227
Add Atmosphere Or Effect dialog box, 327
Add Keys tool, 139
aliasing, in reflections, 349
Align Sub-Object Selection dialog box, 127
Align tool, 127
ambient color, 211
Amount of noise, for volume light, 329
Angle Snap Toggle, 128, 144
animation, 111. *See also* character animation; rigging
    / (slash) button to play, 125
    adding to model, 276
    anticipation and momentum, 131–142
    of ball, 112–117
    blocking out, 131–133, *132*
    of camera, 341–342, *342*
    controlling view, 287–289
    copying keys, 296
    deleting, 286
    Dope Sheet for modifying, 299–304
    playing, 287
        / (slash) button as shortcut, 125
    recording, 113
    refining, 118–129
    rendering, 336
    squash and stretch, 121–123, *122*
    timing for, 123–124
    of XForm modifier, 128–129
animation curves
    editing, 119–121
    reading, 116–118

animation cycle, 114
animation exposure sheets (X-sheets), 115
Animation, Motion Editors
    Track View-Curve Editor, 115
    Track View-Dope Sheet, 300
Animation Playback controls, 16
Animation Time/Keying control, *2*, 3
Animation_Ball_00.max file, 112
Animation_Ball_01.max file, 124
Animation_Ball_02.max file, 129
anisotropic shader, 212, *212*
anti-aliasing, 226
anticipation, adding to knives, **137–138**,
        138
Apple QuickTime movie file format, 337
Application button, *2*, 2, 3, 20
    Import, Merge, 54, *54*, 75, 108, 207
    Manage, Set Project Folder, 59, 112, 131
    New, 22
Application menu, 2
Arch (architectural) & Design material
        (mental ray), 212, 365
    creating, 369–370
    and Multi/Sub-Object material
        (MSOM), 370–372
    templates, 366–368
Architecture Engineering and
        Construction (AEC) tools, 57
ArchModel file, 312
ArchModel project, 59, 93
ArchModel_00.max file, 61
ArchModel_01.max file, 65
ArchModel_02.max file, 68
ArchModel_03 .max file, 70
ArchModel_04.max file, 73
ArchModel_Final.max file, 104, 108
ArchModel_furniture_04.max file, 228
ArchModel_IntroMat_01.max file, 213
ArchModel_IntroMat_02.max file, 220
ArchModel_IntroMat_03max file, 223
ArchModel_LightEnviro_End.max file,
        329
ArchModel_LightEnviro_Start.max
        file, 321
ArchModel_mentalray_Day_End.max file,
        383, *384*
ArchModel_mentalray_Day_Start.max
        file, 379

ArchModel_mentalray_End.max file,
        372, *372*
ArchModel_mentalray_Light.max file, 372
ArchModel_mentalray_Start.max file, 365
ArchModel_Render_Start.max file, 340
arm
    adjusting, 272–274, *273*
    animation, *297*, **297–298**
    creating, **158–161**, *160*
Arrange Elements rollout, 254, *254*
Assign Material To Selection tool, 371
atmospheric effects, lighting for, 321–329
Attach List dialog box, 207
attenuation, for omni light, 318
Auto Key button (N), 113, 121
    deactivating, 124
AutoCAD DWG/DXF Import Options dia-
        log box, *60*, 60
Autodesk 3ds Max® software interface,
        1–18
    command panel, 14–16
        modifier stack, 15, *15*
        object parameters and values, 15
        objects and sub-objects, 16
    file management, 16–18
    Graphite Modeling Tools set, **12–14**,
        13. *See also* Graphite Modeling
        Tools
    time slider and track bar, **16**
    transforming objects using gizmos,
        11, 11–12
    workspace, 1–11
        mouse buttons, *7*, 7
        quad menus, 7–8
        user-interface elements, 2–4
        ViewCube, 6, *6*
        viewport, 4–6
AVI File Compression Setup dialog box, 355
Awning window type, 68

B

back light, 306, *306*
    adding, 315
Baseboard Image Plane.max file, 75
baseboard moldings, *72*, 72–78, *77*
    profile, *74*
bevel, 30–31
Bevel caddy, *30*, 30–31

Bevel modifier, 49
Bevel Values rollout, *50*, 50–51
Bezier vertex, 41, 46
Bias parameter for shadow, 320
BiFold door type, 65
biped, 263
    adjusting head and neck, 274–275, *275*
    adjusting torso and arms, 272–274, *273*
    applying Skin modifier, 275–277
        problem areas, *277*
        testing, 276–277
    associating with Soldier model,
        266–289
    creating and modifying, 266–272, *267*
    mirroring skeleton, 268
    reference position for, *264*
    types, 264–265, *265*
Biped rollout, Modes And Display, *288*, 288
bitmap, adding to material, 216–217
Blinn Basic Parameter rollout, *216*, 216, 230
Blinn shader, *212*, 213
blocking out
    animation, 112
    model, 80–82, *81*
Bones system, 265
boots, 183–187, *184–188*
Border mode, 155, 158, 165, 172
Bounce Ball.avi movie file, 129
bounce count, for light ray, 362, *363*
Bouncing Ball project, 112–117
    adding rotation, 126
    moving ball forward, 124–126
    rendering, 336–338
Bridge Edges caddy, *176*
Bridge tool, 163, 176, 197, *200*
bump map, *222*, 222–223, *223*, 258–261,
    259, 261

C

CAD drawing, importing, 59–61, *61*
Camera viewport, 340
cameras, 338–343
    animation of, 341–342, *342*
    creating, 339, 340
Cap Poly, 164
Cartesian coordinates, 4
Casement window type, 68
cd (candela) value for light, 376
ceiling, clone of floor to create, 71
center of lathe, repositioning, 46
center point, on XForm modifier, 127–128
chaise lounge. *See* couch
chamfer, 34–35, *35*
Chamfer caddy, 34
chamfer time, 32–38

character animation, 291–304
    with dope sheet, 299–304
    freeform, 294–298
        arm movement, *297*, 297–298
        head movement, 294–297, *296*
        run-and-jump sequence, 292–293, *293*
character modeling, 143. *See also* Soldier
    project
    scene setup, 143–146
Character Studio, 289
    collision detection and, 299
    workflow, 263–265
CheckerPattern, 241, 242, 250
child objects, 140–141
Choose Renderer dialog box, *336, 358*, 358
Chrome material, 225, 366–368, *368*
Classic biped type, 264, *265*
clipping planes, 342–343, *343*
Clock project, 20, *56*
    back side, 36
    beginning, 22–24
    bells, 45–48, *47*
    body progress, *31*
    handle, *38*, 38–44
        finished, *44*
    hands, 51–53, *53*
    modeling, 25–38
    numbers, 49–51
    reference photo, *21*
Clock_Bell_Start.max file, 45
Clock_Body_Start.max file, 18, 25
Clock_Handle_End.max file, 44
Clock_Handle_Start.max file, 38
clone, creating ceiling from floor, 71
Clone Options dialog box, 55, *71*, 71, 81,
    145, *145*
Clone Rendered Frame Window tool, 349
collision detection, Character Studio
    and, 299
color, 211
color gradient, on mesh, 278
color map, applying to soldier, 257, *258*
color temperature of light, 376
command panel, 14–16
    displaying, 61
    modifier stack, *15*, 15
    Motion tab, Biped rollout, *267*, 267
    object parameters and values, 15
    objects and sub-objects, 16
    Parameters rollout, for plane, 94
    tabs, *2, 3*
Compact Material Editor, 210
Compression Settings dialog box, 337, *337*
computer-generated (CG) characters, 169
Configure rollout, Map Seams, 236
controllers, in animation, 119

coordinate display area, *2*, 3
coordinate system, 43
copy, 55
Copy/Paste rollout, 270
copying
    animation keys, 296
    keyframes, 113–114
corner vertex, 41
couch, 79–92, *80, 92*
    adding details, *85*, 85–88
    adding softness, 82–84, *84*
    blocking out model, 80–82, *81*
    chaise lounge, *89*, 89–90
    feet, 90–92, *91*
    finished, *88*
    mapping, 213–223, *220*
    materials for, 213–214
        adding bitmap, 216–217
        applying, 214–215, *215*
        bump map, *222*, 222–223, *223*
        for feet, 220–221, *221*
Couch_01.max file, 79
Couch_02.max file, 85
Couch_03.max file, 87
Couch_04.max file, 104, 108
Create Key dialog box, 16
Create Keys For Inactive Footsteps tool, 287
Create Multiple Footsteps dialog box, 292
Create panel
    Doors, Object Type
        Pivot, 65
        Sliding, 67
    Geometry
        Box, 80, 82, 91, 101
        Cylinder, 25, 194
        Fillet, 99
        Outline, 73
        Plane, 22
        Refine, 52, 76, *77, 78*
    Lights, 312, *313*
        Omni, 316, 325, *326*
    Shapes
        Line, 39, 45, 70, 75, 95–96, *96*
        Rectangles, 51
        Text, 49
    Systems, Biped, 267
    Windows, Object Type, Fixed, 68
crossing boxes technique, 21
Crowd system, 263
CSSoldier02.max file, 272
CSSoldier03.max file, 275
CSSoldier04.max file, 278
CSSoldier05.max file, 284
CSSoldier06.max file, 286
CSSoldierComplete00.max file, 292
CSSoldierComplete01.max file, 294

CSSoldierComplete02.max file, 298
CSSoldierComplete03.max file, 299
CSSoldierComplete04.max file, 304
curve, creating smooth from sharp edges, 36
Curve Editor, 114–115, *115*, *118*
    reading curve in, 116
    for timing, 123
Curve, for Knife X, Y, Z Position tracks, 132
Customize menu
    Customization, Units Setup, *58*, 58
    Show UI, Show Command Panel, 61
cycle through keyframes, 114

D

da Vinci pose, 263–264, *264*
Daylight System Creation warning, *379*
Daylight System, in mental ray renderer,
    378–383, *381*
decay, for omni light, 318
default lighting, 306
default renderer, 358
Default Scanline Renderer, 336
Default Workspace, 1
deleting animation, 286
Density parameter, for volume light, 329
Diffuse Bounces value, for Final
    Gather, 362
diffuse color, 211
Diffuse Color Map, 216
direct light, 357
    free, **310–311**
Display menu, Hide Selection, 98
Distribution (Photometric Web)
    rollout, 374
dolly in/out, 340
Door objects
    creating, 64–67, *65*, *66*
    mapping, **228–233**
    parameters, *66*
Dope Sheet, 114–115, 265, **299–304**
Dope Sheet window, *301*, 301–302
    time slider, 302, *302*
Draft mode, for Final Gather, 363
dummy object, 109

E

ease-in, 117, *117*
ease-out, *117*, 117
edge loop, selecting, 34
Edge mode (2), 34
Edged Face mode (F4), 25
Edges tab, Chamfer Settings, 86
Edit Envelopes tool, 278

Edit menu
    Controller, Out Of Range Types,
        115, 115
    Duplicate, Clone, 55
    Group
        Group, *48*, 48
        Ungroup, 214
    SwiftLoop tool, 84
Edit UVs rollout, Open UV Editor, 241
Edit UVWs dialog box, 243, *243*, 250,
    251, *252*
    Tools, Render UVW Template, 255
editable-poly modeling, 19
Element mode, 245
Enhanced Menus workspace, 1
envelopes, 278
    sizing by moving points, *280–281*
Environment And Effects dialog box
    Exposure Control rollout, 374
    mr Photographic Exposure Control
        rollout, 374, *383*
Environment And Effects rollout, 327, *328*
Exclude/Include dialog box, 324, *325*
Exponential parameter, for volume
    light, 329
Extended Parameters rollout, *349*, 349
    Advanced Transparency section,
        352, 352
Extrude Border method, 165
Extrude Edge method (Shift+Move),
    184, 184
Extruder modifier, 49

F

face mask, 207
    creating seams, 247, *247*
falloff, for lights, *309*, 309
Far Attenuation, 318, *319*
Far Clip, 342, *343*
feet
    of biped, envelopes for, *282*,
        282–283, *283*
    of couch, 90–92, *91*
        materials, 220–221, *221*
Female biped type, 264, *265*
FG Precision Presets slider, 361–362, *362*
field of view (FOV), 339
Figure mode, 267
file format, for render output, 333
file management, **16–18**
filename, 18
    for render, 334
fill light, *306*, 306
    adding, 315
filter color, 211

Final Gather
    for luminance, 377, 383
    with mental ray, 360–364
    panel for controls, *378*
Final Gathering rollout, *361*, 361–362
    Advanced settings, 363
Fixed window type, 68
Flip Hinge, 65
floor, **70–71**
    clone
        for baseboard path, 73
        to create ceiling, 71
    creating material, *369*, 369–370
focal length of camera lens, 339
fog light, 321
following through in animation, **139–140**
Footstep Creation rollout
    Create Multiple Footsteps, 287
    Jump, 299
    Run, 292
    Walk, 299
footstep-driven animation, 291
    adding footsteps manually, 299, *300*
    numbering steps, 294
Footstep mode, 287
Footstep Operation rollout, 299
four-viewport layout tab bar, 4–6
frame range, for render output, 333
frames, 112
free camera, 339
free direct light, **310–311**
free spot light, **310–311**
freeform animation, 291, **294–298**
    arm movement, *297*, 297–298
    completing motion sequence, 298
    head movement, **294–297**
Freeze Selection in viewport, 266
furniture. *See also* couch; lounge chair
    folder for, 109
    merging files into room file,
        108–109, *110*

G

Gamma & LUT Settings Mismatch warn-
    ing, 112, 131, 236
General Parameters rollout, for free spot
    or direct light, 311
General Viewport Label menu, Configure
    Viewports, 343
Generic Units, 58, 80
Geometry rollout
    Box, 80, 82, 91, 101
    Cylinder, 25, 194
    Fillet, 99

Outline, 73
Plane, 22
Refine, 52, 76, *77*, *78*
gizmos, for transforming objects, *11*, 11–12
glass material, 230
global illumination, 360
Glossiness value, 370
goggles, 207
   UV unwrapping for, 246, *247*
Graphite Modeling Tools, 12–14, *13*, 26
   Edges
      Bridge, 163, 176, 197, *200*
      Chamfer, 34, 36, 159, 173, 201, *201*
   Edit panel
      Cut, 201, *202*
      SwiftLoop, 28, *28*, 36, *37*, 148, *149*
      Use NURMS, 102
   Geometry
      Attach, Attach from List, 207
      Cap Poly, 155, 164, 172
      Loops, Flow Control, 153, *154*, *155*
      Modeling, Edge mode (2), 29
      Modify Selection panel, 153
      Loop, 29, 32, 36, 173, 178
      Ring, 153
   Polygon Modeling panel
      Collapse Stack, 173, 206
      Convert To Poly, 26, 42, 83, 89,
         101, 104, 148, 324, 371
      Ignore Backfacing, 156
      Use Soft Selection, 193
      Vertex, 152
   Polygons panel
      Extrude, 86, 179
      GeoPoly, 156
      Outline, 28
   Vertices
      Target Weld, 197, 203, *204*
      Weld, 161, 165, *166*
Grid and Snap Settings dialog box, *62*, 62
gross animation, 112
grouping objects, 109
gun holster, *182*, 182–183
   weighting, 284–286, *285*

H
Hammersley SuperSampling filter, 227
handle, for keyframes, 118–119, *119*
head, **193–206**
   accessories, **207–208**
   animation, **294–297**
   creating back, *205*, 205–206, *206*
   mirroring, **206**
   outlining, **196–201**, *197*, *198*
   rounding face, **203**, *203*, *204*
   seams for, *248*
   UV unwrapping for, **245–247**

height
   of door, 65, 67
   of window, 68
helmet, 207
   seams for straps, *248*
   UV unwrapping for, *246*, 246
hiding
   image planes, 32
   objects, 71–72
Hierarchy panel, Pivot, Adjust Pivot, 112
high-polygon-count models, 143–144
highlight color, specular map for
     defining, 261
hotspot, 307

I
image aspect, for render output, 333
image maps, 218
image planes
   adding material, **145–146**, *146*
   hiding, 32
   for lounge chair, 93–94
   for Soldier project, 144–145
image size of render, 333
importing, CAD drawing, **59–61**, *61*
In Place mode, 287–289
Index Of Refr parameter, 349, 351
indirect lighting, 357, 360
InfoCenter, *2*, 2, 3
Initial FG Point Density, for Final
     Gather, 362
instance, 55
Intensity/Color/Attenuation rollout, 314,
     376, 376
   Multiplier, 316
intensity of light, 376–377
interface. *See* Autodesk 3ds Max® software
     interface
Interpolate Over Num.FG Points value, for
     Final Gather, 362
Isolate Selection mode (Alt+Q), 32, 75, 76,
     182, 218
   exiting, 34
Isolate Selection Toggle button, 83

J
jagged edges, anti-aliasing to smooth, 226
Jorgenson, Nastasia, 60
jump cycle, 265, *293*, 302, *303*

K
Kelvin units, 376, 377
Key Controls toolbar, Move Keys tool, 133
Key Entry toolbar, 123
key light, 306, *306*

Keyboard Entry rollout, *22*, 22–23
   for object parameters, 25
keyboard shortcuts
   for sub-object levels, 26
   for viewports, 10
keyframes, 16, 111
   adding, 139
   copying, 113–114
   handle for, 118–119, *119*
   for original biped pose, 276
   for X and Y Position tracks, 125
Knife project
   adding rotation, **135–137**, *136*
   anticipation, **137–138**, *138*
   blocking out animation, **131–133**, *132*
   following through, **139–140**
   trajectories, *134*, 134–135
   transferring momentum to target,
     140–142
knife_animation.mov file, 142

L
Lathe Parameters rollout, Align area,
     Min, 46
lathe technique, 45
Leather.tif file, 224
leg strap, **178–182**, *179–181*
lens of camera, 339
light lister, **329–330**
Light Lister dialog box, *330*
lighting, **305–330**
   in 3ds Max, **306–312**
   for atmospheric effects, **321–329**
   color temperature of, 376
   default, 306
   excluding object from, **324–326**
   free spot or direct light, **310–311**
   indirect, 357
   omni light, **311**, 311–312
   photometric
     in mental ray renderings, **372–378**
     parameters, **376–378**
   for still life in interior space,
     312–318, *313*
   targeted, 374
     direct light, *309*, 309–310
     spotlight, **307–309**, *308*
   three-point, *305*, 305–306
   volumetric, **321–323**, *327*, 327–329, *328*
Lighting/Cameras
   Create Lights
     Daylight System, *379*, *379*
     mr Sky Portal, 381, *382*
   Tools (Lights/Cameras Set), Light
     Lister, 330
Line tool, 39, 70

Live Area Safe Frame, 343
lm (lumen) value for light, 376
lounge chair, *93*, 93–109, *107*
    attaching sides, *98*, 98–99
    base, *103*, 103–106
    cushion, 101–102
    frame, *101*
    image planes for, 93–94
    mapping, 223–227
    materials for, 94, 223–227, *224*
        creating for base, 227, *228*
    splines for frame, 95–100
    straps, 102–103, *103*
LoungeChair_01.max file, 91
LoungeChair_02.max file, 96
LoungeChair_03.max file, 100
LoungeChair_06.max file, 105, 109
low-polygon-count models, 144
lx at (lux) value for light, 376

M

Male biped type, 264, *265*
Manage, Set Project Folder, 17, 20
mapping, 209
    chair, 223–227
    couch, 213–223, *220*
        standard material for, 213–214
    windows and doors, 228–233
mapping coordinates, 217, 218–223
Maps rollout, Standard rollout, 260
Material Editor, 210. *See also* Slate
    Material Editor (M)
material IDs, 230
Material/Map Browser, 210, 211, 213, 257
    Maps, Standard rollout, *217*
    Materials, Standard, 345
    Raytrace map, 231
    for raytrace mapping, 347
materials, 209–233. *See also* Slate
    Material Editor (M)
    adding bitmap, 216–217
    adding reflection, 225–226
    adding to image plane, 145–146, *146*
    for couch, 214–215, *215*
        bump map, *222*, 222–223, *223*
        feet, 220–221, *221*
    for lounge chair, 94, 223–227, *224*
        creating for base, 227, *228*
    mental ray, 212, 364–383
        shaders, 212–213
    types, 211–212
    for windows, 232, *233*
Max 2.5 Star SuperSampling filter, 227
Max. Reflections value, for Final
    Gather, 363

Max.Refractions value, for Final
    Gather, 363
MAXScript Mini Listener, *2*, 3
measurement, units setup for, 58
mental ray
    Final Gather with, 360–364
    lights for, 307
    material, 212
        shaders, 212–213
    photometric lighting in, 372–378
    sampling quality, 358–359
mental ray materials, 364–383
mental ray Rendered Frame window,
    364, *364*
mental ray renderer, 357–359
    daylight system in, 378–383
    NVIDIA, 358
menu bar, *2*, 4
merge, 54–55
    furniture files into room file, *110*
Merge File dialog box, 108, *108*, 207
mesh in 3ds Max, 16
Metal shader, *212*, 213
Mini Curve Editor, 120
Mirror Parameters rollout, Mirror Offset,
    283, *284*
Mirror tool, 147
mirroring, 169
    biped skeleton, 268
    head, 206
mistakes
    in animation, 111
    in seams, undoing, 239
modeling. *See also* Graphite Modeling
    Tools
    editable-poly, 19
    spline, 38
    in sub-object mode, 26–30
modeling ribbon, 26, 32. *See also*
    Graphite Modeling Tools
modeling windows, 4. *See also* viewports
Modified Object track, 129
modifier stack, *15*, 15
Modifiers, Geometry (Parametric),
    XForm, 127
Modify panel, 25
    Advanced Effects rollout, 326
    Atmospheres & Effects rollout, 321
    Directional Parameters rollout, 322
    General Parameters rollout,
        Shadows, 315
    Intensity/Color/Attenuation rollout,
        314, 322
        Far Attenuation, 318, 326
        Multiplier, 316

Modifier List
    Bevel, 50
    Extrude, 70, *71*
    Lathe, *46*, 46
    Symmetry, 206
    Taper, 91
    Unwrap UVW, 236
    UVW Map, 218–219
modifier stack
    Editable Poly, Element, 245
    expanding list of sub-objects,
        39, *40*
    Selection rollout, 52
    Vertex mode, 96
    Rendering rollout, 42
    Shadow Parameters rollout, Object
        Shadows Dens, 317
    Spotlight Parameters rollout, 308, *308*
moldings, baseboard, *72*, 72–78, *77*
momentum, transferring from knife to
    target, 140–142
Motion panel
    Copy/Paste rollout, *270*, 270
    Footstep mode, 292
mouse buttons, 7, *7*
Move Keys Vertical tool, 138
Move tool (W), 94
Move Transform gizmo, 268
moving camera, animating, 341–342, *342*
mr Photographic Exposure Control roll-
    out, 374, *383*
Multi/Sub-Object material (MSOM)
    and Arch & Design, 370–372
    creating, 228–233, *230*

N

n-gon, 155
names
    for files, 18, 334
    for materials, 214
navigation
    in Action View area, 214
    with Point-to-Point Seams, 237
near clipping plane, 342, *343*
Nitros display driver, 314
Noise Filtering value, for Final
    Gather, 363
noise level
    for renderer, 359
    for volume light, 329
normal, 258
normal mapping, 258, *259*, *261*
NURMS (Non-Uniform Rational Mesh
    Smooth), 82–84
NVIDIA mental ray renderer, 358, 365

O

Object Type rollout, AutoGrid, 194
objects
    display in viewport, 8–10, 23
    excluding from light, 324–326
    grouping, 109
    hiding, 71–72
    parameters and values, 15
    parent and child, 140–141
    and sub-objects, 16
    trajectories of, *134*, 134–135
    transforming using gizmos, *11*, 11–12
    viewing frozen, 266
omni light, *311*, 311–312
    creating, 316
Open Mini Curve Editor, 119, *120*
orbit navigation control, 11
Orbit tool, *27*
orthographic views, 4. *See also* viewports
out-of-range animation, 116
Outline caddy, 28
outlining head, **196–201**, *197*, *198*
output, from rendering, 355–356

P

pan navigation control, 10
Parameter Curve Out-Of-Range Types
    dialog box, 116, 125
Parameter Curve Out-Of-Range Types
    feature, 114
Parameter Editor, for Multi/Sub-Object
    material, 228, *229*
Parameters rollout, 115, 211
    for Normal Bump node, *260*
    for plane, 144
    for Wall object, *63*
parent object, 140–141
Paste Posture Opposite tool, 272
Peel rollout
    Expand Polygon Selection To Seams,
        242, 250
    Pelt Map, 243
    Point-to-Point Seams tool,
        236–237, *237*
Pelt Map dialog box, 243, 250
Perspective viewport, 82
    fitting model in, 215
    orbiting around object, 26
    walls in, 63, *64*
Phase parameter, for volume light, 329
photometric lights, 306–307
    in mental ray renderings, 372–378
    parameters, 376–378
photos, as reference materials, 20
Photoshop, 235
piping on couch, 85–88

Pivot door type, 65
pivot point
    for ball, 126
    for ball, XForm modifier for, **127–128**
    Symmetry modifier and, *170*, 170–171
Pivoted window type, 68
Play Animation button, 118
Playback Controls area, 287
playing animation, 287
    / (slash) button as shortcut, 125
Point-to-Point Seams tool, 236–237,
    237, 239
poly count of model, 83
Polygon mode (4), 152
Polygon Modeling panel, Edge mode (2), 32
Polygon sub-object mode, 26
polygons, 16, 155
    selecting, *27*, 179
Polygons panel, Extrude, Extrude
    Settings, *105*, 105
portal, 380
Position controller, 119
pouch, **174–177**, *175*, *176*
primary light, 306, *306*
project workflow, 19–24
Projected window type, 68
projects, setting, **17–18**
prompt line, *2*, 3

Q

quad menus, 7–8, *8*, 32
    Bezier, *40*
quad polygons, for smooth surfaces, 83
quality of renders, 359, *359*, *360*
Quick Access toolbar, *2*, 2, 3
QuickTime movie file format, 337

R

Rays Per FG Point value, for Final
    Gather, 362
Raytrace Basic Parameters rollout, 345
Raytrace map, 226
raytrace mapping, 347–348, *348*
    refractions using, **351–352**, *352*
Raytrace material
    for creating reflection, 345–346, *346*
    refractions using, 348–351
raytraced reflections
    adding to furniture, 353–354
    creating, 345–352
raytraced shadows, 320–321, *321*
Raytracer Controls rollout, 346
Realistic viewport, 314, *315*
recording animation, 113
Rectangular Selection Region tool, 42, *43*

redo command (Ctrl+Y), 2
reference, 55
Reference Coordinate System drop-down
    menu, 44
reference materials, 20–24, 59, *61*
    applying to image planes, 93
    texture mapping onto planes, 145
reference photo, for image planes, *24*, 24
reference position, for bipedal
    character, *264*
reflection
    adding raytraced to furniture,
        353–354
    applying, **225–226**
    for Arch & Design materials, 370
    Raytrace material for, 345–346, *346*
Reflectivity value, 370
refractions
    using raytrace mapping, 351–352, *352*
    using Raytrace material, 348–351
Relax Tool dialog box, 243–244, *244*,
    250, 251
Render Last tool (F9), 215
Render Output File dialog box, 334, *334*,
    337, 355
Render Preview dialog box, 374, 383
Render Production tool, 215
Render Setup dialog box, 331, 337
    Common tab, *332*, 333, 355
        Assign Renderer rollout, 357, *358*
    Final Gather and, 377
    Global Illumination tab, Final
        Gathering rollout, *361*, 361–362
    Renderer tab, 358, *359*
Render UVs dialog box, 254, *255*
Rendered Frame window, 334, *335*
    toolbar, 349
rendered images, folder for, 16
renderers
    mental ray, 357–359
        NVIDIA, 358
    types, **336**
rendering, 331
    Bouncing Ball project, **336–338**
    cameras and, 338–343
    filename for output, 334
    interior and furniture, 353–356
        raytraced reflections, 353–354
    output from, 355–356
    setup, 331–338
Rendering dialog box, 334, *335*
Rendering menu, Environment And
    Effects, Environment And Exposure
    Settings, 231, 374, 383
Rendering rollout, 99–100, *100*
resolution, for render output, 333, 355
ribbon, *2*, 3

rigging, 263–290
    associating biped with Soldier model,
        266–289
    Character Studio workflow, 263–265
roll for camera, 340
rollout, 2, 3
rotation, adding to knives, 135–137, 136
Rotation controller, 119
run cycle, 265

S

Safe Frames (Shift+F), 343, 344
Sample Range parameter for shadow, 320
Save As dialog box, Increment button, 18
saving, 24
    version numbers for, 18
Scale controller, 119
Scale gizmo, 44
Scale key, squash and stretch and, 122
Scale tool (R), 29
    for image map, 219
scene files, folder for, 16
Screen coordinate system, 43
scrubbing time slider, 113
seams
    for head, 248
    mistakes in, undoing, 239
    for soldier body, 249, 249–257
search, in Slate Material Editor, 353
See-Through mode (Alt+X), 25, 34, 237
    for clock handle model, 42, 42
    turning off, 32
Select And Link tool, 66
Select And Move tool (W), 41, 124, 158
    for camera, 340
Select And Rotate tool, 128
Select And Scale tool (R), 44
Select And Uniform Scale tool (R), 36
Select Bitmap Image File dialog box, 216,
    224, 257, 260, 345
Select Bones dialog, 276
Select By Element UV Toggle tool, 253, 253
Select By Name tool (H), 292
Select Camera dialog box (C), 368, 371
Select From Scene dialog box, 276
Select Object tool (Q), 42, 70
selecting
    biped, 276
    model, 251
    objects in viewport, 9
    polygons, 27, 179
Set Tangents To Fast icon, 120
Set Tangents To Linear icon, 126
Shaded + Edged viewport rendering type
    (F4), 266
Shader Basic Parameters rollout, 212
shaders, 212–213

Shading Viewport Label menu
    Lighting And Shadows, Illuminate
        With Scene Lights, 314, 314
    Shaded, 147
Shadow Map Params rollout, 316, 323
shadow maps, 320
shadow studies, 379
shadows
    adding, 323–324
    adjusting density, 317
    importance of, 318
    from omni light vs. spot light, 312
    raytraced, 320–321, 321
    selecting type, 319–321
    types of, 318
shininess, specular map for defining, 261
Show Shaded Material In Viewport tool
    (Material Editor), 217
Size parameter
    for shadow, 320
    for volume light, 329
sizing envelopes by moving points,
    280–281
Skeleton biped type, 264, 265
Skin modifiers, 263
    applying to biped, 275–277
        problem areas, 277
        testing, 276–277
    Parameters rollout, Envelopes and
        Cross Sections, 284, 284
    tweaking, 278–287, 279
Skin Weight Table dialog box, 285, 286
skinning, 264
Slate Material Editor (M), 210, 210–211,
    211, 257, 365
    Active View area, 222
    binoculars icon for search, 353
    Blinn Basic Parameter rollout, 216, 216
    for shiny white material, 371
    Specular Color input socket, 261, 262
    toolbar, Assign Material To
        Selection, 214
Sliding door type, 65, 66–67, 67
Sliding window type, 68
smooth vertex, 41
softness, adding to couch, 82–84, 84
Soldier project. See also biped
    accessories, 173–183
        boots, 183–187, 184–188
        gun holster, 182, 182–183
        leg strap, 178–182, 179–181
        pouch, 174–177, 175, 176
        utility belt, 173, 174
        vest, 177
    animation, 291–304
        arm movement, 297, 297–298
        completing motion sequence, 298

    head movement, 294–297
    run-and-jump sequence,
        292–293, 293
    applying color map, 257, 258
    associating biped with model,
        266–289
    beginning model, 146–167, 168
        arms, 158–161, 160
        elbow bends, 159–160
        fixing, 166–167
        forming torso, 147–158, 148,
            149, 151
        legs, 161–165, 162, 163, 164
        torso armhole, 156
    bump map, 258–261, 259
    completed model, 208
    completing main body, 169–173
        selecting torso top edges, 171, 171
    final render, 262
    final texture map, 256
    fixing details, 166, 166–167, 167
    hands, 188–192, 189–191
    head, 193–206
        accessories, 207–208
        creating back, 205, 205–206, 206
        mirroring, 206
        outlining, 196–201, 197, 198
        rounding face, 203, 203, 204
        image planes for, 144–145
            adding material, 145–146, 146
        joint edges spacing, 167, 168
        neckline adjustment, 193–195,
            194–196
    seams for body, 249, 249–257
    specular map applied, 261
    testing model, 286–287
    unfolding body, 250–257, 256
    UV layout, 254, 254, 255
Soldier_Accessories.max file, 207
SoldierTexture_v01.max file, 236
SoldierTexture_v02.max file, 242
SoldierTexture_v03.max file, 245
SoldierTexture_v04.max file, 250
SoldierTexture_v05.max file, 250
SoldierTexture_v06.max file, 257
Soldier_v01.max file, 147
Soldier_v02.max file, 158
Soldier_v03.max file, 161
Soldier_v04.max file, 166
Soldier_v05.max file, 169
Soldier_v06.max file, 173
Soldier_v07.max file, 183
Soldier_v08.max file, 188
Soldier_v09.max file, 193
Soldier_v10.max file, 207
Speckle Reduction value, for Final
    Gather, 363
specular color, 211

Specular Highlight area, 346
specular highlights, turning off, 316
Specular level of materials, 224
specular maps, 261–262
Spline dialog box, 70
splines, 38–53
    for lounge chair frame, 95–100
    renderability of, 99
spot light, free, 310–311
squash and stretch in animation, 121–
    123, *122*
standard lights, 307
standard materials, *211*, **211**
    adding to Multi/Sub-Object mate-
        rial, *229*
status bar, *2*, 3
Still Life Camera viewport, 316
stock lenses, 339
Structure rollout, *268*, 268
stunt double, 169
sub-object mode
    exiting, 34
    modeling in, **26–30**
sub-object visibility technique, 245
sub-objects, **16**
subdivision, 83
Sunlight light
    Atmospheres & Effects rollout, 327
    General Parameters rollout, Shadows
        section, 323
    in mental ray renderer, 378
SuperSampling filters, 226, 227,
    349–350, *350*
Sweep modifier, 75
Sweep Parameters rollout, 76
SwiftLoop tool, 36, *37*, 84
Symmetry modifier, 169
    pivot point and, *170*, 170–171

T

tangents, 41
    for animation curve, 118
target camera, 339
target direct light, *309*, **309–310**
target node, for light, 307
target spotlight, **307–309**, *308*
Target Weld, 197, 203, *204*
targeted light, 374
templates, Arch & Design material (men-
    tal ray), **366–368**
test render, settings for, 333
text parameters, 49, *49*
texture mapping, 94
three-point lighting, *305*, **305–306**
tiling image map, 218
Time Configuration dialog box, 132, *133*
time-lapse looks, 379

time requirements for rendering, 355
    Reflection Map and, 351
    with refraction, 348
time slider, *2*, 3, **16**, 112, 121
    in Dope Sheet window, *302*, 302
    scrubbing, 113
Title Safe area, 343
toolbar, *2*, 4
topology dependency warning, 245
track bar, *2*, 3, **16**
    animation keys in, *295*
Track Selection rollout, 268
Track View, 114
Track View—Curve Editor, 114–116
Track View—Dope Sheet, 299, 300
trajectories, of objects, *134*, **134–135**
Transform gizmo, *170*
transforming objects using gizmos, *11*,
    11–12
transparencies, shadow response to, 319
truck, 340

U

undo, 138
    last click, 63
Undo Scene Operation command
    (Ctrl+Z), 2
unfolding body, **250–257**, *256*
Uniformity parameter, for volume
    light, 329
units setup, 58
Unwrap UVW modifier, 236
Use Soft Selection tool, 193
user-interface elements, 2–4
User Safe setting, 343
utility belt, **173**, *174*
UV Editor, CheckerPattern in, 241, 242
UV unwrapping, 235, **236–247**
    for head, **245–247**
    steps, *242*, **242–244**, *243*
UVW Mapping modifier, **218–221**

V

version up, **18**
vertex
    quad menu to modify type, *40*
    types, 41
vertex fillet, *97*
vertex weighting techniques, 284
vest, **177**
View hybrid coordinate system, 43
ViewCube, *6*, 6
Viewport Configuration dialog box, Safe
    Frames tab, *344*
Viewport Label menu, 23
Viewport Layout tab bar, *2*, 3, 4–6, *5*

viewports, *2*, 4–6
    changing/maximizing, 9
    Freeze Selection in, 266
    navigation controls, *2*, 3, *10*, **10–11**
    objects displayed in, 8–10, 23
    orbiting in, 27
volumetric lights, *327*, **327–329**, *328*
    creating, 321–323
    parameters, 329

W

walk cycle, 265, *289*
Wall objects, **61–64**
    doorway opening in, 65
    editing, 63–64
    Parameters rollout for, *63*
weighting accessories, **284–286**, *285*
Window Glass object, Opacity value, 323
windows
    creating, 68, *69*
    mapping, **228–233**
    material for, 232, *233*
    Multi/Sub-Object material applied to,
        230–231, *231*
Wireframe view, 237, *238*
wireframe viewport, 23
workspace, **1–11**
    mouse buttons, 7, *7*
    quad menus, 7–8
    user-interface elements, 2–4
    ViewCube, *6*, 6
    viewport, **4–6**
World coordinate system, 43

X

X axis, 4
X-sheets (animation exposure
    sheets), 115
XForm modifier, **127–128**
    animation, 128–129
    Gizmo sub-object of, 128

Y

Y axis, 4

Z

Z axis, 4
Z Position curve, 120
Zoom Extents All Selected tool, 109
Zoom Extents All tool, 23
zoom navigation control, 11
Zoom To Results tool, 353, *354*
zooming lens, 340